Handbook on
Statewide Systems of Support

Acknowledgement

The editors and leadership of the Center on Innovation & Improvement are appreciative of the suggestions made by representatives of the U.S. Department of Education's Regional Comprehensive Centers, U.S. Department of Education personnel, State Education Agency personnel, scholars, and educational leaders who have critiqued this Handbook at various stages, from concept to outline to draft. We are also grateful to the contributors to this volume and those who copy edited the manuscript and designed the publication: Pamela Sheley, Lori Thomas, and Stephen Page.

Center on Innovation & Improvement
121 N. Kickapoo Street
Lincoln, IL 62656 USA
Phone: 217-732-6462
Fax: 217-732-3696

www.centerii.org

The Center on Innovation & Improvement is administered by the Academic Development Institute (Lincoln, IL) in collaboration with its partners, Temple University Center for Research in Human Development and Education (Philadelphia, PA) and Little Planet Learning (Nashville, TN).

Information • Tools • Training

Positive results for students will come from changes in the knowledge, skill, and behavior of their teachers and parents. State policies and programs must provide the opportunity, support, incentive, and expectation for adults close to the lives of children to make wise decisions.

The Center on Innovation & Improvement helps Regional Comprehensive Centers in their work with states to provide districts, schools, and families with the opportunity, information, and skills to make wise decisions on behalf of students.

A national content center supported by the U. S. Department of Education's Office of Elementary and Secondary Education.

Award #S283B050057

The opinions expressed herein do not necessarily reflect the position of the supporting agencies, and no official endorsement should be inferred.

Handbook on
Statewide Systems of Support

Edited by

Sam Redding
Herbert J. Walberg

CENTER ON
INNOVATION &
IMPROVEMENT
Twin paths to better schools.

INFORMATION AGE PUBLISHING, INC.
Charlotte, NC • www.infoagepub.com

Library of Congress Cataloging-in-Publication Data

Handbook on statewide systems of support / edited by Sam Redding, Herbert J. Walberg.
    p. cm.
  Includes bibliographical references.
  ISBN 978-1-59311-882-2 (pbk.) – ISBN 978-1-59311-883-9 (hardcover)
  1. Government aid to education–United States–States–Handbooks, manuals, etc. 2. School improvement programs–United States–States–Handbooks, manuals, etc. 3. Educational accountability–United States–States–Handbooks, manuals, etc. I. Redding, Sam. II. Walberg, Herbert J., 1937-
  LB2825.H236 2008
  379.1'220973–dc22

                                                          2007050129

CONTENTS

PART A
INTRODUCTION AND COMMENTARY

1 Introduction and Overview 3
Herbert J. Walberg

2 Policy to Reinforce Changing State Role 9
Brett Lane

3 A Mountain Beyond Mountains 15
Paul Reville

PART B
EVIDENCE, FRAMEWORK, AND EVOLUTION

4 State Role in Supporting School Improvement 21
Lauren Morando Rhim, Bryan Hassel, and Sam Redding

5 An Evolution in American Education 61
Sam Redding

PART C
PROFILES OF KEY STATES

6   Introduction to Profiles of Key States 85
    Sam Redding

7   The Accountability Roundtable in Alabama 87
    Thomas Kerins, Susan Hanes, and Carole Perlman

8   Performance Contracting in Washington 111
    Thomas Kerins, Susan Hanes, and Carole Perlman

9   Exemplary Educators in Tennessee 141
    Thomas Kerins, Susan Hanes, and Carole Perlman

10 Highly Skilled Educators and Scholastic Reviews in Kentucky...... 167
    Thomas Kerins, Susan Hanes, and Carole Perlman

PART D
THE ROLE OF COMPREHENSIVE CENTERS

11 CII and the Comprehensive Centers' Work with the States 199
    Marilyn Murphy

12 Appraising Instructional Practices in West Virginia 205
    Caitlin Howley

13 From Compliance to Assistance: Building Statewide
    Systems of Support 209
    Barbara Youngren, Jayne Sowers, Gary Appel, and Mark Mitchell

14 Creating a Vision in New Jersey... 215
    Marilyn Muirhead and Ryan Tyler

15 Telling the Story of Improvement in Missouri 223
    *Belinda Biscoe, Stan Johnson, Donna Richardson, Ellen Balkenbush,
    and Patricia Fleming*

16 Working Sma-tah, Not Ha-dah in New Hampshire 235
    Adam E. Tanney

17 Building Relationships in Texas 245
K. Victoria Dimock

18 "Montana-cizing" a Scholastic Review 253
Jennifer Stepanek

19 Building SEA Capacity in Utah 261
Libby Rognier and Mary Peterson

PART E

TOOLS TO STRENGTHEN THE STATEWIDE SYSTEM OF SUPPORT

20 Tools to Strengthen the Statewide System of Support 271

The Allegory of the Garden: Incentives • Capacity •
Opportunities 273

Synopsis of the Framework for an Effective Statewide
System of Support 277

Functions of the State Education Agency 283

Key Documents in aStatewide System of Support 287

Taking Stock 289

Summary Appraisal to Inform Plan to Strengthen the
Statewide System of Support 307

Preparing the Plan to Strengthen the Statewide
System of Support 313

Table of Contents for the Plan to Strengthen the
Statewide System of Support 321

APPENDICES

A Theory of Action of the Framework for an Effective System
of Support 328

B Graphic of the Framework for an Effective Statewide System
of Support 329

PART A

INTRODUCTION
AND COMMENTARY

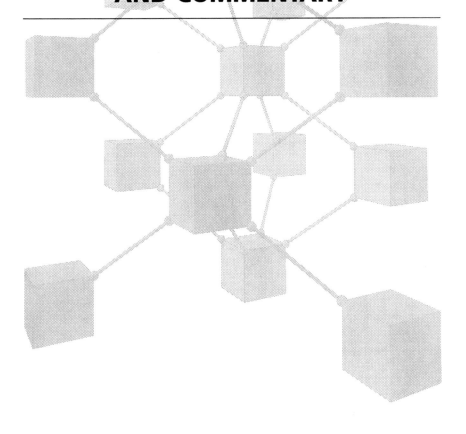

CHAPTER 1

INTRODUCTION AND OVERVIEW

Herbert J. Walberg

As subsequent chapters point out, the No Child Left Behind Act (NCLB) requires states to provide assistance to districts in improving the schools within their purview. Of course, the U.S. Constitution and federal laws leave the control of education largely to the states, and states have long provided support to school districts. In return for federal monies, however, NCLB requires states to provide such help under the statewide systems of support (SSOS) provision of the Act.

The purposes of this Handbook are to survey the research related to statewide systems of support, to present the experience and insights of educational leaders in how such support can best be conducted, and to derive actionable principles for improving schools. It is intended for use not only by the staff of the U.S. Department of Education-sponsored Regional Centers that serve state department staff but also by the staff of school districts and schools.

Also sponsored by the U.S. Department of Education, the Center on Innovation & Improvement (CII) previously developed the *Handbook on Restructuring and Substantial School Improvement* (Walberg, 2007) that became the basis of CII's technical assistance to Regional Centers on this topic. CII

Handbook on Statewide Systems of Support, pages 3–7
Copyright © 2008 The Academic Development Institute and Information Age Publishing
All rights of reproduction in any form reserved.

made available for downloading PowerPoint presentations and web-based seminars ("webinars") based on the previous Handbook.

CII's intended audiences widely employed the previous *Handbook on Restructuring and Substantial School Improvement* and auxiliary materials and found them useful in their technical assistance efforts to disseminate and encourage evidence-based ideas for restructuring and improving schools. With advice from the U.S. Department of Education, scholarly experts, and experienced educators in the Regional Centers, state departments of education, and school districts, the CII staff concluded that what it envisioned as the present Handbook would be similarly useful.

CII clients, it was thought, would benefit from a thorough, coherent presentation of material useful in their work on statewide systems of support. As in the case of the restructuring handbook, however, statewide systems of support is an emerging research topic. Educators themselves have had little experience with statewide support systems relative to, say, school and district governance.

Even so, several previous reports could be drawn upon including the Rennie Center's (2005) *Reaching Capacity: A Blueprint for the State Role in Improving Low Performing Schools and Districts* and the U.S. Department of Education's (2004) *Evaluation of Title I Accountability Systems and School Improvement Efforts*, which provided an early look at national implementation of NCLB provisions regarding statewide systems of support. In addition, many smaller-scale studies could also be synthesized.

Thus, CII planned to compile, analyze, and synthesize the results of the existing studies and reports to provide sound principles and to gather and synthesize the views and experiences of successful educators in the Regional Centers and states as another source of evidence. These efforts, it was hoped, could serve as the basis of protocols and other tools for use in staff development and to evaluate present programs and plan future evidence-based activities. The overall goal was to provide a coherent and practical document on this important topic to facilitate the delivery of high-quality technical assistance.

The rest of this chapter overviews the parts and chapters in this Handbook to give readers a clear idea of its structure and to guide them to the material they will find most useful. This Handbook is sequential and can be read straight through, but, to a large extent, the parts and chapters are designed to stand on their own. They can be downloaded from the CII website along with related PowerPoints and webinars for individual and group study and planning.

Part A: Introduction and Commentary

Herbert J. Walberg, "Introduction and Overview," the present chapter, which presents the purpose, rationale, scope, and overview of the book.

Brett Lane, "Policy to Reinforce Changing State Role." In striving to meet NCLB requirements, states' historical role as compliance and regulatory actors has expanded into more proactive policy activities at the district and school level. State education agencies must be empowered to identify and articulate conditions and policies outside traditional state purview that directly impact school improvement. With federal assistance and school cooperation, states will now be able to design and implement cohesive systems of support.

Paul Reville, "A Mountain Beyond Mountains." The data collected from standards-based state accountability systems is at the heart of closing the achievement gap between educator expectations and student performance. Building the capacity of the states becomes the supreme challenge as states work to oversee restructuring at the district level, and schools strive to adhere to NCLB performance mandates. Research, described in the chapter by Rhim, Hassel, and Redding, creates a theoretical framework of incentives, capabilities, and opportunities, at all departmental levels, to alleviate past tensions and conflicts. From teachers and administrators, to district and state officials; all need to adhere to a new spirit of support and collegiality from which new leaders arise.

Part B: Evidence, Framework, and Evolution

Lauren Morando Rhim, Bryan Hassel, and **Sam Redding**, "The State Role in Supporting School Improvement." States and, specifically, state education agencies (SEAs) have historically focused on promulgating regulations, setting and developing policy, disseminating funds, and collecting data. Under the progressively more high-stakes accountability systems that are a central feature of contemporary education policy, the state's role increasingly includes direct support and technical assistance to districts and individual schools to help them build capacity for meaningful change that will lead to improved academic outcomes. Though the literature related to state education agencies' involvement in school improvement is relatively thin and evolving, it provides a framework to consider how to construct an effective system. Building on research that identifies incentives, capabilities, and opportunities as the central elements of effective systems, this chapter synthesizes the current research on the state role in improving public schools and, in particular, the construction of "statewide systems of support" as defined under No Child Left Behind.

Sam Redding, "An Evolution in American Education." From colonial times to the 21st Century, systematic approaches to educating children have had to adapt to the changing tastes and priorities of localities' diverse populaces. Parents now demand greater control in where and how their children are educated. And the Civil Rights movement, spawned in large measure by *Brown v. Board of Education* (1954), has reinforced our democracy's highest domestic goal—to best educate all of our children to prepare them for the challenging demands of the future. In accordance with NCLB, statewide systems of support require cooperation of the federal government, state departments of education, and district and school staff.

Part C: Profiles of Key States

Thomas Kerins, Susan Hanes, and **Carole Perlman** conducted site visits with the state education agencies in four states, interviewing personnel responsible for the statewide system of support with an interview protocol aligned with the framework presented in this Handbook. They also collected artifacts from the state agency staff and conducted telephone interviews with superintendents and principals in districts served by the statewide system of support. Based on this gathering of descriptive information about each state, the authors provide profiles of the states, the salient features of their statewide systems of support, and the observations and recommendations of the people interviewed.

Part D: The Role of Comprehensive Centers

Marilyn Murphy describes the U.S. Department of Education's system of Comprehensive Centers, both Regional Centers and Content Centers, and explains the role of these technical assistance providers in assisting states with the development and improvement of their statewide systems of support. Following Murphy's introductory chapter, eight Regional Centers describe their work with statewide systems of support over the past two years.

Part E: Tools to Strengthen the Statewide System of Support

A design team of CII staff and consultants, with an eye to the evidence and framework presented in this Handbook and the experiences of the states and Comprehensive Centers, developed a set of tools to guide an SEA in self-assessing its current system of support and planning for its improvement.

REFERENCES

Rennie Center for Education Research & Policy. (2005). *Reaching capacity: A blueprint for the state role in improving low performing schools and districts.* Boston, MA: Author.

U.S. Department of Education. (2004). *Evaluation of Title I accountability systems and school improvement efforts.* Washington, DC: Author. Retrieved from http://www.eric.ed.gov/ERICWebPortal/custom/portlets/recordDetails/detailmini.jsp?_nfpb=true&_&ERICExtSearch_SearchValue_0=ED483058&ERICExtSearch_SearchType_0=eric_accno&accno=ED483058

Walberg, H. J. (Ed.). (2007). *Handbook on restructuring and substantial school improvement.* Charlotte, NC: Information Age.

Herbert J. Walberg *serves as Chief Scientific Advisor to the Center on Innovation & Improvement and is a Distinguished Visiting Fellow at the Stanford University Hoover Institution.*

CHAPTER 2

POLICY TO REINFORCE CHANGING STATE ROLE

Brett Lane

Since the publication of *A Nation at Risk* in 1983, the public's focus on the performance of public schools has steadily increased. The emergence of the standards movement and the 1994 and 2001 re-authorizations of the 1965 Elementary and Secondary Education Act (ESEA) reflect the efforts of the states and the federal government to develop mechanisms to sharpen our collective attention on under-performing schools and to provide, at least in theory, the tools needed to improve student performance in districts and schools. As the focus on under-performing schools intensifies, states and state education agencies are compelled to figure out how they can scale up improvement efforts across growing numbers of districts and schools that have been identified through state and federal accountability systems. The urgent need to close the achievement gap and to improve the educational outcomes of low-income and minority students remains one of the most important challenges and "problems" that we face.

Handbook on Statewide Systems of Support, pages 9–13
Copyright © 2008 The Academic Development Institute and Information Age Publishing
All rights of reproduction in any form reserved.

THE SHIFTING ROLE OF STATE EDUCATION AGENCIES

State education agencies have a unique and vital role in crafting statewide strategies to scale up improvement efforts across multiple districts and schools. The No Child Left Behind (NCLB) Act of 2001 provides a federal mandate for states to develop "statewide systems of support" intended to build the capacity of under-performing districts and schools (albeit within the limits of Title I). Likewise, some state legislatures have been proactive in creating new policy and strengthening the legal footing by which state education agencies can intervene in under-performing schools. It is clear that we have reached the tipping point, and that state education agencies now play a pivotal role in helping under-performing districts and schools to improve, a role that is different and in many ways more difficult than the role they have traditionally played.

Barring a major reshaping of the architecture of ESEA in its next re-authorization, state education agencies will continue their expanded role in providing support to under-performing districts and schools. As a result, state education agencies face a policy implementation challenge leading to the question: How can states provide viable and meaningful support to under-performing districts and schools within current policy and resource constraints? Answering this question becomes increasingly difficult when we acknowledge that state education agencies (and the people who make decisions within those agencies) function within a state of heightened urgency and increased pressure to intervene on the behalf of students.

If state education agencies are to play a major role in crafting support strategies that address the needs of districts and schools, and do so at scale, then it is critically important that states create the right mix of incentives and consider capacity-building strategies necessary to support districts and schools. This would create the opportunities that cultivate sustainable improvement. Rhim, Hassel, and Redding expertly examine how states are addressing these three elements—incentives, capacity-building strategies, and opportunities—which together provide a framework for the types of discussions taking place in states across the country as state officials grapple with improving under-performing districts and schools. In particular, states' differentiation of support services based on individual school needs, states' use of networking strategies to build capacity among districts and schools with similar needs, and the increased focus on the district as the primary entry point are three emergent and promising strategies.

THE CHALLENGES TO DEVELOPING A COHESIVE
STATEWIDE SYSTEM OF SUPPORT

Developing an effective statewide system of support is by no means an easy task, and the states face considerable challenges in this work. In particular, there are three challenges that influence a state's ability to develop meaningful incentives and to mobilize the type of supports and resources needed for improving targeted districts and schools. These challenges are characterized as: (1) negotiating and balancing expectations to monitor and provide support; (2) building organizational cohesiveness around district and school improvement; and (3) addressing external conditions hindering district and school improvement.

Negotiating Expectations to Monitor and Provide Support

As states refine their methods to provide targeted support to under-performing districts and schools, negotiating the proper mix of compliance and support monitoring will be an increasingly important task. Accomplishing this task will require states to have finite resources, time, and personnel capable of crafting support strategies. Also, it is often the case that monitoring and reporting requirements take precedence over providing support to identified schools. While there are historical and very important reasons for states to actively monitor federal funds and to continue to do so, the reality is that in meeting monitoring and reporting requirements, states are often constrained in their ability to devise and implement support strategies. While the 4 percent set-aside of Title I funds designated for state activities is a source of financial support to assist districts and schools, some states are finding it difficult to provide both compliance monitoring and a fully functional statewide system of support with current funding levels. Without fiscal support from federal and state sources, in addition to the 4 percent set-aside, states will be stretched to mobilize the resources needed to develop the high-quality systems of support called for in Title I.

Building Organizational Cohesiveness Around District and School Improvement

NCLB requires that the classification of districts and schools be based on subgroup performance. This should impel statewide systems of support to provide, or at least have access to, expertise in multiple content areas serving students with varied and targeted needs (e.g., English language learners, special education, and Title I). This leads to a simple question: Are state education agencies built to provide targeted and differentiated support to under-performing districts and schools? The answer to this question varies. Some states are better situated than others, but no state has it figured out. A second challenge now arises. How can a state education agency create the necessary internal conditions (e.g., the configuration of offices and ways of working together) so that one of its central functions is to leverage state and federal resources and provide differentiated support to under-performing districts and schools?

States that have tackled this question have come up with a number of different solutions and methods of working together. Common among these solutions is an understanding that the development of a cohesive statewide system of support requires offices (and the individuals in those offices) to collectively relinquish their institutional distinctions and leverage their expertise towards the shared goal of supporting and improving under-performing districts and schools. Clearly, this is easier said than done. Many states, often through federal funding, have built extensive infrastructures focusing on specific populations and areas of expertise. Accessing specialized knowledge so that it supports and aligns with overall school improvement efforts, and doing so without destroying the source and passion needed to advance specialized knowledge, is a tricky endeavor. However, some states are making (or are considering) this shift through significant organizational changes. Organizing around school improvement and leadership, rather than by categorical funding streams, content areas, or grade levels, is more effective.

Addressing External Conditions Hindering District and School Improvement

The third challenge that states face is to acknowledge and articulate the conditions and policies that are outside of the state education agency's sphere of influence, yet dramatically impact the ability of districts and schools to make sustained improvements. Examples of external conditions and policies that are outside agency spheres of influence include low and disparate teacher pay across districts/counties, school funding, unequal placement of highly qualified teachers, and limits on educational alternatives, such as charter schools. More often than not, state education agencies find themselves reacting to external conditions and events (e.g., litigation, budget shortfalls, and shifts in state and federal policy) and adapting their efforts rather than playing an active role as a policy advocate. In some instances the Commissioner of Education and other high ranking officials may have a role in working to change policy and are able to do so, while in other cases state education officials may know exactly what needs to be done to help a school or an entire district, but are powerless to act.

A state system of support cannot be expected to dramatically impact school and student academic achievement if external policy conditions constrain state officials, or their designees, from making decisions that provide the type of support that will actually make a difference. The challenge for states and state education agencies is to find a way to capture the extensive knowledge and expertise of state education officials—especially those who work in the trenches with districts and schools on a daily basis—and to transfer and mobilize this knowledge into specific and feasible policy alternatives and legislation.

CRAFTING POLICY TO SUPPORT STATE EDUCATION AGENCIES

State education agencies are focusing resources and prioritizing their efforts towards developing statewide approaches to support under-performing districts and schools. The framework developed by Rhim, Hassel, and Redding provides an excellent basis for continued discussions and refinement of these support systems. However, the challenges outlined here suggest that the success and viability of states' systems of support rely on (1) the crafting of federal and state policies that reinforce efforts to build a cohesive system of support and (2) the development of external conditions that are conducive to quickly scaling up improvement efforts. While state education agencies are by no means excused from their responsibility to serve schools, it is important to acknowledge that other policy actors (e.g., state legislatures, governors, and federal education policy officials) establish much of the policy environment within which state education agencies exist, and it is these policy actors that ultimately have the ability to alter that policy environment.

Brett Lane *is a managing specialist at the Education Alliance at Brown University and the project director of the Comprehensive School Reform Support and Capacity Building Program. Mr. Lane specializes in education and accountability policy and is currently investigating how education policy is effectively implemented in complex educational systems, focusing on the interactions among state, district, and school leaders.*

CHAPTER 3

A MOUNTAIN BEYOND MOUNTAINS

Paul Reville

One of the strengths of standards-based accountability systems is that the data they provide not only force educators to re-examine their practices, but also compel policymakers to continually confront the gap between their expectations for student achievement and the realities in the field. Performance data motivates the search for gap-closing solutions in practice as well as policy. In practice, the persistent achievement gaps have led us into much deeper discussions about our core business of teaching and learning, to strategize on the improvement of instructional practice, to utilize data to inform practice, and to invest in higher quality professional development.

Meanwhile, policymakers, desperate to find solutions to these same persistent gap problems, are considering measures like wrap-around services to boost student readiness to learn, expanded school time to provide for additional instruction, and early childhood education to ensure that all students enter school prepared to learn. While there isn't yet consensus on which policy and practice strategies are most likely to succeed in closing the gaps and boosting student achievement, it is safe to say that we wouldn't even be talking about these subjects without the pressure applied by our standards-based accountability systems.

Handbook on Statewide Systems of Support, pages 15–18

Another important subject that arises from standards/accountability/ gaps discourse concerns building the capacity of states, and particularly state education agencies (SEAs), to fulfill the implied obligations incurred during the 1990s when states assumed a leadership role in setting standards and holding districts and schools responsible for performance. Although the subject of building "state systems of support" is lately often discussed in the context of the legal obligations mandated by the No Child Left Behind Act (NCLB), there has been an educational and moral imperative to provide such systems of support ever since the states began enacting standards-based reform in the early 1990s. Nonetheless, most states have failed to adequately meet the challenge of providing adequate technical assistance and support as a function of their new accountability role.

These "capacity building" obligations, unforeseen in many states, followed directly from the logic of standards-based reform: if a state was going to publicly "call out" a district or school for "under-performance" then that state was obligated to provide technical assistance and support to help the district/school improve performance. My colleague, Richard Elmore, has described this concept as "reciprocal accountability." Elmore posits, "For every increment of performance I demand from you, I have an equal responsibility to provide you with the capacity to meet that expectation" (2002).

Translated into the world of educational accountability, it goes like this: if the state is going to expect districts and schools to dramatically improve their performance to unprecedented levels where all students attain proficiency, then the states must help educators to accomplish this new demand. Ideally, support should be provided to educators prior to the full demands of accountability taking hold, but at a minimum, once accountability stakes are implemented, the state must stand ready to help.

NCLB makes explicit the new, substantially higher expectations for SEAs by demanding a variety of support functions from the states. However, little effort is made through NCLB to build state capacity. This leaves under-staffed, under-funded education agencies, with a history and culture of compliance monitoring, to suddenly reinvent themselves into leadership agencies. Cast in this new role, they are now expected to provide in-depth support to schools and districts that are striving to achieve policymakers' ambitious proficiency goals for all students.

The NCLB mandates attain urgency by the ever-increasing number of schools and districts identified as needing assistance. This urgency creates a rare opportunity for rebuilding SEAs into potent leadership and support organizations. However, the focus of the new work needs broader definition than simply conducting interventions in poorly performing schools. Rather, these new efforts should be shaped by a conception of the state's role in the general improvement of all schools.

Serving all schools is a tall order, especially in light of the prevailing limits of expertise and financial resources. Even in the narrow field of intervention, SEAs are hampered by constraints. As Sunderman and Orfield (2006) have argued, "…the record on intervention was poor, the amount of funding appropriated under NCLB was small and did not represent additional money but a reallocation of Title I funds."

States will need to curtail certain existing roles, locate and build new school improvement capacity, consolidate current strengths, integrate services, and rely on a variety of outside providers in order to get this job done. At the same time, SEAs will need to cope with persistently glaring capacity limitations of the schools and districts they are trying to serve.

Rhim, Hassel, and Redding's impressive essay describes the new challenge facing SEAs in detail. They review the limited literature on this subject and point to some important considerations, next steps, and cautions in the execution of this work. Their major contribution is to provide a theoretical framework for the analysis of experience and literature in this domain, a framework that offers three significant categories for viewing this work: incentives, capabilities, and opportunities. This framework is a helpful guide for analytical purposes and for planning future policy and practice.

Rhim, Hassel, and Redding's introduction to the challenges of building state systems of support will enable us to move forward to meet this often neglected accountability obligation. With any luck, we will seize the opportunity presented by the urgency of this current predicament (large numbers of schools in need and limited capacity to help) to launch the state education function into a new, more constructive era.

The transformed SEA will need to guide its systemic school improvement work with a clear action plan toward school betterment. The focus of that plan should point to the systemic improvement of instruction, and by extension, on the state's role in improving instruction. How can states assist districts to help schools to help teachers improve instruction? How can teachers, through enhanced practice, help students to learn more?

This new work for SEAs must be informed by current practice that recognizes some SEAs are already doing pieces of this work, even if those pieces are sometimes fragmented and in need of focus and coherence. Advocates for strengthened SEAs will need to confront the political realities of this work. Most SEAs have small to non-existent constituencies. They typically have little political influence and are sometimes regarded as annoying bureaucracies.

Although more and more educators in the field will clamor for SEAs to provide guidance and support "if they expect us to achieve a high standard of proficiency for all students," the reality is still that if you put a dollar on the typical superintendent's desk and ask whether it should go to the district or the SEA, the superintendent will, almost always, and for obvious reasons, favor the district.

Doing this work will undeniably require new resources. There's no avoiding this reality. It's fine to talk about using all kinds of partners to build capacity, but partners need support, too. Certainly, efficiencies can be achieved in the implementation of existing work, but most state agencies are already painfully lean, while their staffs are usually underpaid and overburdened.

SEAs will need to engage in serious new strategic planning to support districts and schools. They'll need to do rigorous and penetrating analyses of current operations coupled with realistic assessments of their respective environments and opportunities. Tough decisions will be required for coordination and prioritizing.

The Rennie Center for Education Research and Policy has identified several key points of entry for this work: leadership development and strategic planning; professional development with particular attention to guidance on curriculum and instruction; and assistance with assessment, especially formative assessment, as well as guidance on data utilization for informing instructional practice.

For most SEAs, this will be risky, experimental work that, at least initially, will not be well supported. Agencies will need to attempt and sometimes fail at this work. Such work will require strong leadership and a robust dialogue with the field, especially with districts that should be the prime customers of new SEA support work. States cannot possibly provide substantial support at the school level because of the sheer numbers, so the district level is the logical place to target capacity-building interventions.

From cultural and organizational points of view, this will be groundbreaking work for many SEAs. SEAs will have to strike a delicate balance between the incentives, opportunities, and capabilities functions that Rhim, Hassel, and Redding describe. In other words, SEAs will have to balance their accountability, regulatory, and technical assistance roles in a new way that focuses sharply on school improvement.

The challenging work described in this volume is certainly daunting, yet an absolute prerequisite if we are to realize the ambitious goal of education reform—all children achieving proficiency. Let's get started.

Paul Reville *is the director of the Education Policy and Management Program at the Harvard Graduate School of Education where he is a lecturer on educational policy and politics. He is president of the Rennie Center for Education Research and Policy, an independent education policy "think tank."*

PART B

EVIDENCE, FRAMEWORK, AND EVOLUTION

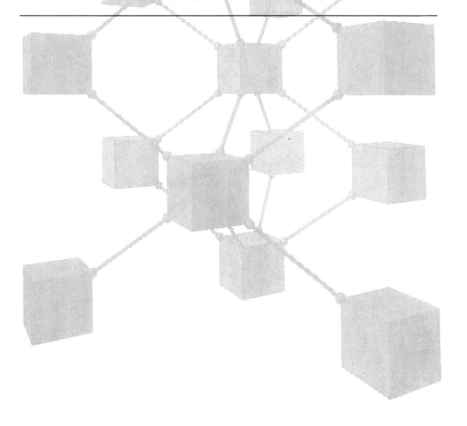

CHAPTER 4

STATE ROLE IN SUPPORTING SCHOOL IMPROVEMENT[1]

Lauren Morando Rhim, Bryan Hassel, and Sam Redding

ABSTRACT

States and, specifically, state education agencies (SEAs) have historically focused on promulgating regulations, setting and developing policy, disseminating funds, and collecting data. Under the progressively more high-stakes accountability systems that are a central feature of contemporary education policy, the state's role increasingly includes direct support and technical assistance to districts and individual schools to help them build capacity for meaningful change that will lead to improved academic outcomes. Though the literature related to state education agencies' involvement in school improvement is relatively thin and evolving, it provides a framework to consider how to construct an effective system. Building on research that identifies incentives, capabilities, and opportunities as the central elements of effective systems, this chapter synthesizes the current research on the state role in improving public schools and, in particular, the construction of "statewide systems of support" as defined under No Child Left Behind.

Handbook on Statewide Systems of Support, pages 21–60
21

INTRODUCTION

> Each State shall establish a statewide system of intensive and sustained sup-
> port and improvement for local educational agencies and schools receiving
> funds under this part, in order to increase the opportunity for all students
> served by those agencies and schools to meet the State's academic content
> standards and student academic achievement standards. (No Child Left Be-
> hind Act of 2001 20 U.S.C.A. § 6301-6578)

Evolution of State Role in School Improvement [2]

States and, specifically, state education agencies (SEAs) have historically
played a very distinct role in public schools. They interpret and enforce policies established by Congress and state legislatures. And, they facilitate data
collection in partnership with district policymakers and school-level practitioners (Hannaway & Woodroffe, 2003; Lusi, 1997). Yet, under increasingly high-stakes accountability systems, the SEA's role is evolving. SEAs are
increasingly being required to provide direct support and technical assistance to districts and individual schools to help them build capacity for
meaningful change that will improve academic outcomes. The emerging
and expanding role of SEAs is especially apparent in the lowest performing
schools (Sunderman & Orfield, 2006).

While being pushed to take a relatively proactive role to improve schools,
SEAs themselves face limits associated with the broader state policy context
that influences their actions. Of note, SEA policies and practices are largely
constrained by their state legislators and their governor. Yet, SEAs are often called upon to testify before legislators and advise their governor on
education-related matters. So, while SEAs have increasing responsibilities
with somewhat limited authority, they do have the potential to influence
their policy context.

The evolution of state systems of support has its roots in the push for
high standards instigated by the 1983 publication of *A Nation at Risk*, which
implored the nation to increase rigor in American public education. The
report set in motion a series of reforms at the state level over the next
two decades, during which most states established academic standards, de-
ployed assessments to measure students' mastery of them, and instituted
consequences for schools that fell short. At the national level, the contemporary standards movement was articulated by the National Education
Goals Panel and codified in 1994 by Congress in the Goals 2000: Educate
America Act. This Act endorsed learning standards and standards-based
assessments as ways to measure progress toward national goals. The reauthorization of the Elementary and Secondary Education Act (Improving
America's Schools) in the same year called upon states to build systems of

standards and assessments and to provide support for schools to improve. The No Child Left Behind Act of 2001 directs that states and, specifically, SEAs functioning as the executive branch of state government responsible for implementing policy, provide a statewide system of support for schools in need of improvement.

States are required to reserve a prescribed percentage of Title I Part A funds (4% in 2007) for school improvement without reducing any local education agency (LEA) Title I funding below the previous year's level. States are required to dedicate 95% of these reserved funds to districts to support improvement efforts at schools identified as low-performing. Five percent is slated to support state responsibilities related to improvement. Though previous authorizations of the Elementary and Secondary Act sought to increase the state's role, and multiple state education agencies were actively engaged in school improvement prior to the Act, NCLB has heightened the focus on the role states can play in support of school and district improvement.

NCLB requires states to prioritize support, providing it

- first to schools in corrective action and schools for which the district has not carried out responsibilities regarding corrective action or restructuring;
- then to districts with schools identified as in need of improvement; and
- then to other Title I districts and schools needing support and assistance.

NCLB defines three means of providing support: (a) school support teams, (b) distinguished principals and teachers from effective Title I schools, and (c) "other" approaches. School support teams are groups of "skillful and experienced individuals" typically including some or all of the following:

- highly qualified or distinguished teachers and principals;
- pupil services personnel;
- parents;
- representatives of institutions of higher education;
- representatives of educational laboratories or regional technical assistance centers;
- representatives of outside consultant groups; or
- other individuals that the SEA, in consultation with the LEA, may deem appropriate (USDOE, 2006, p. 17; NCLB §1117(a)(5)(a)).

As outlined in NCLB, school support teams are charged with assisting schools in need of improvement to (a) review and analyze all facets of the school's operation; (b) collaborate with school staff, LEA staff, and parents to design and implement a school improvement plan; (c) monitor implementation of the improvement plan and provide additional assistance as requested; and (d) provide feedback on a regular schedule.

NCLB defines distinguished educators as teachers and principals who have been "especially successful in improving academic achievement" in Title I schools (§1117(a)(3) and (4)(A)). According to the non-regulatory guidance, "other approaches" to support may include engaging external agencies such as institutions of higher education, educational service agencies or other local consortia, or private providers of scientifically based technical assistance to provide technical assistance and support. In addition, the network of United States Department of Education funded Regional Comprehensive Centers, Content Centers, and Regional Educational Laboratories was created for the purpose of supporting school improvement, including providing assistance to states and districts identified as in need of improvement (USDOE, 2006).

NCLB and related policy guidance outlines the purpose, general structure, and goals of state systems of support. Some scholars and observers, however, regard this framework as a floor rather than a ceiling for the state role in school improvement. For example, some have argued that efforts to improve low-performing schools should be part of a broader coherent strategy to improve all schools, not an isolated initiative (Dwyer et al., 2005; Mazzeo & Berman, n.d.). Others have suggested that SEAs reconsider their existing systems and strive to develop new approaches to help districts and schools achieve the goal of proficiency for all students (Council of Chief State School Officers [CCSSO], 2006). Still others have called for a thorough rethinking of the state's role. Based on their in-depth examination of school improvement in Massachusetts, for example, Reville and others characterize "building capacity to broker and deliver the services educators need to enhance their practice" as "pivotal" to SEAs transitioning from "bureaucratic, compliance-oriented" organizations to "service-oriented organizations" (2005, p. 20). Rather than just a means of complying with federal requirements, these new state roles are viewed by these authors as an appropriate evolution of state leadership and an opportunity for SEAs to infuse a new level of coherence and focus to complex, multilayered state systems of public education. The current expanding role of the state aligns with the history of U.S. education policy in which state, not federal, constitutions recognize education as a public interest (Tyack & Hansot in Sunderman & Orfield, 2006). While NCLB shines a spotlight on state systems of support, these structures arguably represent the evolution of states' responsibility to provide high-quality public education to all of its citizens.

The need for state support and technical assistance is great, and under the existing NCLB accountability framework, the need will most likely continue to grow as more schools and districts are identified as in need of improvement (Dwyer et al., 2005; Reville, Coggins, & Candon, 2005). In the fall of 2006, 8,446 schools and 1,624 districts were identified as in need of improvement according to NCLB. A total of 2,399 districts have at least one school identified as in need of improvement (Archer, 2006a).

To meet this growing need, states must address significant challenges to refine existing support structures and develop new ones (Laguarda, 2003). Most notably, SEAs have limited human and fiscal capacity to provide direct support and training to districts and individual schools (Archer, 2006a; Dwyer et al., 2005; Education Commission of the States [ECS], 2002; Reville, 2004). Stagnating wages, poor working conditions, and low prestige are all reportedly hindering SEAs' ability to compete with local districts to recruit and retain personnel with relevant expertise (Archer 2006a; Institute for Educational Leadership [IEL], 2001; Reville et al., 2005; Reville, 2007; P. Reville, personal communication, June 2, 2007). Consequently, in order to craft and support strong statewide systems of support, SEAs will need to dedicate resources to developing their internal capacity. Observers from researchers to judges have found that SEAs lack the capacity they need to support substantive improvement in schools and districts. A lack of capacity at the SEA level was a key challenge to the early implementation of the standards-based reform movement (Lusi, 1997; Massell, 1998) and, specifically, efforts to infuse accountability into schools (Mintrop & Trujillo, 2005). The spate of fiscal equity and adequacy lawsuits shine a bright light on the role of states in developing and implementing policies that foster high-quality schools across an entire state (Rebell, 2007). For example, in response to a protracted lawsuit filed by students regarding the adequacy of their education dating back to 1997, a Massachusetts Supreme Court judge recently ruled that limited state and district capacity "contributed significantly" (Botsford 2004 in Reville, 2004) to school system deficiencies. In particular, the judge ruled that the systems the state developed to support schools were inadequate (*Hancock v. Driscoll*, Botsford report, 2004, p. 27 as cited in Reville, 2004).

Critics of NCLB question the logic of further expanding the state's role absent corresponding increases in funding (Sunderman & Orfield, 2006). Indeed, SEAs—frequently perceived to be bureaucratic, regulatory agencies rather than sources of substantive support—struggle to leverage the political capital to secure substantive funding increases (P. Reville, personal communication, June 2, 2007). In the absence of additional funds, expanding the state's role related to systems of support will necessitate shifts of human and fiscal resources. Given the limited federal appropriations dedicated to school improvement, states and, specifically, the SEAs will need to do more to reallocate resources. Rather than developing individual programs traditionally driven by specific funding sources (e.g., Title I, bilingual education, special education), SEAs will need to develop cohesive support systems based on a finely honed theory of action about how to stimulate substantive school improvement.

Understanding State Support: Incentives, Capacity, and Opportunity

This chapter presents a synthesis of the emerging literature related to NCLB-defined statewide systems of support and research that preceded NCLB but focused on the role of states in school improvement (American Institutes for Research [AIR], 2006; Archer, 2006 a; Barney & Robyn, 2005; CSSO, 2003; David, Kannapel, & McDiarmid, 2000; Dwyer et al., 2005; ECS, 2002; Hannaway & Woodroffe, 2003; Hanushek & Raymond, 2004; Heck & Weiss, 2005; Holdskom, 2001; IEL, 2001; Laguarda, 2003; Lane & Garcia, 2004; Lane, Seager, & Frankel, 2005; Lusi, 1997; Massell, 1998; Mintrop & Trujillo, 2005; Mazzeo & Berman, n.d.; Reville et al., 2005; Reville, 2004, 2007; Sunderman & Orfield, 2006; Westat, 2006). The literature on state involvement in school improvement is relatively thin and still evolving. A rigorous analysis of the outcomes associated with growing statewide systems of support has yet to be conducted. Therefore, while not rigorous in terms of establishing causal connections, the research provides a framework for SEAs considering how to construct an effective system of support.

In conducting the literature review, we sought to document how states have structured their efforts to support school improvement and identify potentially promising practices. The resulting framework serves as the structure for the case studies of state systems in this volume. State systems of support operate within a broader system driven in part by federal education policy, whereby Congress passes legislation that states are expected to implement. Under NCLB, this system is comprised of its own set of incentives (e.g., loss of Title I funding), capacity building initiatives (e.g., grants), and opportunities (e.g., regulatory flexibility) promulgated to foster action at the state, district, and school levels that supports improved school performance.

The review is not a definitive assessment of the state's role in school improvement, nor an evaluation of the merits of state versus district initiatives, nor a critique of the theory of logic driving the development of state systems of support outlined in NCLB, and it is not a comparison of different states' approaches to providing support. Rather, given the prominent role NCLB assigns states, the literature review is our attempt to synthesize the existing literature for practitioners wrestling with how to develop systems and for researchers interested in examining the effectiveness of the systems.

Building on the work of Bryk, Shipps, Hill, and Lake (1998) on school decentralization, Hill and Celio (1998), in their examination of efforts to "fix" urban schools, propose that successful systemic reform requires three key components: incentives, capacity, and opportunities. Incentives are inducements designed to motivate personnel to change or improve behavior that influences education outcomes. Capacity entails the school's ability to respond to incentives in ways that improve outcomes and includes investment in new ideas, instructional methods, and human capacity. Opportunity represents the environment in which schools operate, particularly policies that enable schools to operate successfully absent "rules that limit and routinize instruction" and limit allocation of staff and money (Hill & Celio, 1998, p. 75). Our review of the literature on the state's role in school improvement and restructuring revealed that these components provide a helpful conceptual framework when contemplating creating effective state support systems.

The sum of these three components is arguably greater than the parts. Research has demonstrated that incentives without capacity cannot spur meaningful and sustainable change, nor can opportunity without incentives and capacity (Elmore, n.d.; Malen & Rice, 2004; Massell, 1998; Mintrop & Trujillo, 2005). At the same time, devoting more resources to capacity-building activities like professional development without changes in the incentive structure appears equally problematic (Elmore, 2002). In considering the literature on the state role in school improvement through the lenses of incentives, capacity, and opportunity, it is essential to consider them as individual legs of a three-legged stool as opposed to separate components that could be applied effectively in isolation.

FUNCTIONS OF A STATEWIDE SYSTEM OF SUPPORT

The literature on the state role in improving schools and districts depicts examples of incentives, capacity, and opportunities that states are providing to schools and districts in need of improvement. The following sections define each component of the framework, introduce examples of strategies being implemented and, where possible, review evidence of successful practices.

Provide Incentives for Change

One way that states can provide support for school improvement is to create incentives for educators to engage in change. Incentives are an important part of the process because without strong motivation to take on the hard work that change entails, no amount of capacity or opportunity can make change happen (Hanushek, 1994). Arguably, the most powerful incentives created by states are those instituted in legislation, which are outside the direct control of SEAs. Nonetheless, as implementers of such legislation, as managers of significant funding programs, and policymaking bodies in their own right, SEAs are in a position to create incentives directly and to enhance—or diminish—the power of incentives established by state legislation.

State-level incentives for improvement come in many forms, described here under the following headings:

- Public disclosure: standards, accountability, and information about results
- Negative incentives: consequences of low school performance
- Positive incentives: contingent funding, autonomy, and recognition
- Market-oriented incentives: changing the "market" structure of public schooling

Public Disclosure: Standards, Accountability, and Information About Results

One of the most significant policy developments over the last three decades has been the widespread adoption of "standards-based reform" by states (Smith & O'Day, 1991). Even prior to NCLB, virtually every state had established a system of standards specifying what students should know and be able to do at different grade levels; instituted mandatory assessments to determine the extent to which students are meeting those standards; and begun reporting the results of these tests publicly. NCLB required all states to take these actions as a condition of Title I funding. NCLB also sought to standardize state practice to some degree with regard to issues such as what grade levels states must test, what kinds of disaggregation by subgroup they must perform, and what information they must report to the public.

Standards, assessments, and information potentially play both indirect and direct roles in a state's efforts to create incentives for performance. Indirectly, they provide the basis on which the state enacts various remedies for under-performance—a subject addressed in the next subsection. More directly, standards, assessments, and information arguably create incentives in their own right for school and district improvement. According to this theory, by revealing the performance of schools and districts, information itself spurs educators to take steps to improve (Hanushek & Raymond, 2004). One study of Michigan's implementation of No Child Left Behind, for example, concluded that the "spotlight that NCLB shines on the performance of schools coupled with the threat of sanctions appears to have worked to persuade schools to systematically improve their own performance, despite the fact that only a handful of schools have been subjected to significant sanctions" (Plank & Dunbar, 2007, p. 4, emphasis in original).

Hanushek & Raymond's comprehensive analysis of NAEP data relative to state accountability systems concluded that "regardless of design flaws," accountability systems have a positive impact on academic achievement and the effect is due primarily to the public disclosure aspect of current systems (p. 414).

The degree to which standards, assessments, and information have this kind of incentive value depends upon a range of policy decisions made by states. In the implementation of No Child Left Behind, it has become clear that states have significant latitude on policies such as:

- the level of rigor of student learning standards;
- the ambitiousness of thresholds set for student proficiency;
- the degree of alignment of state assessments with state standards;
- the strictness of policies regarding student participation in tests;
- the user-friendliness with which results are reported to the public;
- the degree of dissemination of results to the public;

and many other particulars related to standards, assessments, and information systems (Center on Education Policy [CEP], 2006; ECS, 2007c). Changes in these variables can significantly alter the incentive value of accountability systems. And states can significantly increase or decrease the potency of incentives. States, for example, determine the timeline on which to release information about state test scores and determinations of adequate yearly progress. According to an analysis by Manna (2007), states vary widely in the timeliness of this information dissemination. Only five states released their final AYP determinations for 2005-06 prior to July 2006; 15 released them September or later (Manna, 2007, p. 7). Test score availability influences the degree to which test performance serves as an incentive that can shape behavior. If test scores are not released in a timely manner, it is difficult to attach incentives that could influence behavior in a timely manner. An additional concern is the potential for incentives to have unintended or perverse consequences. For instance, high stakes attached to testing can spur cheating, and public reporting can lead to misleading or misrepresented data (Nichols & Berliner, 2007). High-stakes tests also encourage over-identification for special education and rising drop-out rates (Hannaway & Woodroffe, 2003). Effective incentives, therefore, require a larger infrastructure that monitors performance in a manner that can detect unintended consequences.

Negative Incentives: Consequences of Low School Performance

States can also create incentives for change through the remedies they establish for low school performance. Most of the remedies states undertake are capacity-oriented: they aim to provide some sort of help to schools and districts to enhance their capacity to improve. Remedies like these are discussed in the capacity section, below. Other remedies states use are incentive-oriented: they aim, in part, to induce schools and districts to change by threatening some kind of undesirable consequence if low performance persists.

While states generally had adopted some incentive-oriented remedies on their own, NCLB placed some parameters on states' remedies through its "corrective action" and "restructuring" provisions. As with NCLB's requirements for standards, assessments, and information, however, the Act's mandates regarding corrective action and restructuring leave wide latitude for states to determine the power of incentive-oriented remedies (CEP, 2006; Scott, Jennings, & Rentner, 2007). This latitude arises in part because NCLB only specifies a menu of possible corrective action and restructuring approaches, allowing districts to choose how to proceed. In some cases, existing state law has limited the options and sanctions that are actually available to states and districts (DiBiase, 2005). Latitude also exists because NCLB allows states to play a range of roles in overseeing districts' implementation of the remedies. As a result, one early study of 13 states' use of restructuring found that states differ widely in the interpretation of their role in school restructuring, which results in a range of SEA involvement. Some states have chosen more significant involvement in district decision making, such as participating in plan development, modification, and monitoring. On the other end of the spectrum, some SEAs do not collect or review plans and provide little oversight of the LEAs. Of the 13 states surveyed, 7 SEAs were found to have approval processes of varying rigor for all school restructuring plans; 2 collect plans but do not officially approve them; 1 collects plans of only some schools; and 3 do not collect plans at all (DiBiase, 2005).

Positive Incentives: Contingent Funding, Autonomy, and Recognition

Another way states can create incentives for change is by making certain benefits contingent on taking certain actions or achieving certain results. Funding is the most prominent example of such a benefit. States provide about half of all K-12 education revenues, a proportion that has risen steadily for 100 years (NCES, 2005, Table 152). With this increasing control of the purse strings has come increasing potential leverage for states over the actions of districts and schools. A long line of literature on federal grants to states makes clear that contingent grants are a blunt instrument for influencing actions within the federal system (e.g., Beam & Conlan, 2002; Elmore & McLaughlin, 1998), and some of the same challenges are likely to limit the effectiveness of state contingent grants as well. But since states provide a substantially greater proportion of education funding, their potential for impact is greater.

States have also experimented in recent years with using funding to affect individual behavior. Examples of these incentives (currently used in multiple states) are inducements for talented people to enter teaching (e.g., ECS, 2007a; Fowler, 2003), for existing good teachers or new entrants to teach in hard-to-staff schools or demanding subjects (Kowal, Hassel, & Hassel, 2007), for talented leaders to take on the challenge of turning around low-performing schools (Duke et al., 2005), and for high performing teachers based on student outcomes (Podgursky & Springer, 2007).

Funding is just one kind of benefit that could be offered as an incentive. Other possibilities including awarding greater autonomy to schools that achieve desired results, or using non-financial rewards, such as public recognition, to motivate performance. By and large, little evaluation has been conducted of the effectiveness of these incentives, but they remain as tools in states' incentive toolkit.

Market-Oriented Incentives: Changing the "Market" Structure of Public Schooling

Finally, states can seek to create incentives by changing the "market" structure of public schooling. Analysts of education have long theorized that if states broke the "exclusive franchise" (Kolderie, 1990) districts hold on providing public education, they could provide stronger inducements for districts and schools within them to improve. The argument goes that, forced to compete with other districts, independent charter schools, or even private schools for students and funds, conventional public districts and schools will have added motivation to take the steps needed to raise student achievement. In recent decades, states have indeed enacted many policies altering the market structure of public education. Forty states and the District of Columbia now have charter school laws; 43 have provisions allowing inter-district transfers; and 12 have either a law providing publicly funded vouchers to attend private schools, or a law offering some kind of tax credit or deduction related to private school tuition, or both (ECS, 2007b; McNeil, 2007).

Evidence about how much incentive power these measures have has been mixed. While several studies have found positive effects of competition on student achievement (e.g., Hoxby, 2004), the overall research base on the topic is inconclusive (Gill et al., 2001). Hess (2002) suggests that voucher programs' impact on conventional districts is diminished by program design factors, such as the relatively small market share allowed to use vouchers, and the fact that states cushioned the financial impact of voucher choices on districts and individual schools.

As with other kinds of incentives discussed in this section, NCLB imposes some requirements on states and districts with regard to providing public school choice to students whose schools have failed to make AYP for two or more years running. However, as with the other incentives, NCLB leaves states broad latitude in implementing this provision. Research to date has documented that few students are opting to take advantage of these choice options as currently constructed by states and districts (Hannaway & Cohodes, 2007; Olson, 2005; Sunderman, Kim, & Orfield, 2005). Possible explanations for parents not taking advantage of choice options under NCLB are the choice timeline that results in parents being notified of the choice option late in the year relative to the typical school enrollment cycle and parental questions regarding whether AYP is a valid assessment of a school's quality (Hannaway & Cohodes, 2007). The market structure of schooling remains largely a matter of state policy.

Build Capacity to Change

Building district and school capacity—supported by incentives and opportunities—is the core of efforts to help schools improve (Massel, 1998; Mazzeo & Berman, 2006). In an effort to synthesize the research, we separated capacity building into two categories: systemic and local. Systemic capacity building involves state-level efforts aimed at helping schools and districts across a state, including building state education agency capacity and initiatives designed to support research and development or improve the supply of human capital available to schools in general. Local capacity building incorporates the direct support and technical assistance that states or their designated partners provide to specific districts and schools.

Engaging in systemic capacity-building efforts is an acknowledgement that there are often deeply entrenched policies and practices that influence the ability of schools to be successful in educating all children. Examples of system-wide issues include:

- variable-funding levels for public schools,
- statewide teaching shortages, and a
- lack of high-quality teachers in high poverty schools.

Other system-wide issues point to the lack of a common curriculum aligned with state standards and the absence of research-based information about how to address certain learning issues. Addressing systemic issues entails that multiple state entities (e.g., the legislature, the governor, state board of education, and the SEA), or in some cases a consortium of states, work together to develop and implement required changes. Furthermore, while NCLB requires states to focus on schools in need of improvement, systemic capacity building efforts hold the promise of helping all schools (B. Lane, personal communication, May 29, 2007).

In contrast, local capacity-building efforts recognize that chronically low-performing schools may require customized and focused intervention above and beyond the supports that the state makes available to all districts and schools. It is important for states to differentiate those issues that require systemic capacity-building efforts and those that are best addressed through local capacity building (B. Lane, personal communication, May 29, 2007). Therefore, while NCLB defines statewide systems of support primarily as local capacity building, it does not place limits on state systems. As a result, we consider both kinds of capacity building in this section.

Build Systemic Capacity

Three approaches states can use to build systemic capacity are creating and disseminating knowledge, enhancing the supply of human capital, and developing strong data systems. The following subsections define these approaches and introduce examples identified in the literature.

Create and Disseminate Knowledge. To improve, schools and districts need various kinds of knowledge. At the classroom level, knowledge involves specialized content expertise as well as information about approaches to instruction, including instruction of special populations such as students with disabilities and English language learners. Knowledge also involves classroom management, formative assessment, data-driven decisions, and other activities that contribute to student learning. At the school level, knowledge of organizational practices—including change processes that lead to better outcomes—is essential, as is knowledge about best practices, data analysis, and resource allocation. At the district level, officials require know-how regarding governance and management approaches, adoption of data-driven decision making, and other systems that will help school leaders and teachers support best instructional and managerial practices in schools and classrooms.

SEAs are uniquely positioned to stimulate the development and dissemination of organizational practices and specialized content and instructional expertise. Ideally, SEAs could use the power of centralized pooled resources at the state level to invest in new ideas that individual districts and schools, lacking time and resources, would find difficult to support. Reville and his colleagues (2005), for example, suggest that states create a comprehensive "default curriculum" encompassing scope and sequence, pacing guides, sample lessons, recommend texts and materials, and assessments for districts that don't have the resources to develop their own. States are also well positioned to help districts generate and analyze data that should play a central role in school improvement decision making.

There are multiple examples of SEAs creating knowledge for the benefit of all the schools in the state. The state of Michigan is illustrative. It has developed a new "technology" specifically to assist low-performing schools to improve. Based on a select group of highly skilled educators' experiences working with low-performing schools in the state, Michigan developed what they call their "curriculum for school improvement" that includes specific lesson plans for change (Archer, 2006a, p. 5). Referred to as "MI-MAP," the lesson plans are described as a "how-to" guide for turning around failing schools. The MI-MAP is the basis of a two-day training seminar for teams of educators from schools identified for intervention. The curriculum is designed to build local capacity but is an example of a state investing in creating and disseminating knowledge that can benefit schools across the state. This is in contrast to delegating responsibility for developing this expertise to local districts.

Another example of creating knowledge is the New England Compact. In 2001, commissioners from Maine, New Hampshire, Rhode Island, and Vermont formed a collaborative partnership to create and disseminate knowledge. Capturing the potential value associated with a state's (or in this case multiple states') pooling of resources to develop knowledge, the Compact's website notes that "the Compact helps states explore strategies, share knowledge, and establish cross-state activities whose economies of scale and cost-efficiency benefit each state by allowing them to leverage their resources" (New England Consortium, 2007). The Compact has created a common statewide assessment, the New England Common Assessment Program (NECAP), and common grade level expectations (B. Lane, personal communication, May 29, 2007).

Given SEAs' limited resources, it may be unrealistic to expect them, on their own, to serve as laboratories of innovation. Instead, SEAs could invest in research and development carried out by other organizations and take steps to ensure that the growing knowledge base is widely disseminated to schools and teachers. For instance, the Texas Education Agency (TEA) supports the University of Texas Center for Reading and Language Arts (now known as the Vaughn Gross Center for Reading and Language Arts). TEA funding created the Center in 1996 to ensure that Texas educators had access to the instructional approaches they needed to meet the state's accountability goals. The Center conducts scientific research on reading methods and provides technical assistance and professional development to disseminate those methods statewide (http://www.texasreading.org/).

In light of their own capacity limits, SEAs may choose to partner with existing research and dissemination networks such as the 16 USDOE funded Regional Comprehensive Centers and the 5 National Content Centers. These Centers were created specifically to conduct research and provide SEAs with technical assistance informed by evidence-based research findings. The rationale behind the regional network is to develop expertise that reflects unique regional needs. SEAs can then utilize this expertise to bolster state systems of support and, specifically, to disseminate new governance and instructional practices to districts and schools. The five Content Centers were created to centralize research and dissemination of best practices in key priority areas identified by the USDOE (i.e., assessment and accountability, innovation and improvement, instruction, teacher quality, and high school reform); again, this is for the explicit purpose of providing technical assistance to SEAs. In theory, once trained, SEAs share the emerging research with district and school level practitioners.

The potential of SEAs to serve as stimulators of new instructional or governance practices is arguably under-developed. Nonetheless, as states contemplate developing thoughtful and cohesive statewide systems of support, capitalizing on their potential as creators and disseminators of leading edge practices is one powerful role states could play in supporting school improvement.

Enhance Supply of Personnel. Education is intensely dependent upon human capital, and SEAs have developed a variety of initiatives that build the capacity of the entire state system by improving the supply, quality, and training of teachers and school leaders.

Supply of Qualified Teachers. Prior to and now in conjunction with NCLB, states have instituted multiple efforts to improve the supply of qualified teachers. For instance, states have developed credentialing standards and instituted state teacher tests in an attempt to ensure that, at a minimum, all teachers share an established base of knowledge (Darling-Hammond, 2000; Darling-Hammond & Baratz-Snowden, 2005; Fulton, Yoon, & Lee, 2005). In addition, states have passed legislation designed to encourage people to enter the teaching profession. For example, in 1998, the Mississippi legislature adopted the Critical Teacher Shortage Act that allocated scholarships, housing loans, and moving expenses to entice teachers to work in hard-to-staff regions of the state. And multiple states offer loan forgiveness programs for new teachers whereby if they teach in hard-to-staff schools or subjects, they can have their undergraduate loans forgiven (e.g., Florida and Wisconsin; Kowal, Hassel, & Hassel, 2007). A number of states (e.g., California, Georgia, and New York) have also developed programs to encourage teachers to enter the teaching profession as a second career or by way of non-traditional alternative certification routes (USDOE, 2004). All of these approaches aim to improve the quality of teaching within a state and contribute to improving the overall capacity of the states' system of public education.

Supply of School Leaders. Effective school leadership is a key determinant of school success (Leithwood, Seashore Louis, Anderson, & Wahlstrom, 2004; Waters, Marzano, & McNulty, 2003). Similar to efforts to increase the supply of teachers, states have developed training pipelines that potentially benefit the entire state. For instance, multiple states have developed principal leadership academies to recruit and train high-quality principals (e.g., Arkansas, Florida, Iowa, Indiana, Kansas, and Missouri).

Some states have also created innovative programs to train administrators to work in schools identified as in need of improvement. For example in 2004, under the direction of the governor, the Virginia Department of Education funded an innovative partnership between the University of Virginia Curry School of Education and the Darden School of Business. Its purpose is to train experienced principals to be turnaround specialists charged with dramatically changing failing schools in Virginia. The program represents an innovative new approach to training school leaders developed by the executive arm of the state government in concert with the state department of education. Preliminary evidence from schools employing the turnaround specialists has been encouraging: 7 of the 10 previously low-performing schools that employed a UVA turnaround specialist made AYP after a single year (Duke et al., 2005).

Teacher recruitment and retention initiatives, leadership academies, and programs specifically designed to prepare school leaders to work in low-performing schools represent opportunities to improve the overall human capacity for a state education system. Though more diffuse than support and technical assistance provided directly to districts and schools, these initiatives signify a state's long-term commitment to and investment in the overall health of its public schools.

Create Strong Data Systems. Meaningful reporting and data-driven decision making require strong data systems. Yet, many individual districts, and most schools, lack capacity to develop or maintain strong data systems on their own (Palaich, Griffin, & van der Ploeg, 2004). Given that managing data and developing data systems has historically been the primary responsibility of the SEA, ensuring that the state has a strong data system is the natural evolution of the state's role in public schools. Data systems are comprised of student enrollment data as well as state assessment data.

States need accurate data to assess schools and districts for the purpose of implementing incentive systems. In addition, states need to maintain strong data systems to inform their decisions about how to differentiate their local capacity building efforts. In particular, strong data systems are the foundation of accurate needs assessments that enable the state, in collaboration with the district and school, to identify specific areas for targeted technical assistance and develop restructuring plans.

The importance of strong data systems is reinforced by NCLB accountability systems that depend upon accurate and timely data. Strong data systems that track enrollment and outcomes provide teachers, principals, district officials, and state officials with timely, user-friendly data that can inform their decisions. Cumbersome systems that don't provide the end-user with functional information, or fail to do so in a timely manner, undermine efforts to use data to make informed decisions. For instance, a recent report examining implementation of NCLB documented that seven states do not report AYP data to districts until after the following school year starts, thereby undermining schools' ability to use spring assessment data to inform instructional practices (CEP, 2007).

States are and will need to continue to dedicate substantial resources to developing strong data systems to support school improvement (Palaich et al., 2004). Prior to the implementation of NCLB with funding from the USODE, the Maryland State Department of Education was a pioneer in the development of a strong state data system when it created a website designed to help districts and schools conduct data-driven school improvement planning (Palaich et al., 2004). More recently, the Illinois State Board of Education has created a specific plan, the Illinois E-Plan, to help districts record required, as well as requested, data. As part of the plan, the SEA has created a variety of templates for use by districts facing school improvement including plans related to: technology integration, restructuring, and district as well as school improvement (Diaz, 2007).

Whereas traditionally state data systems were created to collect and manage financial, human resources, and programmatic compliance data in separate systems, contemporary data systems need to be integrated and easily cross-referenced. Furthermore, they need to include a wide variety of data including but not limited to:

- state assessments,
- school report cards,
- aggregate and disaggregate longitudinal student performance data,
- attendance/enrollment data, and
- aggregate and individual student-performance data (Palaich et al., 2004).

Systems that permit end users to track individual students are critical to ensuring that data systems can inform decisions at the state, district, school, and even classroom level. State investments in strong data systems need to include careful consideration of the Family Educational Rights and Privacy Act to ensure that efforts to support data-driven decision making don't undermine student privacy rights (Palaich et al., 2004).

Build Local Capacity

Building local capacity incorporates the direct support and technical assistance SEAs provide to districts and schools for the explicit purpose of improving student outcomes. Based on the literature, we categorize statewide system of support local capacity building efforts according to their (a) structure, (b) differentiation, and (c) service delivery (AIR, 2006; Archer,

2006a, 2006b; CCSSO, 2002; David, Kannapel, & McDiarmid, 2000; Dwyer et al., 2005; ECS, 2002; Hoff, 2006; Holdzkom, 2001; IEL, 2001; Laguarda, 2003; Lane, Seager, & Frankel, 2005; Lusi, 1997; Massell, 1998; Mazzeo & Berman, n.d.; Mintrop & Trujillo, 2005; Reville et al., 2005; USDOE, 2006; Westat, 2006). The statewide system of support structure encompasses who provides support and the point of contact between the SEA, or its designee, and the district and school. Differentiation pertains to aligning the type or mode of support with individual district and school needs. Finally, delivery includes the actual type of support that SEAs are providing directly or contracting with other entities to provide.

States are utilizing a number of structures, means of allocating support, and types of support services; yet, the literature provides little evidence regarding what support systems are particularly effective or efficient. Given noted limitations in SEA capacity, identifying effective and coherent practices is critical. The evidence that is available does not identify clear causal connections between particular means of supports and actual student outcomes. The lack of rigorous evidence is due in part to the newness of the construct of statewide systems of support. More problematic is the practical reality that each state has developed its own unique system within a unique larger policy context in which it operates (ECS, 2002). As a result, it will be difficult for researchers to untangle the effects of the many tools states are utilizing. Furthermore, state education policy, and of interest for our analysis, state systems of support, are both works in progress. By the time research has been conducted and published, most systems have already changed. With these limitations in mind, the following sections describe local capacity-building structures, means of differentiating support, where and what types of services are being provided, and practices that have been identified as promising or successful in the research literature.

Capacity Building Structures. The defining characteristic of state accountability systems and consequent approaches to helping low-performing schools is their heterogeneity (AIR, 2006; ECS, 2002; Westat, 2006). The absence of a documented relationship between specific state support structures and improved outcomes precludes identification of an effective or "model" structure. A key determinant of the structure or approach states take to providing support and technical assistance is the SEA's level of internal capacity to provide support, which sets limits on the degree to which SEAs can provide support themselves. The lower the SEA's internal capacity to develop and provide a statewide system of support, the more it will need to identify external capacity that it can support or leverage (CCSSO, 2006). An additional consideration in determining the structure of the state's support system is the state's ability to commit fiscal resources (Reville, 2004). Across the nation, states are constructing support systems based in state education agencies, intermediate units, and partner organizations, or utilizing consultants (AIR, 2006; Archer 2006a, 2006b; CCSSO, 2003; ECS, 2002; Reville, et al., 2005). Within and across these structures, states are deploying distinguished educators and school support teams to work with districts and schools. A recurring theme in the literature is the importance of relevant and ongoing professional development for personnel charged with assisting schools and districts to improve (Dwyer et al., 2005; Reville et al., 2005).

State Education Agency. The state education agency is the entity charged with identifying low-performing schools and constructing, facilitating, and/or supporting the development of systems to support school and district improvement. In some instances, SEA personnel also engage in providing direct support to schools and districts.

A review of all 50 states' systems of supports reveals multiple organizational structures that states are using to deliver support and technical assistance (Westat, 2006). For instance, 32 states provide ongoing assistance but not on-site assistance on a regular basis, and 17 states provide coaching/facilitating to groups of schools and whole districts (Archer, 2006a).

Ongoing assistance is typically delivered by consultants hired by the SEA who serve as liaisons or brokers to schools (Laguarda, 2003). These individuals typically help schools craft and thereafter implement school improvement plans. They can also play a role in assisting schools to understand state policies pertaining to school improvement and accessing resources. For instance, Laguarda documented that in Florida and Vermont, the SEA consultants play a central role in developing improvement plans, identifying resources and technical assistance, and monitoring implementation of school improvement activities. However, there is little documentation regarding the qualifications of these consultants or the relevant value they add to schools or districts.

Some SEAs are opting to build their internal capacity to provide direct support by constructing school support teams or identifying distinguished educators who can be dispatched to schools and districts in need of improvement. Ideally these individuals have experience successfully improving schools. Arizona Department of Education staff members, in part to monitor and control quality, provide support to schools and districts. In addition, Arizona maximizes the value and reach of its personnel by utilizing technology to offer online professional development and training (CCSSO, 2006). In Connecticut, SEA personnel are helping district leaders learn from one another by facilitating meetings to discuss data-driven decision-making (Archer, 2006a).

Research predating NCLB found that in order to effect change, SEA operations should reflect best practices and serve as a role model for district and school reform (Lusi, 1997). If schools are expected to be open to change and the introduction of new practices, SEAs should also be open to change. For instance, SEA personnel may struggle to grant LEAs flexibility if SEA personnel are working in an environment that does not respect the need for flexibility and creative problem solving based on local needs.

Intermediate Agencies. Intermediate agencies serve a variety of purposes and have different names (e.g., Area Education Agencies, Boards of Co-operative Educational Services, Education Service Centers). Intermediate agencies are typically (a) a regional extension of the SEA, (b) a service provider to the SEA but linked to local districts, or (c) a cooperative entity created by local districts to fill a shared need (McIver, 2005). A total of 14 states reported in their consolidated plan that they use intermediate agencies to provide direct support to schools and districts (Archer, 2006a). For example, Illinois, Ohio, and Pennsylvania utilize independent regional agencies that are affiliated with the state department of education to provide services (CCSSO, 2006). In New York, the State Education Department implemented a regional approach to providing support in order to provide flexible and customized services to local districts across a large state in an efficient and effective manner (Lane, Seager, & Frankel, 2005). A key component of New York's regional network strategy for school improvement was identifying existing support systems and building new partnerships that benefit schools. The network is comprised of seven regional centers that compete for contracts to coordinate and provide services to districts and schools identified as in need of improvement. According to a case study of New York's system of support, the state developed the regional network to "leverage and refocus existing resources" (Lane et al., 2005). The decentralized agencies also presumably enable states to customize support based on local needs.

External Partner Organizations. An alternative approach to creating or engaging traditional intermediate agencies is contracting with external partners. As of fall 2006, 19 states reported in their consolidated plan that they use external partners and consultants to deliver their support (Archer, 2006a). These partnerships appear to fall along a continuum according to the degree of control exerted by the SEA (Reville et al., 2005). For instance, New York invites external partners to bid for contracts to provide support. Thereafter, the SEA manages the contracts to ensure that services are provided to schools and districts in need of improvement in line with the broader state system of support. Indiana contracts with both regional and national service providers to assist its districts and schools to improve (CCSSO, 2006). These direct contracts enable states to engage external expertise while retaining a degree of control over the cost and quality of the services provided to schools and districts.

At the other end of the spectrum, some states do not manage the contracts with external providers directly. In California, for example, the state provides eligible schools with funds to hire the individual or group they choose to help them improve. The entity may be a county-wide education office or an entity in the private sector (Archer, 2006a; ECS, 2002). Research on California's model of intervention documented that 20% of the first cohort of schools that volunteered to receive intervention support met the state's growth expectations (Mazzeo & Berman, n.d.).

Private industry is responding to the growing demand for SEA external partners, and industry leaders are wading into the school improvement market. For instance, Standard and Poor's created a School Evaluation Services division that is currently assisting states to analyze their data to more efficiently allocate resources. McKinsey and Company has formed a partnership with the Minneapolis Public Schools to manage and analyze their student performance data (Reville et al., 2005).

Private consultants can play a key role in helping districts build capacity. Multiple states have hired retired superintendents and principals to serve as individual consultants or as members of teams assigned to help districts support schools to change.

Preliminary research indicates that successful partnerships with external providers require goal setting and training at the beginning of the collaboration and ongoing monitoring of performance. Furthermore, regardless of whether technical assistance is provided via contracts with external providers, or negotiated by schools, districts, or the state, great care must to taken to hire quality providers who can be held accountable for providing high quality services (Laguarda, 2003).

Distinguished Educators. NCLB defines distinguished educators as individuals (teachers and school leaders) who have experienced success in low-performing schools and who are recruited to leverage their success to help other districts. The term distinguished educators takes on slightly different meanings in different states and contexts. Alternate titles include peer mentor, school improvement coach, and highly skilled educator (David et al., 2000; Mintrop & Trujillo, 2005; Newman-Sheldon, 2006).

While identifying an adequate supply of distinguished educators can be challenging (Hoff, 2006; Reville et al., 2005), multiple states have tapped into distinguished educators and reported success with this delivery structure (David et al., 2000). Early reports from Pennsylvania indicate that distinguished educators can be effective change agents and, in particular, can build solid bridges between school districts and their SEA (Archer, 2006b).

The Kentucky distinguished educator (DE) program has been identified as positively influencing school outcomes (David et al., 2000). Established in 1994 to assist low-performing schools to improve, the program consists of teams of distinguished educators providing varying levels of intensive technical assistance to schools identified as low-performing according to the Kentucky accountability system. The lowest performing schools receive the most intense support; two full-time distinguished educators are charged with evaluating all school personnel and authorized to recommend removal. To be hired as a distinguished educator, applicants went through a "rigorous multi-step process which led to the selection of a highly motivated group of educators" (David et al., 2000, p. 2). Approximately half of the DE's were teachers, and the remainder were central office administrators. The DEs received two weeks of training and then participated in ongoing professional development with their cohort. During the course of the two-year assignment, the educators attended 60 days of professional development to enhance their skills based on their experiences in the schools in need of improvement. While tasks varied by school, the distinguished educators were credited with providing technical knowledge related to human resource allocation, curriculum and instruction, and leadership.

After two years, 34 of the first cohort of 53 schools met or exceeded their performance goals. In the second cohort, 167 of 188 schools improved, and 85 of these schools exceeded their goals (David et al., 2000). The rate of improvement in the schools assigned distinguished educators exceeded the statewide rate of improvement. An evaluation of the Kentucky distinguished educator program concluded that these specialists were most effective when (1) they worked at the school full-time; (2) were well matched to the school; and (3) stayed at the school for two years (David et al., 2000).

Seven states have created networks of practitioners and school leaders to share best practices. For instance, the Connecticut Department of Education has created cohorts of teams of superintendents, principals, and curriculum specialists from low-performing schools to share ideas and training designed to help them improve their schools (Archer, 2006a). The research on Kentucky's distinguished educator program noted the value of building cohorts of professionals engaged in school improvement and, thereafter, leveraging their expertise to mentor future cohorts (David et al., 2000).

School Support Teams. NCLB identifies state support teams as one tool that SEAs should use to assist schools in need of improvement. These teams are typically comprised of educators and SEA staff (Reville, 2004). The structure, size, scope of work, and means of working with schools and districts varies widely across the states (Archer, 2006a; Dwyer et al., 2005; Laguarda, 2003; Mazzeo & Berman, n.d.; Reville et al., 2005; Westat, 2006). The following examples of school support teams illustrate the variability.

South Carolina requires its lowest performing schools to embark upon a thorough review by a team of state-identified professionals comprised of educators, university faculty, community representatives, and other designated experts. Based on the review of curriculum and instruction, leadership and governance, student outcomes, and professional development, specialists are assigned to help the school implement its improvement plan. If justified by the low performance level, the school may be assigned a distinguished educator to serve as a mentor to the existing school leader. Schools working with school support teams are eligible for multiple grants offered to support school improvement. Of the original cohort of 73 schools identified for participation in 2001-2002, 26 exited the program due to meeting achievement goals (Mazzeo & Berman, n.d.)

In North Carolina, teams of retired or specially designated principals and teachers are hired and participate in a month-long training to enhance their existing content expertise with complementary coaching, leadership, and organizations skills (Reville et al., 2005). The teams are thereafter assigned to work for an entire year with a single school. Multiple analysts identified North Carolina's school support teams as particularly intensive (Laguarda, 2003). Identified schools are required to participate in the program. Teams' work varies by school, but typically the teams help schools develop a school improvement plan, evaluate personnel, provide professional development, serve as mentors and coaches to school personnel, and provide feedback to staff. At the end of the intensive year, consultants hired by the state department of education monitor the schools regularly to ensure ongoing implementation of the improvement plan. In addition to the intensive school support teams, the state offers a second tier of voluntary support that consists of non-resident school support teams that work with multiple schools for a year (Laguarda, 2003).

Coordination Between and Among Statewide System of Support Structures. The aforementioned state system of support structures (state education agency, intermediate agency, external partner, distinguished educator, and school support teams) are presented as distinct structures. In practice, however, most states' systems are comprised of a combination of these structures. There is an inherent risk of inefficiency in a large, multi-layered state system. Developing a coherent and efficient system may depend on effective coordination of multiple strands of support potentially housed in different divisions of the SEA and different entities across a large state. Evidence from the field indicates that regular communication, sharing of information across units potentially unaccustomed to collaborating, and regular reporting of data are central to creating an effective system of support (Dwyer, 2005; Lane, Seager, & Frankel, 2005; Lusi, 1997; Massell, 1998). A key decision that states need to make is whether they will support school improvement directly or work with districts to develop required support systems.

Differentiated Support to Local Districts and Schools. NCLB provides states with a rubric to identify schools in need of improvement. In addition, some states have their own accountability system that may use different metrics to identify schools for state intervention (e.g., Florida and Texas). States are using these metrics as a means to differentiate support to schools and distinguish both in the level of intensity and focus of services provided (ECS, 2002; Archer, 2006a).

At their core, public schools share a common mission, but each school is shaped by the local community, the capacity of its school personnel, its history, and the broader policy context in which the school functions. Consequently, districts' and schools' capacity for change and level of need varies. While there are efficiencies associated with identifying a one-size-fits-all model of school improvement, research and practical experience indicates that there are multiple reasons why schools are unable to fully address the needs of all students, and therefore efforts to help schools improve must be individualized (Dwyer et al., 2005; Holdzkom, 2001; Mazzeo & Berman, n.d.).

States have different thresholds for identifying schools as low-performing and, subsequently, different benchmarks schools must attain in order to exit corrective action or low-performing status (Laguarda, 2003). The diversity of relative standards translates into state assistance programs with different levels of "intervention burden" (Mintrop & Trujillo, 2005, p. 6). In considering how to approach development of local capacity, state education agencies need to assess and differentiate support and technical assistance.

There is relatively universal agreement in the literature on state systems of support that a key task for states is to assist districts in determining their technical assistance and support needs (AIR, 2006; Laguarda, 2003; Mazzeo & Berman, 2006; Reville, 2004). As the keepers of data, states can provide districts with access to data and assist districts in analyzing the data to ascertain specific deficiencies that need to be addressed to increase overall school performance.

As states work to develop systems to support school improvement, a central consideration is the degree to which they will differentiate support based on need and capacity. Reville frames this decision as one between depth of support and breadth of support: states can either provide intense support to a few select schools or minimal support to all schools in need of improvement (2004). While some states are providing assistance to a large group of schools identified as in need of improvement, most are providing intense assistance to a small cohort of high-need schools. Research on differentiated support based on greatest needs in Kentucky, North Carolina, and South Carolina indicates that intense efforts have had positive effects on the lowest performing schools, but that these schools require significant support and involvement (Holdzkom, 2001).

The literature indicates that states are differentiating support according to point of impact (school or district) and intensity and duration of services. Furthermore, the degree to which state intervention is voluntary or involuntary appears to influence the relationship between the state and the district or school. Voluntary participation reportedly builds ownership of change initiatives in schools identified as in need of improvement (Laguarda, 2003). Somewhat related to the notion of ownership is the less tangible but nonetheless influential role of interpersonal relationships between the providers and recipients of technical assistance and support (Holdzkom, 2001). Findings from a case study of the state of New York indicate that successful support requires development of interpersonal relationships between key actors and an ongoing commitment to change, not short-term engagements (Lane, Saeger, & Frankel, 2005).

Differentiate by Point of Impact. The first level of differentiation pertains to the focus of state-provided or sponsored technical assistance and support. One theory of action is that NCLB requires states to support school improvement, and the focus of the support is helping districts support individual school improvement. An alternate approach is for states to support individual school improvement directly. Our review of existing state systems reveals evidence of both approaches (Dwyer et al., 2005; ECS, 2004; Westat, 2006).

The research indicates that school districts are central players in effective and sustainable school reform; consequently, efforts to improve schools should incorporate school districts (Archer, 2006a; Dwyer et al., 2005; McLaughlin & Talbert, 2003; O'Day & Bitter, 2003; Spillane, 1996, 1997, 1998). Of particular note, schools operate within a local context; if districts are not actively engaged in assisting schools to succeed, district policies may actually undermine school-level change efforts (Archer, 2006a). Yet, research indicates that the district's role is somewhat underdeveloped (Laguarda, 2003). While NCLB emphasizes the importance of building state systems of support to help schools in need of improvement, efforts that bolster district capacity may provide long-term dividends by leveraging state capacity to benefit the greatest number of schools.

Multiple states are providing multi-level systems of support in an effort to strategically leverage resources while simultaneously responding to district needs (AIR, 2006). Willingness and capacity to change are considerations that shape differentiation by point of impact (David et al., 2000; Reville et al., 2005).

Differentiate by Intensity and Duration of Services. Low-performing schools are not all the same; consequently, efforts to improve schools must be individualized (Mazzeo & Berman, n.d). Research indicates that states are differentiating according to intensity and duration of services based on level of performance and local capacity. Twenty-three states provide tiered levels of support based on performance (Archer, 2006a). Individualized remedies that address the underlying causes of low-performance (and resonate with school personnel) potentially decrease the chances of state efforts being marginalized at the local level.

North Carolina provides focused intervention to a select group of schools, and 57 of the 60 schools met improvement targets after two years (i.e., 95% success). In contrast, data emerging from Maryland, New York, and California suggest that fewer than 20% of the schools receiving state assistance were able to meet individual improvement goals after a year of intervention by the state (Reville, 2004). The concept of trajectory entails articulating realistic expectations for school improvement based on consideration of the current status of the school and the changes required to meet state and federal accountability goals. Decades of research has documented the process of incremental school improvement (i.e., the process of making a good school great). However, most schools currently identified for corrective action have a long history of poor performance, and incremental change may not be acceptable; a more dramatic change is required to substantively alter the learning environment for the children currently enrolled in the school.

Incremental change is important and arguably the correct strategy for good organizations interested in becoming great ones. According to the literature, however, efforts to turn around organizations that are failing on multiple metrics require more dramatic change to become successful, change that looks different from incremental improvement over time. Consequently, in developing differentiated systems of support, the required trajectory is one of multiple factors to consider.

Differentiation according to duration of support varies from a couple of months to a couple of years. Evidence from multiple states indicates that multi-year cycles of support can prevent "flip-flopping" on and off the state intervention list after short periods of improvement (Laguarda, 2003, p. 17). To diminish fits and starts of improvement, a number of states (e.g., Arkansas, Nevada, North Carolina, and Vermont) provide ongoing technical assistance even after schools meet established goals. However, the intensity diminishes as schools improve enough to be removed from the state list of schools in need of improvement.

North Carolina's approach to differentiation was cited in multiple research reports as a model for differentiation by intensity (Laguarda, 2003; Mintrop & Trujillo, 2005). The state selects up to 20 percent of its lowest-performing schools designated as in need of improvement and requires these schools to obtain assistance from designated school support teams (Laguarda, 2003). The second tier of support includes schools identified as in need of improvement, and they are offered, but not required, to obtain technical assistance from school support teams.

The duration of services may be largely dictated by the root causes of low-performance. In line with evidence regarding the importance of differentiating support based on school-level data, intensity and duration of services will most likely need to reflect individual school's needs and capacities. Lack of apparent authenticity may limit the potential impact of assistance. In reflecting on school restructuring efforts, a principal from Maryland noted, "I don't focus on the restructuring plan. I focus on what the school needs to do. If I don't move to what the kids need, then I'm not going to move the school. [The restructuring] plan is probably there for the state, but not for me. There are parts that are valid. It's a plan of support and action" (CEP, 2005).

Delivery of Support Services. States currently provide a variety of services to local districts and individual schools. Services have typically evolved over time, are program specific (i.e., reading, English language learners, or special education), and generally lack cohesion (Dwyer et al., 2005; Lusi, 1997; Massell, 1998). Multiple organizations have examined and synthesized existing state systems of support (e.g., AIR, 2006; CCSSO, 2006; Reville, et al., 2005). For a state by state summary, see the Center on Innovation & Improvement's website that includes a database of all 50 states' existing statewide systems of support: http://www.centerii.org/centerIIPublic/.

As states develop and refine their state systems of support, they will need to consider whether their focus will be on districts or individual schools, the array of services they will provide, and the allocation of resources in a manner that facilitates sustainable change. USDOE recommends that schools in need of improvement first conduct a needs assessment, then develop a plan for improvement, implement the plan, and then evaluate the implementation of the plan in order to inform future practice. USDOE outlines these tasks as the key responsibilities of school support teams (USDOE, 2001). The delivery of services provided by the state should complement rather than disrupt the recommended cycle of improvement.

Provide Services. The type of services provided by states to build local capacity differ to some degree, but typical services provided by most states are: (a) development of improvement plans, (b) technical assistance related to curriculum and instruction, (c) data training and support for using assessments, (d) leadership development, and (e) support with parent and community involvement (AIR, 2006; Archer, 2006a; CCSSO, 2003; Dwyer et al., 2005; ECS, 2002; Laguarda, 2003; Mintrop & Trujillo, 2005; Mazzeo & Berman, n.d.; Reville, 2004). According to a recent review of state consolidated performance reports, the most common type of service provided to schools and districts is planning. Forty-seven states provide guidance on developing improvement plans, and the means of providing the guidance includes visits by outside evaluators (29 states), outside reviews based on documentation (13), and self reviews (17); (Archer, 2006a). In addition to planning, 17 states provide leadership training, 15 states provide data analysis training, and 19 states provide specific content in professional development (Archer, 2006a).

Reflecting the challenges inherent to organizational change, the case study of the New York system of support documented that some services (e.g., professional development) may be uncomfortable for instructional personnel unaccustomed to collaborating and reflecting on their instructional practices. Nonetheless, the case study revealed that while personnel initially reported being uncomfortable with the process, after participating in multiple professional development meetings, they were engaging in discussions with their peers about strategies to help low-performing schools. The progression of acceptance was perceived to foster broader school improvement goals (Mazzeo & Berman, n.d.)

In an effort to engage stakeholders outside of the school, some states provide training specifically aimed to engage parents and communities. For instance, Illinois uses regional providers to train schools how to reach out to parents and community members to support school improvement (CCSSO, 2006).

In accord with the importance of differentiating support based on need and local context, the actual services that states provide should reflect the documented needs of schools and districts. Once local needs are identified, states can draw from decades of rigorous research regarding best practices. There is not a "best" model or structure of a statewide system of support. Rather, within the broad parameters of planning, states need to customize their services to reflect their schools' and districts' unique challenges and opportunities.

Allocate Resources for Services. Research indicates that funding alone cannot effectively improve failing schools, but there are indications that increased resources can be an important aspect of state efforts to support school improvement (Dwyer et al., 2005; Lusi, 1997; Massel, 1998; Reville et al., 2005). Effective statewide systems of support require resources: resources to build human and fiscal capacity at the state level and, in most cases, resources to build human and fiscal capacity at the district and school level. To reiterate, under NCLB, states must allocate a set percentage of their Title I funds (4% in 2007) to support school improvement. However, use of these funds for school improvement reflects a reallocation rather than an addition of funds. Some states and state legislatures have allocated substantial additional funding that targets failing schools. Giving rise to critics' concerns about the degree to which NCLB can spur increased performance for all students nationwide, some states' school improvement efforts are funded solely by the 4% set aside, existing Title I funded initiatives, and other federal funds (B. Lane, personal communication, May 29, 2007). Given the urgent need for school improvement and the historical reality that public education is primarily a state responsibility, states will most likely have to allocate additional dollars and reallocate existing state dollars to prioritize development of a comprehensive and cohesive statewide system of support (Dwyer et al., 2005).

The research on state support of school improvement is not conclusive, though some observers have asserted that additional resources targeted at schools and districts do correlate with improved student outcomes (Mintrop & Trujullo, 2005). In any case, states need to be strategic about funding streams to ensure that funds are adequate to support change but also that the funds are leveraged to build sustainable systems as opposed to supporting single projects or events. School improvement has been characterized as "a process not an event" (Elmore, n.d., p. 14) and, therefore, additional funds should be allocated to jumpstarting a sustainable process, not just to producing a single event.

Estimates of the cost of developing an effective statewide system of support vary considerably in part due to the variable intervention burden in different states. The literature does not reveal a standard per unit cost to improve schools or districts. While in no way comprehensive, the following are examples of resources allocated to support state systems of support initiatives: (a) California awarded 353 schools $50,000 planning grants to hire external providers in 1999-2000, (b) Nevada awarded schools grants ranging from $70,000 to $100,000 to implement one of 26 approved school improvement models identified by the SEA, and (c) North Carolina allocated $5.7 million to support its two-tiered school assistance team model in 2002-2003 (Laguarda, 2003).

In summary, the literature on state systems of support describes a set of potential tools (delivery) which are provided by a variety of entities (structure), and states are using a variety of strategies to match the tools and providers to districts and schools based on their unique needs (differentiation). States are developing these systems within a broader policy context influenced by incentives developed to encourage or discourage specific practices. The final piece of the three-legged stool covered in the next section is the opportunities that states can create to provide schools and districts with the chance to use their capacity for the purpose of substantive school improvement.

Provide Opportunities for Change

Incentives and capacity are both vital to the change process, but organizations also need to have the flexibility to change (i.e., the third leg of the stool), as proponents of standards-based reform have long maintained (e.g., Smith & O'Day, 1991; National Governors Association, 1986). If rigidities within the system preclude the kinds of reform that schools and districts need to undertake in order to be successful, then incentives and capacity alone will not spur change. Research on change efforts such as the New American Schools comprehensive school reform initiative (Berends, Bodilly, & Nataraj Kirby, 2002) and Edison Schools (Gill et al., 2005) document the importance of giving educators the flexibility to implement significant changes. State legislatures, governors, state boards of education, and SEAs are uniquely positioned to create the conditions to enable change to occur. As a result, states also need to attend to the opportunities that state policy provides for schools and districts to do what they need to do to improve student performance. There are two broad ways in which states have acted to create such opportunities: by removing obstacles that make it difficult or impossible for schools and districts to take necessary steps; and by creating space in which entirely new public schools can open.

Removing Systemic Obstacles for Existing Schools and Districts

Numerous aspects of state policy can stand in the way of educators' efforts to take necessary actions for school improvement, including policies regarding use of funds, staffing, and scheduling. States have taken two approaches to removing this kind of obstacle. First, in the 1980s and 1990s, most states established processes through which school districts could petition the state for waivers or exemptions from state policies. One review found that by "1993, more than 30 states claimed that waivers could be obtained by schools or districts that requested them, noncompetitively and regardless of performance" (Furhman & Elmore, 1995, p. 15). Most other states had some more limited waiver program, with only six reporting a complete absence of waivers (beyond those allowed in emergencies such as natural disasters).

The second path has been to repeal or reduce problematic regulations. In the 1990s, states such as Minnesota, Tennessee, and Texas removed hundreds (or even thousands) of rules from their state codes. Several others created some kind of "formal review or advisory process" to examine existing regulations and propose changes that interfered with the states' new focus on results-based accountability (Fuhrman & Elmore, 1995, pp. 16-17). Florida sought to create new opportunities for change in 1991 by deleting multiple state regulations altogether (Massell, 1998). At least one state, Vermont, established standards that guide state department of education policies, including one requiring that "any rule or law should advance student performance, but not in such a rigid manner as to foreclose alternate means of achieving goals" (State of Vermont Board of Education, 1992, January 21, pp. 3-4 in Lusi, 1998).

The foregoing discussion focused on states as the sources of the obstacles that needed removing. Some constraints, however, come from sources other than state policy (Fuhrman & Elmore, 1995). Federal laws and regulations, for example, may limit the activities educators can undertake, especially when involved in federally funded programs. Collective bargaining agreements between districts and staff organizations can also create obstacles to change (Hannaway & Rotherham, 2006), as can local policies set by school boards (Hill, 2003). In these cases, it is difficult or impossible for states to waive or repeal these rules because they have been set by agencies outside of state control. It is possible, however, for states to use their own policy- and rule-making authority to place constraints on the barriers thrown up by local institutions. One barrier to improvement identified by California's state policymakers, for example, was the set of collective bargaining provisions allowing senior teachers to transfer within school districts until very close to the start of school. This made it difficult for districts to hire and place new teachers on a reasonable timeline. The state enacted new legislation in 2006 that allows principals to hire teachers after April 15 regardless of whether they are seniority-based transfers (Scott & Rhee, 2006). This law is an example of a state policy that prevents local policies from imposing a particular constraint on school principals.

Creating Space for New Schools
Another means that states can pursue to create opportunities for change relates to crafting space for the creation of new schools. States have primarily sought to create this kind of opportunity by authorizing the formation of charter schools, independently operated public schools that receive autonomy from state laws and policies and are held accountable under a limited term contract that can be revoked or not renewed if the school does not perform. Forty states and Washington, DC now have charter legislation, though the particulars vary widely from state to state (Lake & Hill, 2006). Several large districts have launched their own new school-creation initiatives, using state charter legislation in some cases but also creating new schools under their own authority. For example, Chicago's Renaissance 2010 initiative utilizes both chartering and other forms of contracting to replace failing schools with new smaller schools (Chicago Public Schools, 2007).

In addition to enacting legislation that makes chartering possible, states play two other subsequent roles in the charter school process. First, they are in some cases the "authorizers" of charter schools: the entities that decide whether to approve charter applications, oversee charter schools once they are open, and make decisions about charter renewals and revocations. In twelve states, "the state board of education, the state commissioner, or the state department of education may directly authorize charter schools throughout the state" (Hassel, Ziebarth, & Steiner, 2005, p. 7). Other states plays a more indirect authorizing role such as hearing appeals of local denials of charter applications. Second, states generally have many of the same oversight, accountability, and technical assistance responsibilities toward charter schools that they have toward all public schools, such as monitoring their compliance with federal laws on children with disabilities, ensuring that schools administer the required state assessments, and overseeing implementation of NCLB remedies in the event that schools fail to make AYP repeatedly. In all of these roles—legislating, authorizing, overseeing, and assisting—states exert significant influence over the degree to which chartering actually creates opportunities for schools to do things differently.

Much ink has been spilt over how charter schools in general are performing relative to conventional public schools. The research base on this question is generally weak, and the results mixed (Charter School Achievement Consensus Panel, 2006). This debate, however, is largely irrelevant to state policymakers interested in using chartering as a mechanism for creating new opportunities for improved outcomes because the research focuses on relative average performance of all schools within the two "sectors." Of greater importance to state leaders interested in fostering school change is how to craft a chartering approach (legislation, authorizing, oversight, and assistance) that maximizes the likelihood of success. Research on chartering suggests that policy variables such as rigor of the up-front approval process can have a large effect on the success of this strategy for opening up opportunities (Miron, 2005; Arkin & Kowal, 2005).

Chartering is not the only way states can create space for new schools. Based on a successful model in Boston, the state of Massachusetts recently created the Commonwealth Pilot School Model. Pilot schools are public schools that are granted substantive autonomy over their budget, staffing, governance, curriculum, assessment, and the school calendar, under a partnership agreement between the school district and the local teacher union (Massachusetts Department of Education, 2007). In line with the construction of opportunities, the program website asserts that the schools were "explicitly created to be models of educational innovation and to serve as research and development sites for effective urban public schools." Similar to charter schools in Massachusetts, the pilot schools are exempt from district rules and regulations, including collective bargaining agreement work rules. But, unlike charter schools, due to the partnership with the union, teachers in pilot schools are provided union wages, benefits, and seniority within the district. Given the program's stated commitment to research and development, the model is arguably also an example of how a state can create and disseminate new knowledge in order to build both state and local capacity.

EVALUATION OF THE STATE ROLE IN DISTRICT AND SCHOOL IMPROVEMENT

In line with the broad goals of NCLB, effective monitoring and accountability for performance should be built into states' systems of support. In fact, we propose that evaluating school improvement efforts is so central to the success of the system that evaluation should be considered the floor on which the three legs of the stool stand. States have developed relatively sophisticated means to assess schools, but the rubric for assessing actual state systems appears to be relatively underdeveloped (CCSSO, 2006; Dwyer et al., 2005; Reville et al., 2005). Furthermore, according to Reville (2004), states have made varying levels of commitment to studying intervention outcomes; consequently, SEAs are ill equipped to assess the costs or the benefits of various structures and types of support. The manner of assessing outcomes depends upon the state's approach (i.e., incentives, capacity building structure, differentiation, delivery, or opportunities). In addition, it must take into consideration the multiple and potentially confounding variables that may influence school improvement separate from any actions initiated by the state under the auspices of state systems of support.

While acknowledging the challenges associated with isolating the effect of state systems of support, potential metrics for assessing intervention strategies designed to affect both types of trajectories are:

- track sanctions and utilization of incentives;
- track resources dedicated to research and development;
- monitor implementation of new instructional technologies promoted by the SEA and determine impact of the new practices;
- document participation in teacher and leadership training programs (i.e., human capital pipeline) and assess value of training according to teacher and leader success;
- monitor schools receiving SEA support and track annual improvement goals;
- monitor effectiveness of services delivered;
- monitor implementation of changes resulting from services;
- monitor changes to operations and performance of district and schools within the district; and
- track opportunities created by the SEA and evaluate impact of the opportunities on school improvement.

The conventional wisdom related to school change typically projects that real change requires three to five years. Cross-industry research on organizational turnarounds indicates that while some changes may take three to five years, it is inappropriate to wait this long to expect any change or to assess formative changes (Public Impact, 2007). In fact, initial interventions or "early wins" can signal that real change is possible and serve as the catalyst for more substantive long term intervention. Efforts to track the effect of state systems of supports should incorporate regular benchmarks as well as selecting more long-term measures of success based on the specific unit of intervention (i.e., school or district).

CONCLUSIONS

The number of schools and districts not making adequate yearly progress continues to grow. Although the research on this topic is somewhat preliminary and evolving, it indicates that states and, specifically, SEAs are moving toward a triage approach for their systems of support. States are also realizing the need for strong, continuous, district-directed improvement processes to assist schools at all levels of current performance. As districts assume greater responsibility for their schools' improvement, the state is able to focus its support more sharply on the districts and schools in greatest need of remediation. Thus, states must consider the points of impact where a particular district or school needs assistance and differentiate support and services accordingly. Developing and supporting all three legs of the three-legged stool of incentives, capacity, and opportunity (and a secure floor consisting of an effective evaluation process) are essential to constructing a statewide system of support that can bear the burden of substantive school improvement that will benefit all students. Effectively leveraging incentives to motivate behavioral changes in an environment free of barriers to change, and bolstered by capacity, may provide the best prospect for meaningful and sustainable change to schools and districts.

NOTES

1. We are grateful for the thoughtful comments provide by Brett Lane, Paul Reville, and Herb Walberg. While their contributions strengthened our analysis, all errors of fact or omission are attributable to the authors alone.
2. For more information about the history of the evolution of the state role in school improvement, please see the Redding chapter in this Handbook.

REFERENCES

Archer, J. (2006a, September 13). Building capacity. *Education Week*, pp. S3-S12.

Archer, J. (2006b, September 13). Pennsylvania: To help struggling districts, the state provides teams of top-notch educators for two years. *Education Week*, pp. S18-S19.

Arkin, M. A., & Kowal, J. (2005). *Reopening as a charter school.* Washington, DC: Center for Comprehensive School Reform and Improvement.

Baltimore Public School System. (2007). *BCPSS teacher stipends.* Retrieved April 10, 2007, from http://www.bcps.k12.md.us/Careers/PDF/Stipend_Flyer.pdf

Barney, H., & Robyn, A. (2005). *School improvement, interventions and technical assistance.* Washington, DC: RAND Education. Retrieved March 20, 2007, from http://www.rand.org/pubs/working_papers/WR257/index.html

Beam, D. R., & Conlan T. J. (2002). Grants. In L. M. Salamon (Ed.), *The tools of government: A guide to the new governance.* New York: Oxford University Press.

Berends, M., Bodilly, S. J., & Nataraj Kirby, S. (2002). *Facing the challenges of whole-school reform: New American Schools after a decade.* Santa Monica, CA: RAND. Retrieved December 8, 2005, from http://www.rand.org/publications/MR/MR1498/

Bryk, A. S., Shipps, D., Hill, P. T., & Lake, R. (1998) *Decentralization in practice: Toward a system of schools.* Chicago: The Chicago Consortium on School Research.

Center on Education Policy. (2007). *Educational architects: Do state education agencies have the tools necessary to implement NCLB?* Washington, DC: Author.

Center on Education Policy. (2006). *From the capital to the classroom: Year 4 of the No Child Left Behind Act.* Washington, DC: Author.

Charter School Achievement Consensus Panel. (2006). *Key issues in studying charter schools and achievement: A review and suggestions for national guidelines.* Seattle, WA: National Charter School Research Project, University of Washington.

Chicago Public Schools. (2007). *Chicago Public Schools: Renaissance 2010.* Retrieved March 30, 2007, from http://www.ren2010.cps.k12.il.us/

Childress, Elmore, & Grossman (2006). *How to manage urban schools.* Harvard Business Review. Boston, MA.

Council of Chief State School Officers (2006, September). *State support to schools in need of improvement.* Washington, DC: Author. Retrieved March 13 from: http://www.ccsso.org/content/pdfs/SSSNI_FINAL.pdf

Darling-Hammond, L. (2000). *Solving the dilemmas of teacher supply, demand, and standards: how we can ensure competent, caring, and qualified teacher for every child.* New York: National Commission on Teaching and America's Future. Retrieved April 12, 2007 from: http://www.nctaf.org/documents/supply-demand-standards.pdf

Darling-Hammond, L., & Baratz-Snowden, J. (2005). *A Good Teacher in Every Classroom: Preparing the Highly Qualified Teachers Our Children Deserve.* San Francisco: Jossey-Bass.

David, J., Kannapel, P., & McDiarmid, G.W (2000). *The influence of distinguished educators on school improvement. A study of Kentucky's school intervention program.* Lexington, KY: Partnership for Kentucky Schools.

Diaz, M. (2007). *Meeting the challenge of statewide systems of support.* Chicago: Learning Points Associates.

DiBiase, R. W. (2005). *ECS policy brief: state involvement in school restructuring under No Child Left Behind in the 2004-05 school year.* Denver, CO: Education Commission of the States. Retrieved March 26, 2007, from http://www.ecs.org/clearinghouse/64/28/6428.pdf.

Duke, D., Tucker, P. D., & Higgins J., (2005). *What were the accomplishments of the VSTSP principals? Executive summary of two major research studies, 2004-2005.* Available: http://www.darden.virginia.edu/uploadedFiles/Centers_of_Excellence/PLE/VSTSP_%20Executive_%20Summary.pdf

Dwyer, C, with, Bormand, J., Cevoen, L., Fafard, M. B., Frankel, S., Harvell, C., Keirstead, C., Lane, B., Lopez, J, Lusi, S., Seager, A., & Zarlengo, P. (2005). *Leadership Capacities for a Changing Environment: State and District Responses to the*

No Child Left Behind Act of 2001. Providence, RI: Education Alliance at Brown University.

Education Commission of the States. (2002). *State Intervention in Low-Performing Schools and School Districts*. Denver Colorado: Author.

Education Commission of the States. (2004). *ECS Report to the Nation: State Implementation of the No Child Left Behind Act*. Denver, Colorado: Author.

Education Commission of the States (2007a). *Incentives for Teacher Recruitment and Retention in High-Priority Districts*. Retrieved April 15, 2007 from: http://mb2.ecs.org/reports/Report.aspx?id=1268

Education Commission of the States. (2007b). *School choice state laws: 50-state profile*. Retrieved March 26, 2007, from State policies for school choice database: http://www.ecs.org/ecsmain.asp?page=/html/educationIssues/Choice/ChoiceDB_intro.asp

Education Commission of the States. (2007c). *ECS Report to the Nation: State Implementation of the No Child Left Behind Act*. Denver, CO: Author. Retrieved April 13, 2007 from: http://www.ecs.org/html/special/nclb/reporttothenation/reporttothenation.htm

Elmore, R. F., (n.d.). *Knowing the right thing to do: School improvement and performance-based accountability*. Washington, DC: National Governors Association.

Elmore, R. (2002). *Bridging the gap between standards and achievement*. Washington, D.C.: The Albert Shanker Institute.

Elmore, R. & McLaughlin M.W. (1988). *Steady work: policy, practice, and the reform of American education*. Santa Monica: RAND.

Finnigan, K. & O'Day, J. (2003). *External support to schools on probation: Getting a leg up?* Chicago, IL: Consortium on Chicago School Research.

Fowler, R.C. (April 22, 2003). *The Massachusetts Signing Bonus Program for New Teachers: A model of teacher preparation worth copying?* Education Policy Analysis Archives, 11(13). Retrieved April 15, 2007 from http://epaa.asu.edu/epaa/v11n13/

Fuhrman, S. H. & R. F. Elmore. (1995). *Ruling out rules: The evolution of deregulation in state education policy*. New Brunswick, NJ: Consortium for Policy Research in Education.

Fulton, K., Yoon, I., & Lee, C., (2005). *Induction into learning communities*. New York: National Commission on Teaching and America's Future. Retrieved April 12, 2007 from: http://www.nctaf.org/documents/NCTAF_Induction_Paper_2005.pdf

Gill, B, Timpane, M., Ross, K., & Brewer, D. (2001). *Rhetoric versus reality: what we know and what we need to know about vouchers and charter schools*. Santa Monica, CA: RAND.

Gill, B. P., Hamilton, L. S., Lockwood, J. R., Marsh, J. A., Zimmer, R. W., Hill, D., et al. (2005). *Inspiration, perspiration, and time: Operations and achievement in Edison Schools*. Santa Monica, CA: RAND.

Hannaway, J., & Cohodes, S. (in-press). *Miami-Dade County: Trouble Even in Choice Paradise in The No Child Left Behind Remedies: Safe? Sensible? Effective?* (eds. Frederick M. Hess and Chester E. Finn, Jr.), Washington, DC: American Enterprise Institute Press.

Hannaway, J. & A. J. Rotherham. (2006). *Collective bargaining in education: negotiating change in today's schools.* Cambridge: Harvard Education Press.

Hannaway, J., & Woodroffe, N. (2003). *Policy Instruments in Education.* Review of Research in Education, 27, 1-24.

Hanushek, E. A. (1994). *Making schools work.* Washington, DC: Brookings Institution Press.

Hanushek, Eric A., & Raymond, Margaret E., (2004). The Effect of School Accountability Systems on the Level and Distribution of Student Achievement. *Journal of the European Economic Association.* April–May, 2004, 2(2–3): 406–415.

Hassel, B.C., T. Ziebarth, & L. Steiner. (2005). *A state policymaker's guide to alternative authorizers of charter schools.* Denver: Education Commission of the States.

Heck, D. J. & Weiss, I., (2005, Janaury). *Strategic leadership for education reform: Lessons from the statewide systemic initiatives program.* CPRE Policy Briefs. Philadelphia, PA: Consortium for Policy Research in Education.

Hess, F. (2002). *Revolution at the margins: the impact of competition on urban school systems.* Washington, DC: Brookings Institution.

Hill, P. T. (2003). *School boards: Focus on school performance, not money and patronage.* Washington, D.C.: Progressive Policy Institute.

Hoff, D. J. (2006). Kentucky: The state expands its' distinguished educator' program to districts, including their school boards. *Education Week.* September 13, 2006, pages S14-S15.

Holdzkom, D. (2001). *Low-performing schools: So you've identified them, now what?* Charleston, WV: AEL: Retrieved March 24 from: http://eric.ed.gov/ERIC-Docs/data/ericdocs2/content_storage_01/0000000b/80/0d/d9/5c.pdf

Hoxby, C. (2004). School choice and school competition: evidence from the United States. *Swedish Economic Policy Review.* 10(2): 11-67.

Institute for Educational Leadership. (2001). *Leadership for student learning: Recognizing the state's role in public education.* Washington, DC: Author.

Jacobson, L. (2006, September 13). New Mexico: The Baldrige continuous-improvement program is prescribed by the state as a cure for troubled schools. *Education Week*, pp. S16-S17.

Kober, S., Stark Renner, D., & Jennings, J. (2006). *Hope but no miracle cures: Michigan's early restructuring lessons.* Washington, DC: Center on Education Policy.

Kolderie T. (1990). *Beyond choice to new public schools: Withdrawing the exclusive franchise in public education.* Washington, DC: Progressive Policy Institute. Retrieved March 26, 2007, from http://www.ndol.org/ndol_ci.cfm?kaid=110&subid=134&contentid=1382

Kowal, J., Hassel, E. A., & Hassel, B. C. (2007). *Case studies of innovative compensation plans for hard-to-staff schools and positions.* Naperville, IL: Learning Point Associates.

Kowal, J. K., & Hassel, E. A. (2006). *Turnarounds with new leaders and staff.* Washington, DC: Center for Comprehensive School Reform and Improvement.

Kowal, J., Hassel, E. A., & Hassel, B. C. (2007). *Case studies of innovative compensation plans for hard-to-staff schools and positions.* Naperville, IL: Learning Point Associates.

Laguarda, K. G. (2003). *State-sponsored technical assistance to low-performing schools: Strategies from nine states.* Paper presented at the Annual Meeting of the American Educational Research Association, Chicago, IL.

Lake, R. J., & Hill, P.T. (2006). *Hopes, fears, and reality: A balanced look at American charter schools in 2006.* Seattle, WA: National Charter School Research Project, University of Washington.

Lane, B., & Garcia, S. (2004). State-level support for comprehensive school reform: Implications for policy and practice. *Journal of Education for Students Placed at Risk, 10*(1), 85-112.

Lane, B., Seager, A., & Frankel, S. (2005). *Learning into a statewide system of support: New York State's regional network strategy for school improvement.* Providence, RI: Education Alliance at Brown University.

Leithwood, K., Seashore Louis, K., Anderson, S., & Wahlstrom, K. (2004). *How leadership influences student learning.* Prepared for The Wallace Foundation. Retrieved from http://www.wallacefoundation.org/WF/KnowledgeCenter/KnowledgeTopics/EducationLeadership/HowLeadershipInfluencesStudentLearning.htm

Lusi, S. F. (1997). *The role of state departments of education in complex school reform.* New York: Teachers College Press.

Manna, P. (2006). *State implementation of No Child Left Behind's remedies for troubled schools and districts.* Retrieved March 26, 2007, from http://www.aei.org/docLib/20061130_MannaPaper.pdf

Massachusetts Department of Education (2007). *2007 guidelines for Commonwealth Pilot Schools option.* Malden, MA: Author. Retrieved June 14, 2007, from http://www.doe.mass.edu/sda/redesign/guidelines.html?section=bg

Massell, D. (1998). *State strategies for building capacity in education: Progress and continuing challenges.* CPRE Policy Briefs. Philadelphia, PA: Consortium for Policy Research in Education.

Mazzeo, C., & Berman, I. (n.d.). *Reaching new heights: Turning around low-performing schools.* Washington, DC: Author.

McIver, M. (2002). *Education services units: Initiating, sustaining and advancing school improvement.* Aurora, CO: Mid-Continent Research for Education and Learning. Retrieved April 12, 2007, from http://www.mcrel.org/PDF/SchoolImprovementReform/5031TG_EducationServicesAgencies.pdf

McLaughlin, M., & Talbert, J. (2003). *Reforming districts: How districts support school reform.* Seattle, WA: Center for the Study of Teaching and Policy, University of Washington.

McNeil, M. (2007, February 13). Utah gov. signs broad voucher law. *Education Week.* Retrieved March 26, 2007, from http://www.edweek.org/ew/articles/2007/02/13/23utah_webupdate.h26.html

Mintrop, H., & Trujillo, T. (2005). Corrective action in low-performing schools: Lessons for NCLB implementation from state and district strategies in first-generation accountability systems. *Education Policy Analysis Archives, 13*(48), 1-30.

Miron, G. (2005, April 11-15). *Strong charter school laws are those that result in positive outcomes.* Paper presented at the annual meeting of the American Educational Research Association, Montreal, Canada.

National Governors Association. (1986). *Time for results.* Washington, DC: Author.

National Center for Education Statistics. (2005). *Digest of educational statistics*. Washington, DC: Author.

New England Compact. (2007). Alexandria, VA: Education Development Corporation. Retrieved June 15, 2007, from http://www.necompact.org/

Nichols, S. L., & Berliner, D. C. (2007). *Collateral damage: How high-stakes testing corrupts America's schools.* Cambridge, MA: Harvard Education Press.

O'Day, J., & Bitter, C. S. (2003). *Evaluation study of the immediate intervention/underperforming schools program and the high achieving/improving schools program of the Public Schools Accountability Act of 1999: Final report.* Palo Alto, CA: American Institutes of Research.

Odden, A. R., & Picus, L. O. (1992). *School finance: A policy perspective.* New York: McGraw-Hill.

Olson, L. (2005, March 16). NCLB choice option going untapped, but tutoring picking up. *Education Week, 24*(27), pp. 1, 20.

Palaich, R. M., Griffin Good, D., & van der Ploeg, A. (2004, June). *State education data systems that increase learning and improve accountability.* Chicago: Learning Points Associates.

Plank. D., & Dunbar, C. (2006). *Michigan: Over the first hurdle.* Retrieved March 26, 2007, from http://www.aei.org/docLib/20061130_PlankPaper.pdf

Podgursky, M.,& Springer, M. G. (2007). Teacher performance pay: A review. *Journal of Policy Analysis and Management, 26*(4).

Rebell, M. (2007). Professional rigor, public engagement and judicial review: A proposal for enhancing the validity of education adequacy studies. *Teachers College Record, 109*(6), 1303-1373.

Reville, P. S. (2004). *Examining state intervention capacity: How can the state better support low performing schools and districts?* Boston, MA: Rennie Center for Education Research & Policy.

Reville, P. S. (2007). *Key components of a statewide system of support: State example and resources.* Boston, MA: Rennie Center for Education Research & Policy.

Reville, P. S., Coggins, C., & Candon, J. (2005, Spring). *Reaching capacity: A blueprint for the state role in improving low performing schools and districts.* Boston, MA: Rennie Center for Education Research & Policy.

Public Impact. (2007). *School turnarounds: A review of the cross-sector evidence on dramatic organizational improvement.* Lincoln, IL: Center on Innovation & Improvement.

Rice, J. K., & Malen, B. (2003, December). The human costs of education reform: The case of school reconstitution. *Educational Administration Quarterly, 39*(5), 635-666.

Scott, C., Jennings, J., & Rentner, D. S. (2007, March). *What now? Lessons from Michigan about restructuring schools and next steps under NCLB.* Washington, DC: Center on Education Policy.

Scott, J., & Rhee. M. (2006, November 15). Common sense in teacher hiring. *Education Week.* Retrieved March 30, 2007, from http://www.edweek.org/ew/articles/2006/11/15/12rhee.h26.html

Smith, M., & O'Day J. (1991). Systemic school reform. In S. H. Fuhrman & B. Malen (Eds.), *The politics of curriculum and testing* (pp. 233-267). Bristol, PA: Falmer Press.

Snipes, J., Doolittle, F., & Herlihey, C. (2002). *Foundations for success: Case studies of how urban school systems improve student achievement.* Washington, DC: Center for Education Policy.

Spillane, J. P. (1996). School districts matter: Local education authorities and state instructional policy. *Educational Policy, 10*(1), 63-87.

Spillane, J. P. (1997). A cognitive perspective on the LEA's roles in implementing instructional policy: Accounting for local variability. *Education Administration Quarterly, 34*(1), 295-315.

Spillane, J. P. (1998). State policy and the non-monolithic nature of the local school district: Organization and professional considerations. *American Education Research Journal, 35*(1), 33-63.

State of Vermont Board of Education. (1992, January). *Policy statement on deregulation.* Montpelier: Vermont Department of Education.

Sunderman, G. L., Kim, S & Orfield, G., (2005) *NCLB meets school realities: Lessons from the field.* Thousand Oaks, CA: Corwin Press.

Sunderman, G. L., & Orfield, G. (2006). *Domesticating a revolution: No Child Left Behind reforms and state administrative response.* Cambridge, MA: The Civil Rights Project at Harvard University.

Tyack, D., & Hansot, E. (1982). *Managers of virtue: Public education leadership in America, 1829-1980.* New York: Basic Books.

U.S. Department of Education. (2006, July). *LEA and school improvement, Non-regulatory guidance.* Washington, DC: Author.

U.S. Department of Education. (2004). *Alternative route to teacher certification.* Retrieved March 25, 2007, from http://www.ed.gov/admins/tchrqual/recruit/altroutes/report.pdf

U.S. Department of Education. (2001). *School improvement report: Executive order on actions for turning around low-performing schools: First annual report.* Washington, DC: U.S. Department of Education. Retrieved July 12, 2006, from http://www.ed.gov/offices/OUS/PES/lpschools.pdf

Waters, T., Marzano, R. J., & McNulty, B. (2003). *Balanced leadership: What 30 years of research tells us about the effect of leadership on student achievement.* Aurora, CO: Mid-Continent Research for Education and Learning.

Westat. (2006). *Statewide systems of support profiles.* Rockville, MD: Author.

Lauren Morando Rhim *is a senior consultant for Public Impact and a member of the Scientific Council for the Center on Innovation & Improvement.*

Bryan Hassel *is co-director of Public Impact, a national education policy and management consulting firm based in Chapel Hill, NC, and a member of the Center on Innovation & Improvement's Scientific Council.*

Sam Redding *is the director of the Center on Innovation & Improvement.*

CHAPTER 5

AN EVOLUTION
IN AMERICAN EDUCATION

Sam Redding

The idea of a "statewide system of support" for the improvement of public schools represents the turning of a page in American education. Consistent with the direction of most states since the 1980s, the No Child Left Behind Act of 2001 (NCLB), and its predecessor act (the 1994 reauthorization of the Elementary and Secondary Education Act—Improving America's Schools), codified a stronger role for states in school and district improvement. To satisfy federal funding requirements under Title I of NCLB, a state must provide a statewide system of support to aid the improvement of schools and districts toward the goal of all students achieving proficiency on state standards-based assessments in reading, mathematics, and science by 2013–14.

The state government may play a broad role in school improvement by passing laws, allocating resources, and reorganizing education-related agencies. But the state's education agency (SEA) remains the center of gravity for school and district improvement. The SEA continues to perform many functions, and the statewide system of support is only one of them. The statewide system of support is the SEA's vehicle for assisting districts and their schools in filling gaps between actual and desired performance. This requires the system of support to include coordinated components for assessing current district and school operations and performance, determining need, delivering services, and monitoring progress. However, state support reaches beyond the SEA, as the SEA designates intermediate ser-

Handbook on Statewide Systems of Support, pages 61–81
Copyright © 2008 The Academic Development Institute and Information Age Publishing
61

vice centers, consultants, universities, and partnering organizations to serve in the system. Under NCLB, the statewide system of support must include school support teams that focus on specific schools and districts and distinguished educators who serve as consultants to the schools and districts. Also under NCLB, the system of support performs triage, dealing first and foremost with districts in greatest need of improvement. As the number of schools in need of improvement has escalated, states have realized the importance of the districts in guiding the improvement of their schools.

Reconciliation of Competing Philosophies

A cursory scan of the evolution of schooling in America over the past two centuries reveals that a statewide system of support is both a significant departure from the past and a logical progression. A historical perspective elucidates the competing philosophies of education that NCLB attempts to reconcile, placing national agendas of equity and quality alongside its investment in state authority for public education. At the district level, a democratic preference for organic, local variation is central to the family prerogative in childrearing.

National actions, such as federal legislation and Supreme Court decisions, provide convenient milestones that trace the evolution of American public education, and reflect as much as they dictate changes in the country's notions about its schools. Whatever the origins of changes in public schooling, the effects are played out school by school, teacher by teacher, and family by family. The relationships among the federal government, the states, districts, schools, teachers, and families remain reliable indices of the health of our public school system and its prospects for success.

HISTORICAL PRECEDENTS AND TRENDS

National Encouragement, Local Responsibility, Family Prerogative

Even before the U.S. Constitution was ratified, Congress (under the Articles of Confederation) expressed a national philosophy of education when, in the Northwest Ordinance of 1787, it asserted that "religion, morality, and knowledge, being necessary to good government and the happiness of mankind, schools and the means of education shall forever be encouraged" (Beard & Beard, 1944). Two years earlier, Congress passed the Land Ordinance of 1785. The Act required surveyors in the Northwest Territory to lay the entire region stretching north of the Ohio River to the Great Lakes into township grids of thirty-six 640-acre sections, and to reserve the 16th section for the "maintenance of public schools." National encouragement and means for the operation of schools preceded even the establishment of schools themselves in this section of the country, and the national government provided at least the opportunity for school formation.

The U.S. Constitution, of course, makes no claim for schooling within the enumerated powers of the national government (Article 1, Section 8), reserving for the states or their people responsibility for education under the Tenth Amendment. In keeping with the intent of the Northwest Ordinance, the federal government would forever encourage schools and the means of education, but would not provide or assume responsibility for the operation of schools. An educated citizenry was important to a democratic society, and the states and their citizens would determine how schools would be formed, supported, and operated. In large part, the states left the matter to their citizens. For nearly a century, the people took the lead, with most states relying upon charitable and religious sponsorship of schools for poor children. Meanwhile, affluent families retained tutors for their children or sent them to private schools. Many families provided their own education for their children, which in some cases was considerable and in other instances little or none at all. Families retained ultimate discretion in the type and amount of education their children received. State systems of education and publicly financed schools emerged slowly through the nineteenth century, the pace of their development varying by region and state.

The principal purpose of education, in the eyes of America's founders, was to contribute to the morality and civic responsibility of the masses, a counterweight to the anarchy and excess that many feared would arise from a populace left free in the great experiment of democracy (Jeynes, 2007). Further, Thomas Jefferson and others advocated for high-quality colleges so that the country's elite would not choose to be educated in foreign lands. Higher education, still grounded in the classics, was intended to liberate the parochial mind in preparation for scholarship and civic leadership. While most early American institutions of higher education were private and church sponsored, state universities were established in locales where private colleges were not within reach, including the University of Georgia (1785), University of North Carolina (1789), University of South Carolina (1801), Ohio University (1802), University of Maryland (1807), and Miami University (1809). State-supported universities arose prior to state-supported elementary and high schools.

What we presently think of as vocational, career, or professional education—preparation for the workplace—was, in the first century of American history, obtained through the family passing on its occupation, apprenticeships in crafts and trades, and study under master practitioners in professions such as law and medicine. Only the ministry required advanced academic preparation, though frontier churches, especially the Baptists and similar sects, removed that barrier to clerical occupation from a doctrinal belief in direct access to spiritual revelation and scriptural interpretation. This was also a necessary response to the inadequate supply of seminary-trained clergy.

Through the first half of the nineteenth century, private (usually sectarian) charity schools sprang up across the country providing basic literacy and moral guidance for children of the poor (Jeynes, 2007). Likewise, subscription schools enabled families of meager means to pay for each subject taught to each child, typically with daily or weekly rates that allowed children to work on family farms or in family shops while attending school as time permitted. Subscription schools also solicited support from local people of means whose financial assistance lessened or removed the burden on families. In rural areas, the family remained the chief provider of education for their children, subsidized in some cases through the voluntary contributions of their neighbors. The Bible served as the primary text. The Sunday school movement, spawned in eighteenth-century England and brought to America by the Methodists and other English sects, provided a day of learning for children who worked the farms the rest of the week. Whether through voluntary attendance in charity schools or Sunday schools, investment in subscription schools, or devotion to homeschooling, each family made its own choice about the education of their children.

The Common Schools and State Education Agencies

The seeds of what we now think of as state systems of public education were planted in the decades preceding the Civil War and given impetus by the war and its aftermath (Jeynes, 2007). The common school movement in the early nineteenth century provided the philosophical groundwork for state systems of public education. Joel Spring (1990) argues that the common school movement was distinct in three respects: (a) all children were educated in a common schoolhouse; (b) the school was an instrument of government policy; and (c) state agencies were necessary to control local schools. Centralizing school authority with the state, regulating and standardizing local school operations, and promoting national values in place of regional and sectarian values were in many ways antithetical to the colonial and early American traditions of charity, religious, and subscription schools. Protestant Christian sects, especially those of mainline churches, found the common schools compatible with their own values and traditions, however, and were largely supportive of the movement.

In 1806 and 1816, the Ohio legislature allowed for the organization of schools that would be supported by rents from lands (including the sections provided in the Northwest Ordinance) and tuition (Spring, 1990). New York was the first state to establish a Secretary of Schools (1812), and Massachusetts created a Board of Education and secretary in 1837. The New York plan encouraged and supported education for poor children through the private charity schools, a plan that proved inadequate for the increasing numbers of immigrant children. Massachusetts had provided taxation to support schools and enacted legislation to facilitate the creation of public schools even before the creation of the state Board of Education in 1837.

Onto this seedbed of public schooling, educators including Horace Mann and Henry Bernard promulgated a vision of "common schools," providing for non-sectarian but decidedly Christian (and Protestant), tax-supported schools to fulfill the national desire for a moral and responsible citizenry while also instilling in each generation a common devotion to American principles of democracy that would supersede the pluralistic tendencies of parochial upbringings, especially for immigrants (Fraser, 2001). The common school was also intended to provide avenues of opportunity for poor children, alleviating the undemocratic division of society between the haves and have-nots. Furthermore, tax-supported, common schools would ensure greater teaching quality through the state regulation that would accompany public financing. State teaching institutions (normal schools) arose to satisfy the states' regulatory requirements and supply the common schools with faculties. The first teacher institute was founded by Samuel Hall as a private institute in Concord, Vermont, in 1823. In 1839, Henry Barnard and Emma Willard established a private teacher-training institute in Hartford, Connecticut. Horace Mann opened the first public teacher institute the same year in Lexington, Massachusetts.

The common school movement met with resistance on several fronts (Fraser, 2001; Jeynes, 2007). Religious groups, including Catholics and Lutherans which had organized schools of their own, often with instruction in languages other than English, and Protestant churches with a non-establishment tradition, feared the homogenizing effects of common schools that would not educate children in their religious sect. Defenders of slavery and advocates of personal choice in the use of alcohol looked to the abolitionist and temperance convictions of Mann and other leaders of the common school movement with alarm. Especially in the West, parents rejected what they perceived as government usurpation of family responsibilities and choices. These parents had grown attached to their church-supported and subscription schools which were locally controlled, community based, and responsive to community concerns. Here, teachers were members of parents' parishes and neighborhoods, so teachers were familiar to the parents.

In 1855, the Illinois legislature passed laws to establish a standardized system of common schools, six years after it had first approved state funding to supplement the scattered and disparate local, public schools that had evolved from church-operated and subscription schools. To focus our lens on a typical local situation, we might look at Jacksonville in the center of the state (Doyle, 1978). Jacksonville's first "colored school" was established in 1865, with financial support from black and white citizens. It was located in an African American church building that was later sold to the school district to ensure its continuation when the city formalized its district in 1867. The school district then included five, six-grade schools for white children, one school for black children with only grades one and two, and a high school for the few white children who advanced to this level. This district system was formed to coordinate individual schools that were already in place and that operated alongside the Lutheran school and Catholic school. Thus, what we now know as a school district often emerged from a background of charity schools, parochial schools, country schools, and subscription schools, especially in the Midwest and West.

Schools for an Urban/Industrial Nation

The Civil War proved to be a watershed in American acceptance of common schools and public financial support for schools, addressing the palpable need for national unity, education of freed slaves, and assimilation of the accelerating stream of non-English-speaking immigrants. American education leaders looked favorably upon the Prussian system of teacher institutes, and fell sway to the philosophy of the Swiss Johann Pestalozzi, who professed that schools could mirror the nurturing aspects of the family. Leaders continued to place moral formation as the chief purpose of schooling. America's own McGuffey Reader, a series of grammar school primers and readers created by Pennsylvanian William McGuffey, sold more than 100 million copies in the nineteenth century and joined the Bible as basic text in American schools. The McGuffey Reader taught children to read while also conveying lessons of morality and character.

In the post-Civil War period, America became increasingly urbanized and industrialized. As a result, populations became more densely concentrated, and people of different national and religious backgrounds lived in greater proximity to each other. Common schools advanced immigrants' learning of English and acquainted them with the history of their new homeland. Likewise, common schools familiarized children of rural families, recently arrived in the cities for employment, with an urban culture that was foreign to them. In line with the thinking of European social reformers, including the Italian Maria Montessori, schooling was viewed as a way to rescue the wandering children of the streets whose parents were now working long hours away from home in the factories. As child labor laws limited children's exploitation and long days in factories, a means for socializing them became more acutely necessary. School enrollments in cities expanded exponentially, and city school districts became more systematized than the states in many respects.

The skills required in an industrialized workplace were not skills children acquired from their families while growing up on the farm or in the family business or trade. Thus, business and government leaders recognized the economic necessity of vocational and occupational training, a new dimension to America's tradition of moral and civic education for the masses. This stood apart from the classics-based intellectual education of the elite. In 1853, the Illinois legislature passed resolutions in support of industrial instruction, and in 1857 Justin Smith Morrill, a Vermont congressman, introduced federal legislation to issue grants of land to states to provide financial support for agricultural, industrial, and military training. President James Buchanan vetoed the legislation. Not to be deterred, Morrill introduced similar legislation in 1862, and President Lincoln signed into law the Morrill Land Grant act of that year. The grants of land awarded to the states provided financial support to existing colleges, including some private colleges, and fostered the creation of new colleges. A Second Morrill Act (1890) required segregated states to split the land grant revenues equally between white and black institutions, greatly benefiting African American colleges that had taken root after the Civil War.

As America was transformed from a rural, agricultural society into an industrial, urban society, institutions reflected the same transformation—from organic, local, and familial to organized, national, and bureaucratic. The progressive movement in the political and economic spheres had its corollary in education, with the philosophy of John Dewey and others providing underpinnings for scientific management, teacher organization, curriculum reform, and testing and measurement (Fraser, 2001).

Expanded Educational Opportunity

As recently as 1915, only 13.5% of adult Americans held a high school degree (U.S. Census Bureau, 2006). Not until 1970 did the census report that half (54%) of adult Americans held high school diplomas (U.S. Census Bureau, 2000). In 1970, only 11.2% of adult Americans had earned a college degree. While these percentages—54% with high school degrees and 11% with college degrees in 1970—seem anemic to us today, the percentages had tripled over the past half century. As schooling expanded into high school and college for more Americans, the year of kindergarten was added as the entry point. Community colleges entered the scene in the nineteenth century and evolved into extensive, statewide systems in the 1960s and 1970s, providing access to advanced training and an affordable step on the ladder of higher education for millions of Americans. By 2003, 85% of adult Americans had finished high school, and 27% held four-year college degrees (Stoops, 2004). Over the span of three generations, America added kindergarten (and later preschool) to the beginning years, high school became nearly universal, and college became the route of choice for the masses rather than an opportunity reserved for the few.

In 1925, the Supreme Court, in *Pierce v. Society of Sisters*, established precedent for a balance between parental prerogative and the interests of the state by declaring that a state could not require children to attend a public school, but could mandate that children of a certain age attend some school and could regulate the schools to ensure an acceptable quality of education. In particular, the court said that states have an interest in socializing children to citizenship through schooling. This case was brought to court to contest an Oregon statute, based on common school principles, that sought to reduce parochialism by requiring public school attendance. With the Court making the distinction between a state requirement that children attend school, which it approved, and a state requirement that children attend a public school, which it found unacceptable, compulsory attendance laws were established throughout the country.

The First World War, the Great Depression, and the Second World War diverted national resources and attention from education. These difficult times also fostered new appreciation for the advantages of education. Education historians (Berrol, 1982; Cremin, 1962; Ravitch, 1974) provide evidence that student achievement actually increased during the depression, as families saw school as a path to a better life for their children, the work ethic was strengthened by necessity, and the college-educated were drawn to teaching as a stable source of employment. School budgets were cut during these years, focusing curricula on basic subjects and contributing to community involvement in support of their schools.

The G. I. Bill of 1944 paved the way for more than seven million veterans to attend college by providing financial support to individual students to attend the college of their choice. This resonated with the national tradition of encouragement and support for education, without federal direction, in the operation of the schools. This distinction between federal encouragement of education for individuals and direct federal support for and influence over the operation of schools was evidenced when Congress later rejected President Truman's push for federal funding of education and also defeated President Eisenhower's first plan to fund school construction.

When the Russians launched an unmanned orbital satellite in 1957 (Sputnik), Americans were shocked to see that its Communist foe was capable of such a technological achievement. Political leaders concluded that America's schools were not keeping pace with Russia in preparing the scientists and engineers that would keep the country safe during the Cold

War. Studies revealed that the number of American high school students taking foreign language and advanced math and science courses had been in steady decline (Jeynes, 2007). While conservatives blamed progressive education theory and low standards for the decline, liberals pointed to the stagnant investment in education, including low teachers' salaries and inadequate school facilities. President Dwight D. Eisenhower found common ground between these divergent critiques in proposing both increased federal financial assistance and higher standards in science, math, and language as a matter of national defense. In 1958, the National Defense Education Act authorized a billion dollars over four years for both public and private schools to: (a) purchase equipment for language, math, and science; (b) sponsor graduate fellowships in areas related to national defense; and (c) provide student loans in math, science, and language.

Veterans went to college after World War II and also produced the "baby boom," an influx of children into the public schools that required more teachers and more school facilities. Standards stiffened, and scores on college admissions tests such as the ACT and SAT climbed to their historic peak in the mid-1960s (Ravitch, 2000).

The era from the First World War through the Second World War also altered the national consciousness about matters of race and opportunity, fueling the civil rights movement of the 1950s and 1960s. Americans of all creeds and colors had fought in the great wars, and people of all backgrounds had descended into hardship during the depression. They emerged from these experiences with a new understanding of their obligations to one another. Furthermore, they recognized the importance of educational opportunity to the improvement of individual prospects and to the overall strength of the nation and economy. Cold War challenges contributed to a national resolve and a striving for unity.

President Harry S Truman, son of a border state, signaled the post-World War II awakening by forming the President's Committee on Civil Rights in 1946, speaking to the National Association for the Advancement of Colored People in 1947, and advocating a civil rights plank at the Democratic Convention in 1948. Not to be outdone, the Republicans, the party of choice for most African Americans since the Civil War and subsequent constitutional amendments granting them full citizenship rights, proposed civil rights legislation in their presidential campaign of 1948.

When the Supreme Court declared in its 1954 decision *Brown v. Board of Education* that segregated schools were inherently unequal and therefore unconstitutional, the federal government's role in education took a dramatic turn. In addition to "encouraging" education, the federal government would now take a stand on education policy as it related to the rights of individuals and groups. School desegregation became a chief goal in the broader civil rights agenda of national leaders such as Martin Luther

King, Jr., and Ralph Abernathy, both Baptist preachers who made the moral case for equality to accompany the constitutional grounds provided by the Supreme Court. President Eisenhower demonstrated the federal government's willingness to intervene when state education policies and actions ran counter to the requirements of the Brown decision by sending federal troops to Little Rock, Arkansas in 1957, to oversee orderly desegregation of schools.

In the wake of *Brown v. Board of Education*, Congress and the executive branch found the new door of equity open to them, passing legislation and crafting regulation to both extinguish de jure segregation and compensate African Americans for its injurious effects. President John F. Kennedy issued executive orders in the early 1960s to ensure equal access to college education and job opportunities through what became known as "affirmative action," a policy further strengthened by President Richard M. Nixon. Under President Lyndon B. Johnson, Congress passed the Civil Rights Act of 1964, the Elementary and Secondary Education Act of 1965, and the Bilingual Education Act of 1968, all aimed at eliminating racial discrimination and compensating for the disadvantage of poor, minority, and non-English-speaking segments of society.

The Coleman Report, named for its chief author James S. Coleman, then a professor at Johns Hopkins University, was the published findings of the Equality of Educational Opportunity Study. It was commissioned in 1964 by the Department of Health, Education, and Welfare in response to the Civil Rights Act of that year. Congress now sought guidance in investing resources strategically to offset the disadvantages of poverty and segregation. The Coleman Report found that the level of educational resources was less predictive of academic attainment than family background, teacher characteristics, and social context. Coleman's subsequent work (Coleman, 1988; Coleman & Hoffer, 1987) established the importance of social context to education and set in sharp relief the contending influences of educational resources, educational practices, and family background. *Brown v. Board of Education* not only signaled the end of de jure segregation but, along with the civil rights movement gathering steam at the time, alerted America to the under-education of many segments of society.

The Elementary and Secondary Education Act (ESEA) of 1965 brought the federal government to the stage as a significant player in what had been primarily a state and local enterprise. At the same time, ESEA strengthened the role of the state relative to local boards of education by channeling funds through state agencies (Spring, 1990). Proponents justified ESEA as a tool for compensatory education, a way to redress historical injustices and overcome the disadvantages of poverty suffered by children of all ethnic backgrounds. ESEA included a variety of formula grants, including Title I, which required state educational agencies to administer and monitor the distribution of these funds. Recognizing that channeling new resources to districts and schools through the state educational agencies placed increased demands on the SEAs themselves, ESEA included Title V, known as Strengthening State Educational Agencies, which provided funds and guidance to build the capacity of the SEAs. This influx of financial support for state administration, research, evaluation, and data management prompted a significant growth in the staff levels and operational capacity of the SEAs. The Education Consolidation and Improvement Act of 1981 later consolidated Title V and more than 30 other separate programs. ESEA (1965) also established the National Institute of Education (NIE) which later became the Office of Educational Research and Improvement, both predecessors to the Institute of Education Sciences (2002), all of which promoted education research.

The 1970s enlarged the scope of national attention to inequalities with the Title IX (1972) prohibition of unequal allocation of resources and program opportunities between the sexes and the Education for All Handicapped Children Act's (1975) assurance of educational opportunity for children with disabilities. The Education for All Handicapped Children Act extended public education to more than six million children previously kept at home or in institutions without the advantage of schooling. The massive extension of public education to more and more Americans for more and more years of their lives is the central theme of the twentieth century, with the inclusion of children with disabilities, the growing numbers of poor children (black, Hispanic, and white), the added kindergarten year (and later preschool), and the universal expectation of high school. The century also gave rise to the community college system, adult education, and financial assistance for college attendance.

Equity and Quality

In 1980, Congress, at the urging of President Jimmy Carter, authorized the formation of the U.S. Department of Education. The new department was carved from the U.S. Office of Education (then part of the Department of Health, Education, and Welfare), gave education a national platform and provided the federal government a cabinet-level bureaucracy devoted to schooling. President Ronald W. Reagan's National Commission on Excellence in Education asserted in *A Nation at Risk* (1983) that America's pursuit of equity in education must be matched with regard for quality. *A Nation at Risk* showed that our students' academic performance was unfavorably contrasted with students in other nations. The effective schools research (see, for example, Edmonds, 1979) that emerged in the years just prior to *A Nation at Risk* had already demonstrated that school practices varied, and that some schools did a better job than others in achieving satis-factory results with similar populations of children. This conclusion echoed Coleman's findings. The scores on college entrance exams had declined steadily since the mid-1960s; SAT results descended during those years to their low point in 1980. Scores on most national and state tests fell similarly during this same span of years (Ravitch, 2000).

A Nation at Risk called for higher standards of learning for America's school children. Literacy arose in the 1980s as a chief area of concern, with Jonathan Kozol's *Illiterate America* (1985) sounding the alarm over basic lit-eracy and E. D. Hirsch Jr.'s *Cultural Literacy* (1987) expanding the definition of literacy to include acquisition of core knowledge. In 1988, the federal government responded with Even Start, a program to promote family lit-eracy. Learning standards became one means for dealing with both the shallowness of curricular content and the decline in student achievement.

The heightened concern for standards in learning that came in the wake of Sputnik in the 1950s coincided with Benjamin Bloom's series of publica-tions (Bloom, 1956; Kratwohl, Bloom, & Masia, 1964). Bloom's research explicated a taxonomy of educational objectives, inaugurating an era of ed-ucation science in which the structural content of schooling was wedded to academic purpose and behaviorist principles of learning. While the nation evolved during the next two decades toward the expansion of educational opportunity and compensation for the disadvantages of poverty and racial discrimination, the standards movement re-emerged in the 1980s. In the wake of *A Nation At Risk*, Bloom's concepts of objectives and mastery, along with quality management techniques borrowed from the business world, provided fertile ground for standards-based education.

In the 1990s, the states' governors looked ahead to the new century and set national goals for education (National Education Goals Panel, 1995). These goals were codified in 1994 in Congress's Goals 2000: Educate Ameri-ca Act, which endorsed learning standards and standards-based assessments as ways to measure progress toward national goals. The reauthorization of the Elementary and Secondary Education Act (Improving America's Schools) in the same year called upon states to build systems of standards and assessments and to provide support for schools to improve. President Clinton in 1996 signaled a return to basics with his recommendation to end social promotion and advance students based on the merits of their accom-plishment. At the same time, the Clinton administration extended school-related programming to after-school hours with the 21st Century Commu-nity Schools program, and provided funding for a national system of Parent Information Resource Centers. Both programs encouraged the education system's ties to community organizations. In 1998 the Reading Excellence Act emphasized the importance of direct instruction and phonics in read-ing instruction, presaging the recommendations of the National Reading

Panel (2000). The 1990s closed with comprehensive school reform spreading research-based models of effective school practice across the country. Fueled by federal dollars, the states erected standards-based curricula and assessments.

Reassertion of Family Prerogatives

As the steamroller of standardization advanced during the 1980s and 1990s, American families reasserted their traditional claim to ultimately determine their children's education, or at least to custody of a reservoir of choice. Homeschooling, charter schools, school choice, private schools, and an array of commercial educational services and products (summer camps, tutoring services, publications, and software) all served as opportunities for families to exercise their prerogatives in their children's education. Perhaps in response to these challenges, or possibly borne of the same winds, public schools sought stronger ties with parents through "parental involvement" strategies.

By the first years of the new century, nearly 2 million children were being homeschooled (Barfield, 2002). Twenty years earlier, homeschooling was barely a blip on educators' radar screens. A desire for moral and religious teaching, once the hallmark of American education, propelled many of these families to educate their children at home, as did the concern over the quality of academic preparation in the public schools (Mayberry et al., 1995). Studies of homeschooling families show that, on average, their annual income is substantially below that of neighboring families attending public schools, due in part to the fact that one parent is at home and not in the workplace (Golden, 2000). Homeschooled children outperform their public and private school counterparts on tests of academic achievement (Mayberry et al., 1995) and have not shown signs of negative social effects (Barfield, 2002). The evidence of superior learning by homeschooled children is unrelated to differences in socioeconomic status (Mayberry et al., 1995; Ray & Wartes, 1991). Homeschooling families compensate for their children not being in school by enrolling them in youth activities, forming associations among themselves, and seeking private instruction to supplement the lessons given by the parents (Orr, 2003).

The public school establishment provided parents with options within the public school system, first with magnet schools and inter-district cooperative programs (especially in rural areas), and then more profoundly through the creation of charter schools and opportunities for parents to select the public school their children would attend. Charter schools had the added attraction of injecting variation into an education system that was growing ever more standardized. Charter schools were freed from many of the regulations the state and district imposed on regular public schools, allowing their creators to adopt specific foci and pursue innovative directions. Both charter schools and public school choice contributed an element of competition into public schooling. The effects of market forces were thought to improve the regular public schools that might lose students when parents were given the option of sending their children elsewhere. President Bill Clinton, an advocate of charter schools and public school choice, encouraged federal legislation to support the creation of charter schools and pilot projects to experiment with public school choice. By 2001, more than 2,000 charter schools were operating in 34 states and the District of Columbia (McLarty et al., 2001); this number doubled by 2006, with more than 4,000 charter schools in 40 states and the District of Columbia (Center for Education Reform, 2007). While studies have yet to demonstrate conclusively that either charter schools or public school choice produces improved academic performance, their adherents contend that improved learning outcomes is only one justification for education options for families. The freedom to choose their children's schools means that parents must be pleased with the choice or they will make another one. The tradition of family prerogative is honored in the process. Other proponents of school choice hold that limiting the choice to public schools removes many of the reasons that parents desire an alternative to the public schools and protects the public school system from true competition (Chubb & Moe, 1990).

National Direction, State Primacy, Family Options

By 2001 when the Elementary and Secondary Education Act was reauthorized as No Child Left Behind (NCLB) under the new administration of President George W. Bush, America was determined to achieve both equity and quality in public education. Having extended educational opportunity by the expansion of school years and embracing every segment of the population, the nation had come to realize that access to education was not enough. Achieved learning varied too widely from group to group and from school to school, indicating that opportunity was not equal for all. Standards and their concomitant assessments provided a measure of progress, and under NCLB progress would be measured for each group of students. These standards are an attempt to close the achievement gap between ethnic groups, between rich and poor, between children with disabilities and those without, and between English language natives and English language learners. By 2014, all students were to become proficient in their states' learning standards.

While No Child Left Behind merged equity and quality into the same policy formulation, it also paid tribute to the family prerogative by providing public school choice for children in failing schools. Further, it required failing schools to offer free tutoring provided by state-approved organizations outside the school system. The federal government also expanded its support for charter schools.

To assist schools in reaching the achievement goals of NCLB, Congress in 2002 passed the Education Sciences Reform Act. The Act created the Institute of Education Sciences (IES) which promoted scientifically based research as the guiding principle in adopting curriculum, instructional methods, and operational procedures in schools. IES's What Works Clearinghouse posted on its website the results of random-assignment, controlled studies to guide educators in improving schools.

Perhaps the greatest effects of No Child Left Behind were to affirm the state's position of primacy in school improvement and to make states accountable for closing the achievement gap. In keeping with provisions in its predecessor act, states were required to adopt learning standards, to annually test students to determine their proficiency in meeting the standards, and to address gaps in performance among ethnic and income groups. NCLB also addressed achievement gaps between native English language students and English language learners, and between students with and without disabilities. Most states were already on board with standards-based learning by the time NCLB was enacted, but the federal legislation brought the remaining states into line. It established learning standards as common currency in American public education, and focused attention on disproportionate representation of student groups in both performance categories (proficient or not proficient) and educational programs (opportunities for advanced courses, for example).

NCLB further strengthened the role of the state in school improvement by reinforcing the concept of "statewide systems of support" introduced in the 1994 reauthorization of the Elementary and Secondary Education Act (Improving America's Schools). The purpose of the statewide system of support is to help schools and districts make adequate yearly progress toward the goal of all students achieving proficiency on state standards-based assessments in reading, mathematics, and science by 2013-14.

Adequate yearly progress (AYP) is determined by the percentage of students in the school or district who score at or above a proficient level on the state's annual standards-based assessment in reading, mathematics, and science. Further, AYP is calculated for various groups of students—minority groups, children in poverty, children with disabilities, and children who are not native English speakers, for example. Each of these groups must also make AYP. Schools and districts not making AYP for two consecutive years fall into "improvement status," and are required to offer public school choice to parents and to provide students with after-school tutoring from an external provider. Should there occur two more years of inadequate progress, the district or school is subject to corrective action such as a change in leadership or curriculum. The state determines the corrective action for the district, and the district determines the corrective action for the school. The district remains under corrective action until it attains AYP for two consecutive years. The school, however, moves from a year of corrective action into restructuring, a two-year process in which the district develops a restructuring plan for the school in the first year and implements the plan in the second year. Restructuring options include conversion to a charter school, contracting the school's operation with an educational management organization (EMO), replacing most of the school's staff, replacing the leadership and some staff, or turning the school over to the state. A school may no longer be subject to the sanctions if it achieves AYP for two consecutive years, and it may return to sanctions if it again fails to meet AYP in two consecutive years.

NCLB codified the relationships between the federal government and the states that had evolved over several decades of efforts to balance equity and quality, opportunity and outcomes. In doing so, the state was placed in a pivotal position in school improvement, and its relationship with districts and schools was altered. While NCLB and corresponding state statutes and policies have laid down a structural and technocratic grid-work for progress, including systems designed to support districts and schools in their improvement, the hard work of school improvement will be shouldered teacher by teacher, school by school, with parents exercising their prerogatives inherent to the American traditions of schooling.

NCLB has turned the state spotlight onto schools where significant portions of students are not meeting state proficiency standards. Getting more students over the bar becomes the chief goal of these schools, and their success is measured accordingly. But what of the great majority of students (60% - 80% in most states) who are meeting and exceeding state standards? Their parents no doubt want more from their schools than mastery of minimum competencies, and they may want more choice in placing their children in schools and programs that best match their values and their children's interests and talents. Family prerogative is not satisfied by simply allowing parents to remove their children from schools in which too many students are failing to achieve lower-order standards. Parents will inevitably elevate their expectations for higher and broader definitions of school success. As statewide systems of support are increasingly successful in turning around low-performing schools, states may feel more pressure from their citizenry to raise their sights and provide greater opportunity for the students who have crossed the bar.

Tensions may arise from a system of public education that narrows the purpose of schooling to proficiency on minimal standards in basic subjects within typically high-poverty communities, while expanding the curriculum, programs, and choices elsewhere. Concern will shift from the school to the needs of the individual student, and the statewide system of support will evolve in response.

IMPLICATIONS FOR STATEWIDE SYSTEMS OF SUPPORT

Accretion of Purpose

As statewide systems of support are now evolving within each state, the relationship between the state and its local districts and schools is also changing. Historically, schools typically emerged first, then districts formed to systematize schools within a local region. State departments of education then arose to monitor district compliance with state legislation regulating districts and state rules attached to state funding. As the role of the federal government grew, state policy incorporated the requirements that accompanied federal funds and federal laws. In short, state departments of education enforced district compliance with state policies, which were increasingly influenced by federal actions. The statewide system of support, however, changes the state role from one of regulation to one of active assistance for the improvement of schools. This change in purpose, or, more precisely, accretion of purpose, has created the tensions concomitant with any systemic change, both for states and for districts and their schools. As the titans of federal, state, and district bureaucracies vie to assert or preserve their relative positions of power, the deep-rooted American ideal of family prerogative in children's education struggles to avoid suppression.

The landscape of American education, especially as it applies to statewide systems of support, is far more complex than a trichotomy of federal, state, and district organization may suggest. Within each state, subunits of the state education department (intermediate service units) are gathered up in a wide net of statewide systems of support. These include: (a) autonomous and semi-autonomous regional organizations; (b) university-based programs and consultants; (c) private and commercial organizations; (d) various professional associations; and (e) family advocacy groups. The interplay among these organizations is critical to the functioning of a statewide system of support, and the relationships among them evolve in response to new stresses and opportunities that arise.

Under NCLB, the district (LEA) is the first provider of technical assistance to schools not making adequate yearly progress, and statewide systems of support are realizing the importance of building district capacity to fulfill this purpose. Effective models for district systems of support will emerge, and the statewide systems of support will foster their development, while also serving as brokers in matching district needs with a variety of service providers equipped to assist them. Statewide systems of support will help establish productive relationships between districts and service providers and oversee the resulting activities and results.

Changing Rules and Changing Behaviors

Behavior is key to school improvement. Changing behavior, a challenge everywhere under the best of circumstances, can come about with prudent reward systems. A regulation-compliance approach restricts the venue of change to the external environment, inattentive to the learning and motivation of the people for which change is sought. This narrow approach is inconsistent with social learning theory (Bandura, 1989) which emphasizes the influences of the person and the person's behavior as well as the environment in learning. The person interprets the environment, behaves in ways that alter the environment, and in some instances exercises choice among alternative environments, all actions influenced by the person's sense of efficacy in meeting the task. Bandura summarizes the influence of models (think of parents, teachers, principals, superintendents, and all players in the statewide system of support) serving as "instructors, motivators, inhibitors, disinhibitors, social facilitators, and emotion arousers" (1989, p. 17). In short, the statewide system of support may encourage change in ways far more complex and potent than by the presentation and attempted enforcement of the desired ends.

Social systems, including school systems, consist of people playing interrelated roles in pursuit of common ends. Systems are improved by making their organization more efficient and by building the capabilities of the people within them. Regulation can change organizations, but an effective change agent, such as a statewide system of support, must also offer incentives, build capabilities, and provide opportunities for the people within the system to learn and change (see Bryk, Shipps, Hill, & Lake, 1998; Hill & Celio, 1998; see also Rhim, Hassel, & Redding in this volume). A regulatory-compliance approach to change is useful in identifying the regulator's desired outcomes, but does not in itself address the incentives, capacity, and opportunities that influence and enable each person's and each system's response. Thus, compliance may be feigned, and true change eluded. Playing the game is substituted for achieving the goal.

When tracing the historical outlines of American public education, the viewpoint is high and wide, interpreting trends through national and state movements. A more productive view to understand the place of a statewide system of support may be achieved by sighting the telescope from the other end—focusing on the child within the family, the family within the community, the child within the classroom, and the teacher within the school. What incentives, capacity, and opportunities are provided to the child, the parent, the teacher, the principal, the superintendent, and the local school board to encourage learning and change?

CONCLUSIONS

A statewide system of support may be seen as a logical evolutionary progression in American education history, but it is anything but a linear path. While the general trend in locus of authority has been away from the local and toward the national, the state is central in that transfer of power, exercising pressure in both directions. In many ways, NCLB is both an assertion of national direction in education and a consolidation of responsibility with the state. Its provisions for public school choice and supplemental educational services, and the continued federal support for charter schools, keep alive family prerogative (in the form of options) in children's education that is foundational in our nation. The pursuits of equity and excellence, rather than competing tensions, are now joined in an accountability system that makes the learning outcomes for each subgroup of students a factor in determining the overall quality of the school, the district, and the state. Ultimately, the learning of each student will be the measure of success, and even in schools making yearly progress, each student's progress will be the paramount benchmark. But first, attention is rightfully directed toward the schools where the most students are in need of rescue, and for those students time won't stand still.

The preceding chapter elucidates, from a macro-perspective, the place of incentives, capacity, and opportunities in a statewide system of support. Other chapters show how these features affect the behaviors of state personnel, superintendents, principals, teachers, students, and parents. A successful statewide system of support has a rightful place for the people it intends to influence, at each level of the system, beginning with the child, the parents, and the child's teachers. Beyond regulatory compliance, a successful statewide system of support will offer incentives, build capabilities, and provide opportunities for change in the desired direction, mediated by personal interpretations, choices, and behaviors. The successful statewide system of support will also honor the ability of parents, teachers, administrators, and local boards of education to make choices, alter environments, and discover their own efficient routes to desired ends, while providing incentives, capacity, and opportunity for them to do so.

REFERENCES

Bandura, A. (1989). Behavior analysis. In R. Vasta (Ed.), *Annals of child development: Vol. 6.* Greenwich, CT: JAI Press.

Barfield, R. (2002). *Real-life homeschooling.* New York: Fireside.

Beard, C. A., & Beard, M. R. (1944). *A basic history of the United States.* New York: Doubleday, Doran.

Berrol, S. (1982). Public schools and immigrants: The New York City experience. In B. J.Weiss (Ed.), *American education and the European immigrant, 1840-1940* (pp. 31-44). Urbana: University of Illinois Press.

Bloom, B. S. (Ed.). (1956). *Taxonomy of educational objectives, the classification of educational goals – Handbook I: Cognitive domain.* New York: McKay.

Bryk, A. S., Shipps, D., Hill, P. T. & Lake, R. (1998). *Decentralization in practice: Toward a system of schools.* Chicago: The Chicago Consortium on School Research.

Center on Education Reform. (2007). Retrieved March 11, 2007, from http://www.edreform.com/index.cfm?fuseAction=stateStats&pSectionID=15&cSectionID=44

Chubb, J. E., & Moe, T. M. (1990). *Politics, markets, and America's schools.* Washington, DC: Brookings Institution.

Coleman, J. S. (1966). *Equality of educational opportunity.* Washington, DC: U.S. Department of Health, Education, and Welfare.

Coleman, J. S. (1988). Social capital in the creation of human capital. *American Journal of Sociology, 94,* S95-S120.

Coleman, J. S., & Hoffer, T. (1987). *Public and private high schools: The impact of communities.* New York: Basic Books.

Cremin, L. A. (1962). *The transformation of the school progressivism in American education, 1876-1957.* New York: Knopf.

Doyle, D. H. (1978). *The social order of a frontier community: Jacksonville, Illinois, 1825-1870.* Urbana, IL: University of Illinois Press.

Edmonds, R. (1979, October). Effective schools for the urban poor. *Educational Leadership, 37*(1), 15-24.

Fraser, J. W. (2001). *The school in the United States: A documentary history.* New York: McGraw-Hill.

Golden, D. (2000, February 11). A class of their own: Home-schooled kids defy stereotypes, ace SAT test. *Wall Street Journal,* p. 1.

Hill, P. T., & Celio, M. B. (1998). *Fixing urban schools.* Washington, DC: Brookings Institution.

Hirsch, E. D. (1987). *Cultural literacy: What every American needs to know.* Boston: Houghton Mifflin.

Jeynes, W. H. (2007). *American educational history: School, society, and the common good.* Thousand Oaks, CA: Sage.

Kratwohl, D. R., Bloom, B. S, & Masia, B. B. (1964). *Taxonomy of educational objectives, the classification of educational goals– Handbook II: Affective domain.* New York: McKay.

Kozol, J. (1985). *Illiterate America.* New York: Anchor Press/Doubleday.

Ray, B. D., & Wartes, J. (1991). Academic achievement and affective development. In J. Van Galen & M. A. Pitman (Eds.), *Homeschooling: Political, historical and pedagogical perspectives* (pp. 43-62). Norwood, NJ: Ablex.

Mayberry, M. J., Knowles, G., Ray, B., & Marlow, S. (1995). *Homeschooling parents as educators.* Thousand Oaks, CA: Corwin Press.

McLarty, T. F., Panetta, L., Bowles, E. B., & Podesta, J. D. (2001). *A record of accomplishment.* Little Rock, AR: William J. Clinton Foundation.

National Commission on Excellence in Education. (1983). *A nation at risk: The imperative for educational reform.* Washington, DC: U.S. Government Printing Office.

National Education Goals Panel. (1995). *The national education goals report: Building a nation of learners.* Washington, DC: U.S. Government Printing Office.

National Institute of Child Health and Human Development. (2000). *Teaching children to read: An evidence-based assessment of the scientific research literature on reading and its implications for reading instruction.* Report of the National Reading Panel. Washington, DC: U.S. Government Printing Office.

Orr, T. (2003). *After homeschool.* Los Angeles: Parent's Guide Press.

Ravitch, D. (1974). *The great school wars.* New York: Basic Books.

Ravitch, D. (2000). *Left behind: A century of failed school reform.* New York: Simon & Schuster.

Spring, J. H. (1990). *The American school, 1642-1990.* White Plains, NY: Longman.

Stoops, N. (2004). *Educational attainment in the United States.* Washington, DC: U.S. Census Bureau. Retrieved June 23, 2007, from http://www.census.gov/population/www/socdemo/educ-attn.html

U.S. Census Bureau. (2000). *Educational attainment: March 1970.* Retrieved June 23, 2007, from http://www.census.gov/population/www/socdemo/education/p20-207.html

U.S. Census Bureau. (2006). *Facts for features.* Retrieved June 22, 2007, from http://www.census.gov/Press-Release/www/releases/archives/facts_for_features_special_editions/007276.html

Sam Redding *is director of the Center on Innovation & Improvement.*

PART C

PROFILES OF KEY STATES

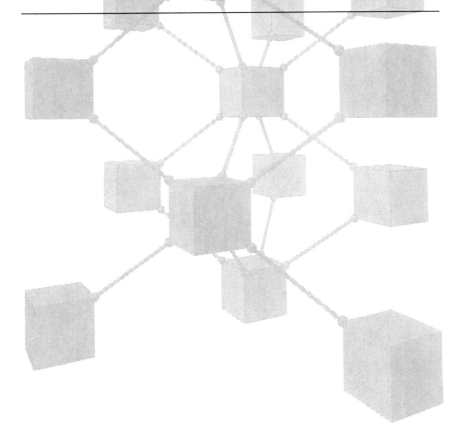

CHAPTER 6

INTRODUCTION TO PROFILES OF KEY STATES

Sam Redding

The *Handbook on Statewide Systems of Support* was developed in 2006–07, a time when every state was stretching and straining to form an array of district and school improvement efforts into a coordinated system of support. States wanted a conceptual framework for how to perceive this system, and they deserved evidence of what was likely to succeed. They also wanted to know what other states were doing, what they were learning, how they were progressing. Concrete examples of SEA experiences, explicit strategies, and the lessons learned by SEA personnel would add flesh to the skeleton of a framework and a real-life validation of researchers' best deductions.

Knowing that no "perfect system" was yet in place, CII sought to explore, in depth, the evolution of systems of support and the emergence of promising practices in a small set of states. With recommendations from the U.S. Department of Education and Regional Comprehensive Centers, CII approached a handful of states that exhibited illustrative elements of what might become an optimal statewide system of support. Four of these states agreed to tell their stories.

CII recognizes that many other states are developing effective systems of support, are already finding success with particular strategies, and have

Handbook on Statewide Systems of Support, pages 85–86

their own stories to tell. In time, all of these stories are worth telling, and we can learn from each of them. For now, CII appreciates the tremendous energy the staff of four SEAs devoted to the creation of the profiles that are provided in this Handbook. Beyond devoting time and thought to this enterprise, the SEA staff approached the endeavor with admirable trust and openness. They have generously shared their experiences for the benefit of their counterparts in the other states.

Three CII consultants took the lead in working with the SEAs in Alabama, Kentucky, Tennessee, and Washington, to prepare the chapters that follow this introduction. Thomas Kerins, Susan Hanes, and Carole Perlman all brought to this task vast experience as high-level administrators in both LEAs and SEAs, Tom and Carole in Illinois, and Susan in Georgia. They approached this assignment with an understanding of the evidence and framework included in this Handbook and a great appreciation for the challenges facing SEAs.

Tom and Susan visited each SEA, spending two days interviewing SEA staff, following a comprehensive interview protocol that was aligned with this Handbook's framework for an effective statewide system of support. They gathered mountains of documents from each state. They followed each visit with telephone calls and e-mail correspondence with the SEA staff. They submitted drafts of their chapters to the SEA staff to check for accuracy. Only savvy veterans of SEAs, with the personal attributes to enlist the trust and openness of their interviewees, could accomplish what Susan and Tom have accomplished in bringing these profiles to fruition.

Telling the story of the statewide system of support from the perspective of the SEA personnel who are daily immersed in this work gives us a unique window into the thinking of these people. But CII also wanted to know how the statewide system of support was perceived by the districts and schools that had received its services. In each state, Carole Perlman interviewed, via telephone, two district superintendents and two school principals who had received services from the system of support. This client perspective adds a necessary dimension to understanding how support from the state plays out in the communities meant to benefit from the services. Carving time from the busy schedules of superintendents and principals is no mean task, and Carole's persistence, tact, and methodical attention to the requirements of the protocol resulted in "views from the field" that enrich these state profiles.

CHAPTER 7

THE ACCOUNTABILITY ROUNDTABLE IN ALABAMA

Thomas Kerins, Susan Hanes, and Carole Perlman

The information included in this profile of Alabama's statewide system of support is derived from an on-site visit of the Alabama State Department of Education (SDE), the state's education agency, by two of the authors, telephone interviews with district superintendents and school principals by the third author, and artifacts provided by the SDE.

INTRODUCTION

This section provides background on the state's development of a system of support, the factors SDE personnel have determined to have the greatest impact on school improvement, and the lessons SDE personnel have learned along the way.

Handbook on Statewide Systems of Support, pages 87–110
87

Evolution of the Statewide System of Support in Alabama

The evolution of the Alabama system of support began more than a decade ago. From 1996 to 1998, five former Alabama Teachers of the Year were selected as Special Services Teachers to assist schools in changing their practices in order to meet improvement goals. The SDE provided limited coordination of the work of the Special Services Teachers, and the change they initiated in the schools was not consistently sustained.

Between 1998 and 2001, the Special Services Teachers approach merged with a system in which cross-functional teams provided assistance directly to non-Title I schools identified for improvement. Each section within the SDE designated members to serve on each of 11 teams. Each team had a designated team leader who directed the assistance efforts within a specified region. There was limited collaboration among teams and regions. Furthermore, resources were not uniformly shared or used. Each team leader employed a different approach to assisting schools. Some teams included local district (central office) personnel in assistance efforts while others did not.

Concurrent with the system of cross-functional teams that assisted non-Title I schools, the Federal Programs Division within the SDE established and ran a separate program to provide support to Title I schools. For a while, an Intervention Team was assigned to "take over" schools that exceeded a specified number of years with low achievement, but this approach ended in 2003. The Title I assistance efforts operated independently from the non-Title I initiatives, and there was little communication between the programs or within them. Sporadic improvement was seldom sustained, as personnel turned over, and the SDE support programs operated with little consistency across regions and applied no accountability measures to mark their progress.

From 2001 to 2005, members of the SDE's Classroom Improvement Field Services unit served as the primary contacts for non-Title I schools in improvement. The Special Services Teachers were coordinated under the direction of an SDE School Improvement Liaison and eventually renamed as PEER Assistants. They received monthly training and updates related to current accountability requirements and shared successful strategies and resources for assisting non-Title I schools in improvement. A school improvement handbook was developed, and coordinated training on the development of school improvement plans was provided to schools. The SDE Federal Programs Division continued a separate program of support for Title I schools in improvement.

The most significant change in the Alabama SDE occurred from August 2005 to June 2006 when the Accountability Roundtable (ART) was formed

(See Figure 7.1—The Accountability Roundtable). The Deputy Superintendent charged the directors of the two programs (Classroom Improvement and Federal Programs) to work as a unit. Subsequently, the Alabama Reading Initiative—with more people working in the field than the other two programs—was included in order to address the overlap of services.

As part of this new effort to unify and coordinate SDE support services, the State's federal Title I assistance program merged with the PEER Assistance Program and the new group was renamed "peer mentors." Beginning in 2005, all schools in improvement received coordinated assistance from a unified delivery system. Collaborative teams conducted regional trainings to train schools to develop their school improvement plans. All districts in improvement status made AYP and moved into delay, meaning their status stayed constant rather than progressing toward corrective action. A majority of schools in improvement status made AYP and also moved into delay. This success was credited to increased collaboration and the requirement that all districts in improvement status (or those with schools in multiple

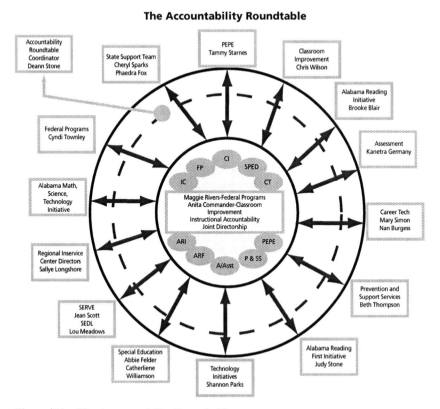

Figure 7.1　The Accountability Roundtable.

years of school improvement status) hire a school improvement specialist who received on-site coaching from select members of ART. During this process, ART designed a new approach based on lessons learned from past efforts and successes from other state initiatives. This approach shifted support efforts from schools to districts.

The establishment of the Accountability Roundtable was critical to the progress of the Alabama system of support. This Roundtable grew out of a need to provide a coordinated, seamless system of continual technical assistance and support. Representatives from the 11 regions meet the third Wednesday of every month to share information with the Roundtable about the schools and districts in their regions that need assistance. The imperative to spend time in planning is recognized by the Department. Prior to the development of the Roundtable, the staff in the 11 regions operated independently.

Beginning in July 2006, a state support team—consisting of two school improvement leaders, eleven regional school improvement coaches (RSICs), and 13 peer mentors was empowered to provide on-site coaching to school improvement specialists serving in 64 districts. The districts were either in improvement status, had schools in multiple years of school improvement, or participated at the request of the superintendent. The state support team also provided assistance to 24 schools in year 3 or more of school improvement status.

Special education and other federal programs later joined the Roundtable. In August 2006, the Alabama Reading Initiative (ARI) principal coaches joined the state support team. For the first time, ARI principal coaches and regional school improvement coaches conducted collaborative district meetings to eliminate the duplicate central office meetings and address proposed, continued, and revised assistance efforts. The Alabama Math, Science, and Technology Initiative joined the unified efforts in April 2007. Thus, over time, disparate state programs evolved into a unified system, coordinated through the Roundtable.

Factors That Contribute to Improvement and Services That Address Them

Leadership. The Professional Education Personnel Evaluation (PEPE) is Alabama's state required personnel evaluation procedure. The guiding philosophy is that well-trained administrators positively affect instruction and academic achievement of students. The initial training and continuing updates help administrators and participants see the value of "good instruction." SDE's professional development training, which is reviewed by the Roundtable, requires principals to attend with their faculty, including mathematics, science, and reading faculty, to focus leadership on instructional improvement. New superintendents, as part of the development of their own professional development plans, learn instructional leadership skills, including how to use their own data for decision-making.

Alabama's Leadership Academy for principals and potential principals, which began in 2000-2001 for low-performing schools, has evolved into a New Principals Academy serving new principals in all member schools rather than only schools in improvement. Beginning in April 2007, all LEAs will have the opportunity to attend a state conference where sessions will focus on building the capacity of districts to support continuous improvement within their schools.

Persistent, Coordinated Support. The work of the Roundtable diminishes duplication of efforts and adds coherence and coordination to the system of support, especially with the inclusion of subject matter specialists. Staff members from each section of the SDE participate in the Roundtable and in support planning. SDE's Listening Posts program sends state directors to districts to listen to issues and questions from local educators. They meet with the local superintendents and central office personnel; then bring issues back to the SDE. This process facilitates the continuous improvement of the statewide system of support.

The Roundtable's development and use of improvement plans proved key for coordination efforts. Local personnel are coached and supported as they develop continuous improvement plans. The SDE's Committee for Accountability and Accelerating Student Learning (CAASL) examines the pace of local improvement. The Roundtable reduced individual silos within the state department: Reading, science, math, technology, school improvement, and school principal coaches now coordinate their consulting assistance with local staff. Regional inservice centers, although based within universities, provide professional development using this same consistent approach.

Data-Driven Decision Making. SDE staff members understand the importance of data, but they are just reaching the point where information such as disaggregated trend results can be provided to teachers for classroom planning. Principals have been utilizing disaggregated school data for several years for school improvement planning, but Alabama realizes the importance of getting better information to teachers. The Department will construct a data warehouse beginning with 2005 results and progress from there.

Lessons Learned

Lesson 1—Planning is required. "If you fail to plan, you plan to fail." Even more so, the Alabama SDE staff believes you have to plan to plan—scheduling is critical when so much time is spent at Roundtable meetings. The message to local personnel—they must know that their plans should clearly illustrate where they want their schools to be in terms of student learning.

Lesson 2—Leadership matters. Individuals with leadership abilities were placed on the Roundtable. With continuing experience, their leadership ability has grown significantly.

Lesson 3—Champions are essential. New initiatives must have a "champion" on the ground. Support from the top is necessary, but each initiative within the system also needs a champion who tends to the quality of its operation and connects it with the larger system. Alabama SDE staff members are quick to point out that the Roundtable does not do the work of school and district improvement, but it does set the direction of the work and assists with implementation.

FUNCTIONS OF A STATEWIDE SYSTEM OF SUPPORT

This section organizes the information provided by Alabama SDE personnel into the evidence-based framework described in the chapter "State Role in Supporting School Improvement."

Provide Incentives for Change

Public dissemination of school and district assessment scores results in some public accountability pressure, but its effectiveness is sporadic and depends on the district. In theory, the threat of penalties, such as restructuring, could be an incentive for districts to improve; in practice, such penalties have not been imposed by the SDE. Staff are working on a new approach that would fully implement rewards and sanctions as outlined in Alabama's improved plan.

The Department's system of financial rewards to districts or schools for improved results is based on performance. The response from districts has generally been positive, except among districts making progress but unable to submit successful funding proposals.

Another major incentive is the selection of Torchbearer schools, recognizing high performance among Alabama's high-poverty public schools. To be considered for recognition, schools must have: (1) at least 80% of the student population receiving free or reduced meals, (2) at least 70% of students score at Levels III or IV on all sections of the Alabama Reading and Mathematics Test (ARMT), (3) students who score above the 50th percentile in reading and in mathematics on the Stanford Achievement Test, 10th Edition (SAT 10) (4) at least 98% of grade 12 students pass all required subjects of the Alabama High School Graduation Exam (AHSGE), (5) an average dropout rate below the state average.

While the SDE does not offer incentives to principals or teachers to work in low-performing schools, some districts do. The Governor's Congress on School Leadership is considering recommending such incentives.

Build Capacity to Change

Build Systemic Capacity

Create and Disseminate Knowledge. Several newsletters disseminate information on school improvement. *Table Talk* is a bimonthly newsletter disseminated by the Roundtable to members of the SDE. As an example of the kind of information transmitted by this newsletter, a recent article notified SDE sections that "School Improvement Checkpoints will be occurring in the eleven regional inservice center areas. These checkpoints are local reviews of school improvement plans and will be held by the Regional School Improvement Coaches with assistance from members of the Roundtable." Regional inservice centers—based in universities—publish occasional newsletters. For example, the East Alabama Regional Inservice Center (EARIC), based at Auburn University, discusses professional development activities tied to local improvement plans. Regional school improvement coaches develop and disseminate newsletters to districts within their regions, providing notification of current training opportunities and plans for future training. Finally, the Educational Research Newsletter contains articles that discuss research on how to work with struggling first-grade readers who are English language learners.

Enhance Supply of Personnel. Universities in Alabama offer alternate routes to certification for professionals from fields other than education who aspire to be principals and teachers. The SDE has an official connection with teacher pre-service institutions through new standards that require teacher education institutions to assure that teachers know and are able to implement state initiatives. Universities receive feedback from Novice Teacher Evaluations and the Evaluation of the Teacher Education Programs (with results published in a Report Card). There are consequences if the graduates of the teacher education programs do not perform at the established standard. University professors are offered an opportunity to go through the PEPE Training to evaluate their pre-service teachers.

The Governor's Congress of School Leadership might bring needed training and requirements for principals. In addition, standards for new teachers are being reviewed by the Governor's Commission on Teacher Quality so that teachers will be better prepared for teaching.

Alabama has over 1,000 National Board Certified Teachers. The state plans to leverage the knowledge and expertise of these teachers in school improvement efforts. Annual grants are provided to the eleven Regional inservice centers so that training is delivered and developed to continue to increase the pool of National Board Certified Teachers.

In 2008, the Continuous Improvement Residency Program will provide training and support for district-based peer mentors.

Build Local Capacity

Capacity Building Structures.

Coordinate Structures and Roles. Deann Stone was the Accountability Roundtable coordinator at the time CII conducted interviews with the SDE; she was subsequently promoted to director of federal programs. The role of the Accountability Roundtable coordinator is to facilitate continuous communication in a seamless system of support for ongoing school and district improvement.

State Education Agency. When the Roundtable first began to meet in July 2005, section directors and representatives discussed methods to control the overlap of services. They also focused on how school improvement plans served to increase student learning. They decided to meet for eight days each month—two days a week during the first four weeks of each month. They set aside time for each section to share its purpose. The directors and representatives found they had activities in common and there indeed was overlap. Roundtable meetings enabled them to become aware of activities and developments throughout the SDE. They then moved into identifying the components of school improvement and the roles each program or office would play in school improvement.

Districts annually submitted their improvement plans to the SDE and were reviewed by one section of the SDE. In 2005, the Department formed 11 three-member teams, including everyone on the Roundtable, to review these plans. Some of the Roundtable members, prior to this event, did not feel that the school improvement plans necessarily made a difference; some had never even seen these plans. That attitude changed during this review when staff provided feedback, including specific achievement targets for the district. Currently, Regional School Improvement Coaches hold annual checkpoints within the region to build the capacity of LEAs to review plans. The SDE requires only schools and districts that do not meet 100% of goals to develop a plan. Schools identified as in "improvement status" must have an approved plan within 90 days after the release of state data.

Members of the Roundtable would be the first to say that collaboration among SDE and partners in the statewide system of support is difficult, but it helps the local staff. They also say that collaboration at the SDE is a "work in progress." Since much of the initial time-consuming work has been completed, meeting time for the Roundtable has been reduced to four days a month—the first and third Wednesdays and Thursdays of each month.

How effective is the Roundtable? Staff believe that the process has been very effective and point to the fact that local districts are using the SDE approach as a model within their own system to provide a more efficient approach to improvement activities. The Alabama SDE has been able to establish among Roundtable colleagues that when they have a Request for Proposal, or a plan requirement, that there must be a connection with the district's improvement plan for it to be approved. For example, there might be an opportunity to apply for technology funds, but any district's proposal must show how the acquisition of these funds would assist the district in its already identified needs stemming from its improvement plan.

Asked how the U.S. Department of Education and its Regional Comprehensive Center might assist Alabama with its statewide system of support, the SDE staff responded that help with methods to evaluate the system of support, including criteria to apply to the evaluation, would be useful.

Intermediate Agencies. Eleven regional inservice centers throughout Alabama provide professional development and are connected to universities. They are funded by the SDE but operate under the direction of the universities. These inservice centers have a representative on the Roundtable. The 11 inservice centers correspond to the 11 areas in which the SDE hires regional school improvement coaches (RSICs). Some coaches are housed in the regional inservice center offices and some are not.

External Partner Organizations. SERVE (www.serve.org) is a university-based Regional Education Laboratory at the University of North Carolina, Greensboro. Its mission is to promote and support continuous improvement of educational opportunities for all learners in the Southeast region of the country. It is one of 10 Regional Educational Laboratories funded by the U.S. Department of Education's Institute of Education Sciences. SERVE has a representative on the Roundtable and provides research to support the Alabama Pyramid of Strategies.

The A+ Best Practices Center (http://www.bestpracticescenter.org/about/history.html) was established in mid-1999 as a public/private partnership to focus on improving student achievement by raising the quality of teaching through professional development. This Center works with the Roundtable and regional staff, providing both materials and training.

SDE staff admit that much work needs to be done over the next few years with external partners as the Roundtable itself gains traction. For example, the SDE is collaborating with the Alabama Education Association to advance online professional development for teachers. The SDE is working with the non-profit Hope Foundation with regard to effective leadership training. Also, universities could be better connected to the system. The SDE plans to review the Voluntary Partnership Assistance Team concept that Kentucky uses to broaden the partnership between the SDE and the business community. Finally, the SDE plans to work more with the principals' and superintendents' associations.

Distinguished Educators. Alabama does not use the term "distinguished educators," choosing instead the terms "peer mentors" and "regional school improvement coaches" for people who assist schools and districts with improvement. Peer mentors serve schools in year four or more of school improvement status. The RISCs work with districts on a regional basis. Members of the Roundtable serve as the interview and selection team for choosing the 12 peer mentors and 11 RISCs. Many of the candidates have been recommend by the districts for this assignment and training. Most of them remain district employees, though the State reimburses the district. In essence, they are on loan from districts to assist other districts. Others may be retired educators or merit employees of the SDE.

The focus of training for both these groups is LEA improvement, not just school improvement. These individuals undergo two weeks of initial training each August by Department staff. There is also monthly ongoing professional development throughout the year. Everyone receives the same basic training; they then customize their work plan according to the needs of their districts.

According to the SDE staff interviewed, "professional development in Alabama has evolved from a 'sit and get' mentality to long-term, focused school improvement." Every educator must have a personal plan for continuous learning. The philosophy of the SDE is that while only 10% of training is retained if the content is not applied, 90% will be retained if professional development includes a coach working side-by-side with the trainee to apply what has been learned.

The SDE assigns members of both groups—peer mentors and RISCs—to particular regions. Some are assigned to schools, while others work in collaboration with districts to help identify reasons why AYP was not met. Each peer mentor works full time, assigned to no more than two schools, and is on site in each school each week. SDE's intent is to build capacity at the district level so central office staff can write better plans for improvement. Change at the school level requires continuous district support.

The SDE evaluates the peer mentors and RSICs at mid-year and at year end. This appraisal presents task statements, such as "The RSIC provides on-site support, coaching, and guidance to local education agencies though the local school improvement specialist or other designated personnel." Each task statement is followed by four specific indicators, a request for evidence (examples listed), and a rating by someone from the Accountability Roundtable that ranges from 0 (does not meet standards) to 3 (exceeds standards).

SDE staff believe the use of practitioners who are familiar with successful improvement strategies strengthens their approach. One interviewee commented that: "They have talent and keep the focus on what is most important at the school. They bring practical connections to research-based ideas...they bring meaning to education jargon." The incorporation of practitioners in the statewide system of support also symbolizes the movement of the SDE from a compliance agency to a problem-solving, service-oriented agency. The peer mentors and RSICs develop training materials for the 67 local school improvement specialists. These 67 specialists are hired by troubled districts and trained and supported by the SDE.

Alabama staff would look to the U.S. Department of Education and the Regional Comprehensive Centers for more information about what other states are doing successfully with their systems of support.

School Support Teams. In Alabama, the state support teams include the regional coaches, peer mentors, ARI partners, AMSTI math and science specialists, regional inservice center directors, ARI reading coaches, local school improvement specialists, and SDE staff assigned to regions. The mission of this collaborative is to build capacity among school and district staff so they can more effectively diagnose their needs and develop meaningful plans to meet those demands.

All schools identified as low-performing schools may voluntarily join the Alabama Math, Science, and Technology Initiative (AMSTI). Math and science teachers in these schools receive up to 120 hours of high-quality, subject- and grade-specific professional development. The two-week summer training equips the teachers with improved skills and materials. Schools that participate in the training also receive on-site teacher mentoring and subject-related teacher coaching from AMSTI-trained leaders. Universities that host the regional inservice centers provide access to a cadre of regional mathematicians and scientists to coach participating teachers in their classrooms and deepen content knowledge.

Differentiate Support to Local Districts and Schools

Alabama's state assessment test provides one way to determine which districts and schools most need assistance. SDE is encouraging local staff to review data in different ways rather than just examining AYP, however, and to consider data for all students and each student. To determine specific local needs, Alabama uses their Pyramid strategies (See Figure 7.2), system support visits, school assistance, and LEA collaborative meetings. The Continuous Improvement Pyramid of Strategies begins with (I) *Building a Case for Instructional Change,* and then goes to (II) *Planning for Instructional Change,* to (III) *Implementing Instructional Change,* and finally (IV) *Motivating for Change.*

Continuous Improvement Pyramid of Strategies

Figure 7.2 Continuous Improvement Pyramid of Strategies.

The Pyramid is designed primarily for use by the school assistance staff and provides a framework and examples of proven strategies. The Pyramid focuses initially on the broad school-wide data, then ultimately brings analysis, planning, methods, and motivation to the individual classroom and students.

- The top of the pyramid, *Building a Case for Instructional Change*, contains methods for analyzing and using data to affect student learning. The data analysis process is designed to reveal strengths and weaknesses in the curriculum over time, as well as current individual student achievement performance. Alabama staff believes that these data—when presented to faculty—are a powerful tool in leading the school to understand both grade level curriculum and individual student learning needs.

- *Planning for Instructional Change* begins with the development of a specific plan for teaching the Alabama Course of Study Standards. This is a precursor for the monthly benchmarking tests—one of several sources of data used for monitoring and responding to student learning needs. Student score profiles from the previous year's assessments, as well as classroom mastery/non-mastery profiles on monthly common assessments, bring individual information on the progress of each student into focus for classroom teachers. Subsequently, a connection is made to meaningful professional development through the school improvement plan.
- *Implementing and Monitoring Instructional Change* means that school leaders implement research-based strategies that will improve student achievement. Personnel such as Peer Mentors in the schools serve daily to ensure through observation, modeling, and coaching that the designed approach to higher learning is supported. As mentioned earlier, Alabama utilizes SERVE and SEDL (Southwest Educational Development Laboratory) to provide the evidence-based research for schools to use.
- *Motivating for Change* is specific to the needs and culture of each school. The Peer Mentor seeks the support of community and other stakeholders in encouraging a positive climate for students and staff regarding school academic accountability/improvement issues.

"Even if AYP is made, if there are some students who did not meet standards, more needs to be done," said one interviewee, stating the SDE's direction. The SDE intends to add more kinds of data to use for decision-making, for example, direct writing. The ideal planning template should include all assessments. Alabama has mostly summative data, but would like some type of formative assessments for local staff to voluntarily use during the year that would be consistent across the state and in line with Alabama learning standards. As with most states, Alabama staff are concerned about placing too much emphasis on "dead data" that are not timely for use in the local improvement process.

In July 2006, the SDE held a Summit with required attendance for all systems identified as in improvement and for systems with one or more schools in year four or more of improvement. RSICs and SDE staff trained 57 LEAs during this Summit. The Summit provided training to five-member LEA teams for the development of school and LEA plans. All training session materials and presentations were shared on a School Improvement Resource Kit CD. In addition to the School Improvement Summit materials, the CD includes data analysis modules, an online tutorial for school and LEA plan development, and research-based strategies and tips.

Based on district requests, the May 2007 Summit was open to all districts to build improvement capacity, not just the districts in academic trouble. Open to all and with attendance voluntary, 80 of Alabama's 131 districts were represented at this year's Summit. By region, the Summit focused on the cycle of improvement. For three days, regional coaches, key specialists, and SDE staff worked with district personnel to identify priority goals and action plans.

Alabama piloted an instructional review process in 31 schools during the 2006–2007 school year. Alabama is one of a consortium of states under the leadership of the Council of Chief State School Officers (CCSSO) that is searching for a consistent method to diagnose needs and provide support in nine Essential Elements: Curriculum, Classroom Evaluation/Assessment, Instruction, School Culture, Student/Family/Community Support, Professional Growth/Development/Evaluation, Leadership, Organizational Structure/Resources, and Comprehensive/Effective Planning. Under these nine elements there are a total of 66 indicators. Each indicator under each element is evaluated on a four-point rubric: (1) indicator not evident, (2) some aspects of this indicator were evident, but they are not systemic, (3) the school has developed a strategy to address this indicator and has made substantial progress towards implementation, and (4) this indicator is evident and the school and the district continually adjust the implementation plan to improve the indicator's impact on quality learning.

For example, among the five indicators under the second Essential Element (Classroom Evaluation/Assessment) are these two: 2.4—Performance standards are clearly communicated, evident in classrooms, and observable in student work; and 2.5—Samples of student work are analyzed to inform instruction, revise curriculum and pedagogy, and obtain information on student progress.

Each school receives a report profile which displays a summary of findings. Those schools with an Essential Element rating of 2 and below receive suggestions about resources and recommendations for strategies to improve identified weaknesses. The overall conclusion for one school was that: "In the areas of Classroom Evaluation/Assessment and Professional Growth, Development and Evaluation, while there is some evidence of progress, the school received overall scores of Level Two, indicating the need for more consistent implementation. Evidence gathered during the visit indicates that substantial progress has been made in the areas of Instruction, School Culture, and School Leadership. It is suggested that the few indicators within those elements that received scores of Level Two may warrant the faculty's future focus."

Alabama has aligned these recommendations with SDE resources. This is another example of how the SDE is moving from compliance to instructional strategies to improve student learning.

Differentiate by Point of Impact. Alabama's system of academic standards, assessments, and accountability is a "single" system that applies to all LEAs and all schools irrespective of their receipt of Title I funds. All LEAs and schools are subject to the state's definition of AYP for achievement of all students and the following subgroups: (1) economically disadvantaged students, (2) students from major racial and ethnic groups, (3) special education students, and (4) limited English proficient students.

All LEAs and schools are identified for rewards and sanctions on the same basis. All schools that do not meet or exceed their annual measurable objectives are subject to progressively more stringent sanctions; however, schools that do not receive Title I-Part A funds are not required but may choose to implement requirements for public school choice and supplemental educational services.

The purpose of the system of rewards and sanctions is to support and encourage schools so that all students meet or exceed proficiency on the state's academic content and student academic achievement standards. Alabama's system of rewards and sanctions values progress; it rewards systematic progress even if the progress is not sufficient to meet AYP, and it applies to LEAs and schools. Alabama employs one or both of the following criteria to identify schools and LEAs for academic recognition and/or rewards:

- The school or LEA "significantly" closed the achievement gap between subgroups of students and made progress toward AYP. "Significantly" will be defined based on year-to-year analyses of test scores and with input from the state's Accountability Advisory Committee.
- The school or LEA made AYP for two or more consecutive years.

Principals and teachers who are highly effective and have been instrumental in closing the achievement gap and/or making AYP will be identified to serve as peer consultants on the State Support Team.

Alabama's system of sanctions for schools identified for improvement adheres to the following principles:

- Sanctions should result in increased learning opportunities for students.
- The state's primary response to schools that are not making academic progress should be intensive support to their instructional programs.
- Sanctions should establish a priority for state support to LEAs as they provide appropriate levels of school improvement guidance beginning in the first year of failure to make AYP.
- The magnitude of sanctions should reflect the magnitude of the need for academic improvement.

Districts with schools with multiple years (4 or more) of needing improvement must hire a school improvement specialist at the district level. Last year, 42 LEAs were required to identify a school improvement district person. Peer mentors are assigned to schools with four or more years of needing improvement status. Alabama staff reported that one district originally believed that the assignment of a peer mentor was a sanction, but by the end of the school year it regarded the peer mentor as a reward.

Differentiate by Intensity and Duration of Services. The Pyramid of Strategies is used along with district and school data to address identified weaknesses. The Roundtable provides support in the identified areas. For example, ARI has funded and trained a school level reading coach in every school with a K–3 configuration. Presently, grades 4–12 are becoming a priority. Now there are coaches for adolescent literacy. Since adolescent content-area literacy has become the next major area of concern, schools are asked to commit to required activities for content literacy across the curriculum and through grade 12. This year 14 high schools have been targeted for reading emphasis in the content areas.

Deliver Services to Districts and Schools

Alabama has a consistent strategy for providing differentiated services to districts according to how they fail to meet AYP. Failure to meet AYP is generally divided into two groups: those well below adequate yearly progress goals and those not making AYP for a specific subgroup of students. Local staff start with the Pyramid of Strategies since the first part of that approach is to view the data; then, they develop a plan based on the data. The coaches work with the districts and these plans to differentiate resources provided to the districts. For example, the Alabama Reading Initiative (ARI) uses AYP information as just one piece of information to identify areas for improvement. Alabama staff are deeply committed to data-driven decision making not only at the state level but also for each school. Through their training and the Roundtable approach, they have taken the jargon about "data-driven decision-making" and made it a real part of their improvement system.

Provide Services. SDE's services, including skills-based training, are customized for the districts. The services are needs-based and not part of a top-down approach from the SDE. Staff is trained to collaborate and provide support. If a RSIC cannot support the need, they can return to the Roundtable for ideas and support.

RSICs are trained not to do the work but to help the districts understand how they can accomplish tasks to meet their needs. Though the term "building capacity" is part of recent education jargon, SDE staff have learned that unless they do build the capacity of the central office, principals, and school improvement teams, the RSICs will have to return in subsequent years to address the same problems. The Alabama mantra is "Build trust, make connections, support, support, support."

How is this support accomplished? Most of the training for SDE staff becomes the basis for training for district personnel. Their training emphasizes building capacity, including how to supply support without doing all the work, how to emphasize improvement and not compliance, how to deal with principals, and how to develop communication skills. Even with all this, Alabama staff would like to see if there are technological approaches that could strengthen the level of communication among the SDE, their service providers, and the school districts.

Specifically, the peer mentor builds capacity at the school level and the State helps districts develop capacity to support schools. Districts are enabling schools to seek support from them rather than from SDE. School staff need to be convinced that the district office, not the state department, is their first line of support. "Previously, perhaps the State has played the role of enabler by working directly with schools."

With regard to the Regional Comprehensive Centers, Alabama would like their role expanded so that state staff can provide training directly to districts. "The State does not have the number of personnel to deliver all the kinds of necessary training," observed one interviewee.

Allocate Resources for Services. Alabama has various grants and other financial resources that schools can apply for, such as monies for extended day programs, technology, and summer schools. However, the SDE believes districts need more guidance on research-based effective programs to make more appropriate use of these funds—especially at the middle and high school levels. Staff hope that the Regional Comprehensive Centers can identify and provide focus on research-based effective programs.

Provide Opportunities For Change

The SDE has a template for school improvement that provides local educators with a broad outline to frame their reflections as they plan how to improve student learning. Within the following framework, districts have the flexibility to implement significant changes within their systems. This flexibility provides districts the opportunity to change in ways that fit their contexts and needs. The framework:

1. Describes evidence-based strategies the LEA will use to strengthen the core academic programs in school.
2. Includes actions the LEA will take to ensure improvement in student achievement. A schedule for the LEA to review school progress is included.

3. Commits to plan and spend not less than 10% of the Title I funds received by the LEA for the professional development needs of the instructional staff.
4. Identifies causes for failure to obtain AYP. The LEA role in assistance to schools to obtain AYP is described in detail.
5. Addresses the LEA role in directing the teaching and learning needs in all schools. Describes in detail why the prior planning of the LEA did not bring about increased student achievement.
6. Describes the LEA role in establishing extended learning activities.
7. Describes the technical assistance provided by the Department of Education. A plan for the collaboration between the SDE and the LEA is addressed.
8. Identifies LEA strategies to promote effective parental involvement in the school.

EVALUATION OF STATE ROLE IN DISTRICT AND SCHOOL IMPROVEMENT

SDE staff have evaluated their statewide system of support within the past year, but this evaluation effort has been based on perception and process data about the effectiveness of the collaborative efforts of the state support team. The appraisal process mentioned earlier in this report is a key component of the evaluation effort. While Alabama does not have "hard data" at this point, it does have formal feedback from RSICs. In addition, there are "listening post" opportunities offered to all superintendents for voicing concerns as well as positive comments.

The Roundtable provides feedback to the RSICs and the peer mentors on a continuous basis. The RSICs in the field feel comfortable in providing honest feedback about improvement efforts. The interviewees believe that their process to date is effective—though not sufficiently effective—since they would like to use student assessment data as a key component of the evaluation process of their system of support. The SDE plans on beginning this component during the 2007–2008 school year. Subsequently, they will identify a set of strategies that work no matter where they are applied.

The SDE believes that while their present website contains data to assist in school improvement planning, they are looking at a more systematic way to display state, district, and school longitudinal data that will provide a foundation for establishing the "hard data" necessary for a more comprehensive evaluation.

VIEWS FROM THE FIELD

The information in this section is a synthesis of interviews with a district superintendent, two assistant superintendents, and two principals who had received service from the Alabama statewide system of support.

Factors That Contribute to Improvement and Lessons Learned

When asked what factors most contributed to their increases in student achievement, the principals and superintendents interviewed most often cited:

- Alignment of state standards, curriculum, instruction, and assessment.
- Using data to determine needs and guide planning.
- Targeting professional development to address those needs.

Other factors included new leaders, the creation of an LEA roundtable patterned after the state Roundtable, increased parental and community involvement, a safe environment, the adoption of a comprehensive school reform model, and instituting a continuous improvement model for all schools in a district, not just those that fail to make AYP.

When asked what lessons they had learned in working with the statewide system of support to achieve district and school improvement, the superintendents and principals noted the following:

Lesson 1—Articulated planning. Articulation from one grade and school to the next is crucial. One district gathered K-12 staff from a cluster of schools, all in a room at the same time, to celebrate strengths, identify weaknesses, and plan how to address those weaknesses.

Lesson 2—Help from the SDE. Get help from the State. The peer mentors, professional development, and walkthroughs provided by the State were instrumental in raising achievement.

Lesson 3—Learning culture. Establish a learning culture where school staff and parents maintain a focus on, and responsibility for, students attaining state academic standards.

Lesson 4—Professional development based on data. High quality professional development is essential to address needs identified through examination of data.

Lesson 5—Effective use of data. Examine data carefully, particularly disaggregated data and cohort data over time. Use data to spark discussion among school and district staff and as a basis for constructing improvement plans.

Lesson 6—Planning. "You must have a plan." Continuously monitor the implementation of school improvement plans. Walk-throughs can provide valuable information on the extent to which elements of the plan are actually being carried out.

Lesson 7—Shared leadership and decision making. Shared leadership and shared decision making, whether in the form of local roundtables or discussions among faculty members, lead to better plans and critical buy-in.

State Policies—Incentives and Opportunities

The principals and superintendents agreed that they were affected by the pressure of public accountability in response to a school's assessment scores, and that the effects were positive. One principal spoke of the special recognition given to Torchbearer schools and schools coming out of improvement, "Releasing results to the media is a motivator, and you don't want your name in the media for something negative." For one of the schools, the threat of reconstitution ultimately had a positive effect, though the initial reaction was negative. That school's principal commented: "When hit with the possibility of reconstitution, many people wanted to give up. Ultimately we said we have to get going."

Both principals reported that financial rewards and the attendant recognition had a positive effect; as one pointed out, "It always gives us something to shoot for, and every school needs money." The superintendents similarly lauded the system of financial rewards, though one expressed regret that schools with continually high performance were passed over.

Although the state does not reward administrators to work in low-performing districts and schools, one of the districts negotiates contracts with principals to provide financial incentives for improved student achievement. The other superintendent said she was thinking about providing incentives for teachers in low-performing schools, but "I'd have to rob a bank to do it."

One of the superintendents reported occasionally obtaining a waiver to provide emergency certification; the other district has not requested waivers from the State. Both superintendents praised alternative routes to teacher certification for people with degrees in other fields for the purpose of easing shortages of science and mathematics teachers. Although one principal reported that alternative certification had no effect on his school, the other principal felt that the alternatively certified teachers at his school—constituting nearly 80% of the entire faculty—were not well prepared, and that student achievement suffered as a consequence.

Building Local Capacity

Two especially useful resources provided by the SDE are data and the SDE website. All interviewees reported extensive use of disaggregated State assessment data in creating their district and school improvement plans. Data for individual students are also available at the site in a conveniently usable form. The website receives high praise: "Everything's on the website.... We can actually go in there and plug in our data and produce the graphs and charts we need and track our data over time." Online staff development, curriculum guides, and lesson plans have been extensively used. Having materials readily available has proved invaluable: "When we pushed for common curriculum...there was only one hard copy in the library for 20 teachers. With the online version, everybody can print it out and keep it in their classroom."

Both superintendents said their districts had help from state staff in constructing and reviewing improvement plans. "Working with people like the Accountability Roundtable Coordinator gave us the opportunity for the staff in our central office to work better with our schools. We felt that we were really on target in what we could help them to do. That gave us some immediate success, which allowed [the school staff] to buy into the program." In addition, regional meetings provide valuable information and training, as well as an opportunity to discuss mutual problems with colleagues from other districts and learn from their experiences.

Services Received From the Statewide System of Support

Professional development is a key area of State support, delivered by way of intermediate service centers, peer mentors, online training, and state conferences. "The State is constantly providing opportunities. All we need to do is call," one local administrator said. The local administrators describe the professional development as being ongoing, of very high quality, and tailored to their specific needs.

"I think our state has been very timely in how they have addressed issues that have come up. For example, data meetings. How do we conduct those? How do we talk with our teachers? Whenever we have gone to them, they have connected back with us with really good suggestions that are not too overwhelming at the district level."

The administrators were lavish in their praise of the peer mentors. As one principal put it, "From [the time the peer mentor came to the school], I cannot say enough about the service provided by the State department." The mentor, who was assigned to the school for a whole school year, assisted with professional development, monitoring instruction, creating data reports, and planning. The school had three site reviews to assess implementation of the school improvement plan and give suggestions for improvements. The peer monitor "had an impeccable record of school improvement and being able to assist with and foster change. To say the least, she was a helpful person.... People had no problem confiding in her. The information and professional development she brought back to us was just unreal." The only negative was that the peer mentor was only there for a year. One of the principals found the position so worthwhile that he used his school's NCLB funds to hire a peer mentor after state funding ran out.

The State Roundtable has been a boon to the superintendents and principals, so much so that the districts instituted their own roundtables consisting of representatives from curriculum and instruction, special education, bilingual education, safety and security, and other departments. District roundtable members create the district improvement plan, work together to solve problems, and help with development of school improvement plans. They also participate in statewide planning summits.

"We're lucky—the best thing our state department did was implement this LEA roundtable. It's been a tremendous amount of support and we know exactly whom to call when we need what... I don't mean to be ugly, but I've been in this a long time and I remember when I used to call the state department and I'd get passed around from department to department. Well now, when I call up there, if I can't get somebody, somebody will call me before the day is out and I can talk to a real person and get an answer." A colleague added, "The main thing is everybody being organized and on the same page. For instance, if we had a professional development plan, there would be four entities that wanted to see it. Now there's only one entity for monitoring. One superintendent described the Roundtable as "a great example of leading by example."

All of the administrators interviewed mentioned how easily accessible help was from the SDE office and regional centers. They do not hesitate to call the state department or their intermediate service center with questions or requests.

One principal observed, "Most people look at state intervention or state assistance as a negative thing. On the contrary, I cannot say anything but positive things for the state department of education and their efforts to improve schools. They're committed to it and even now they call and check and follow up behind us to make sure everything's running right. I cannot say enough for that." The administrators interviewed clearly see the State as a partner in improvement rather than simply an agency that monitors compliance with state regulations.

NCLB Sanctions and Provisions

Each of the districts and schools reported in these interviews has offered supplemental educational services, which they all viewed as somewhat effective, depending on the provider. Another principal responded that the program "could ultimately be very effective" if the program could be implemented earlier in the school year; due to budget timelines, he is currently unable to get it operational until the end of the first semester.

Few students availed themselves of choice under NCLB, so there was little effect on student achievement, though one of the principals felt he lost some of his best students.

Neither of the principals' schools was subject to restructuring, but one of the superintendents had restructured a middle school in his district. A new principal was named and although no teachers were removed, a number chose to leave after one year. Achievement improved under the new principal's leadership.

Suggestions for Evaluation of Statewide Systems of Support

Suggested criteria for evaluation were increased achievement, accessibility, accuracy of information provided, and extent of collaboration and communication with districts and schools. In the view of a local superintendent: "I think they need to listen to their school systems and see what the greatest needs are, and those are going to vary. See how well the districts are taking advantage of what they're putting out there. Sometimes the delivery is so difficult. That's one of the reasons Alabama has been so successful; they work *with* us, not *at* us. When we made suggestions, they listen to us. We call our state department a lot because we want to know what they're thinking about. If they weren't doing a good job, we wouldn't be communicating."

ACKNOWLEDGEMENTS

We would like to sincerely thank the following staff from the Alabama State Department of Education for their time during our interviews and for their time in providing us with important supporting documents: Ruth Ash, Deann Stone, Gloria Turner, Barbara Walters, Brooke Blair, Katherine Mitchell, Judy Stone, Christine Spear, Debbie Webster, Laura Hartley, Kathleen Knight, Lee Berry Scott, Joanne Cain, Pam Lackey, Reeda Betts, Anita Buckley Commander, Maggie Rivers, Sherrill Parris, Cheryl Sparks, Cyndi Townley, Rita Fentress, and Phaedra Fox.

We would also like to thank the following local educators who gave generously of their time to talk with us:

William Hines, superintendent and Mary Bess Powell, assistant superintendent, Escambia County Schools, Brewton, AL
Byron McGlathery, principal, Davis Middle School, Huntsville, AL
Polly Moore, assistant superintendent, Tuscaloosa County Schools, Tuscaloosa, AL
Chuck Willis, principal, Smith Middle School, Birmingham, AL.

Thomas Kerins *is program director at the Center on Innovation & Improvement, where* **Carole Perlman** *and* **Susan Hanes** *are both technical advisors.*

CHAPTER 8

PERFORMANCE CONTRACTING IN WASHINGTON

Thomas Kerins, Susan Hanes, and Carole Perlman

The information included in this profile of Washington's statewide system of support is derived from an on-site visit of Washington's Office of the Superintendent of Public Instruction (OSPI), the state's education agency, by two of the authors, telephone interviews with district superintendents, their designees, and school principals by the third author, and documents provided by the OSPI. The OSPI is hereafter referred to as the State Department of Education (SDE).

INTRODUCTION

This section provides background on the state's development of a system of support, the factors SDE personnel have determined to have the greatest impact on school improvement, and the lessons SDE personnel have learned.

Handbook on Statewide Systems of Support, pages 111–138

Evolution of the Statewide System of Support in Washington

The following is a brief history of school and district accountability in Washington State:

- 1993–1998: The Commission on Student Learning (CSL) was charged with creating a proposal for an accountability system for the state legislature.
- 1999–2006: The Academic Achievement and Accountability Commission (A+) was created to further develop the statewide accountability system from CSL. Several proposals were presented to the legislature between 2000 and 2004; the only recommendation enacted was the provision of funds for a voluntary focused-assistance program for struggling schools. The A+ Commission created annual performance goals in reading and mathematics for grades 4, 7, and 10; on-time graduation rates; and unexcused absence rates. The A+ Commission also set Washington Assessment of Student Learning (WASL) cut scores to meet standards in reading, mathematics, writing, and science.
- 2000: The state legislature enacted a policy requiring students in the Class of 2008 and beyond to demonstrate proficiency on state standards in reading, mathematics, and writing. Science became a requirement beginning with the Class of 2010. Students in the Class of 2008 and beyond were also required to complete a High School and Beyond Plan and Culminating Project.
- 2001: The School Improvement Assistance (SIA) program was initiated and funded with the mission to help build capacity for schools and districts to improve student achievement through the use of a continuous school improvement model; the first cohort included 25 schools.
- 2004: District Improvement Assistance (DIA) Program was initiated; the first cohort included 29 districts.
- 2006–2007: The state board of education was charged with proposing a statewide accountability performance system to the legislature. The legislature requested consideration be given to the following performance improvement goals: criteria for successful schools and districts, criteria for schools and districts where intervention is needed, possible state interventions, and performance incentives and review of assessment report system with a focus on special circumstances and unique populations.

By state law, the Superintendent of Instruction cannot intervene in districts without legislative approval. The voluntary nature of school improvement in Washington evolved from the above policies over the last 15 years.

Although assistance and intervention programs were well underway when NCLB began, NCLB provided the objective criteria to identify failing schools. Currently, the only state interventions available through NCLB are to defer programs or reduce administrative funding and authorize students to transfer from a school not meeting Adequate Yearly Progress (AYP) to a high-performing school. There is no state authority available for any other interventions provided through NCLB.

The Washington SDE staff believes that one key lesson learned in the early stages of educational reform was the critical role of the local superintendent, central office, and school board. With the primary emphasis being the school as the unit of change, there has been significant improvement over the three years of the program in several of the components of school improvement as measured by the Nine Characteristics of Effective Schools.

However, mobility of staff, principals, and central office leadership can negatively impact the sustainability of gains over time since successful strategies and research-based practices may not be continued and reinforced as new staff and leaders embark on different initiatives or are not knowledgeable about the school's work in the School Improvement Assistance program. It has become increasingly clear that building the capacity of the school district to oversee, support, and lead improvement in district schools within a systemic framework is essential to sustained improvement.

Factors That Contribute to Improvement and Services That Address Them

Readiness to Benefit the School or District

Washington uses a system of external facilitators who are paid by the state to provide direct services to school systems. School Improvement Assistance (SIA) and District Improvement Assistance (DIA) program administrators hire primarily central office administrators and principals as external, part-time school and district facilitators. SIA partners with the Association of Washington School Principals to provide leadership training and direct feedback to the leadership in schools in improvement. DIA partners with Washington Association of School Administrators (WASA) to provide leadership training and feedback for superintendents and district leadership teams.

In addition, resource guides are produced to assist the external facilitators and local staff. The Nine Characteristics of High Performing Schools (June 2007 Second Edition, http://www.k12.wa.us/research/pubdocs/NineCharacteristics.pdf) is a research-based framework for school improvement in Washington. Each of the studies that served as the basis for this guide was analyzed to determine which characteristics were found most often among high performing schools. Performance was usually measured in terms of high or dramatically improving scores on standardized tests, often in spite of difficult circumstances such as high levels of poverty. In every case, there was no single factor that accounted for the success or improvement. Instead, the research showed that high performing schools tend to have a combination of common characteristics.

Another resource is the document Characteristics of Improved School Districts (October 2004). This report focuses on improved school districts and their characteristics and actions. Because school districts are complex systems within the contexts of states and communities, the SDE staff points out that the strategies discussed in their studies may not be applicable in other settings. Therefore, they should not be considered prescriptions to follow but rather ideas to consider. An analysis of the studies identified 13 common themes which have been clustered into four broad categories: Effective Leadership, Quality Teaching and Learning, Support for Systemwide Improvement, and Clear and Collaborative Relationships.

The *School Improvement Planning Process Guide* (January 2005, 3rd ed.) is written as a planning document that leads the principal and school community through a cycle of continuous improvement. The guide provides a variety of processes, resources, and graphic tools to engage all stakeholders to develop deeper, sustainable second order change in each school. The SDE in partnership with WASA produced a companion guide for districts, *School System Improvement Resource Guide*, to assist districts with their improvement efforts.

Cohesiveness of School and District Leadership

Washington enters into a two-year Performance Agreement contract with participating SIA schools that identifies how the school, school district, and the SDE will support the successful implementation of the school's improvement plan. However, prior to the development of a plan for improvement, the district, school staff, and the SDE consider ways in which the district can support the school and staff during the planning process. Together they complete the Performance Agreement and submit it to the SDE with their school improvement plan at the end of the first year of the program. High schools participating in school improvement must submit the Initial Performance Agreement to the State by October 31st. The initial high school agreement is reviewed throughout the year and builds the foundation for the district performance agreement to be completed the following spring.

The agreement is organized around a template of 30 district commitments and 8 state commitments—with the option of additional actions to be requested by the district. The template serves as a guide for dialogue between the district and the state. Any of the parties may edit, delete, or add items to maximize district support to the school's plan. Participants consider types of evidence that would demonstrate support for each of the agreed-upon commitments. Examples of the district's written commitments include:

- The district will designate a district level administrator with decision-making authority to provide direct support to the school as a member of the School Improvement Leadership Team.
- The district will ensure that all programs, policies, and practices are continually assessed on the basis of their impact on student learning at the school.
- The district agrees to provide data to the school to guide instructional decisions, to monitor results, provide for equity, accountability, and for consideration in the allocation of resources.
- The district agrees to increase the assignment of reading and/or math specialist time to the school.
- The district agrees to provide supplemental funding for specific professional development activities for instructional staff or for time for staff collaboration and planning based upon strategies identified in the school improvement plan.

Examples of the SDE commitments are:

- The SDE will provide a part-time school improvement facilitator who will work with the school district, school, and the School Improvement Leadership Team to develop, implement, and monitor a school improvement plan consistent with guidelines established for schools participating in SIA.
- The SDE will provide funding to support the identified objectives of the school improvement plan that may include the payment of stipends for the Improvement Leadership Team members, staff planning, professional development, and other allowable school improvement activities.

Fidelity to Creating a Sense of Accountability

SDE staff believes that improvement efforts should be school-based but district supported. The State requires a minimum commitment of three years for a school to receive state support. A recent state approval letter to the Kennewick school district noted the Performance Agreement commitments between the district, school, and the State that have been made to support the successful implementation of the school improvement plan. The Performance Agreement will be reviewed annually based upon student performance.

- Through site visits, reporting, and regular communication with principals and school improvement facilitators, state staff will monitor the status of the Improvement Plans and Performance Agreements.
- State staff will work with district staff and the leadership team of the school if adjustments are necessary.
- Two independent evaluations of the School Improvement Assistance Program have clearly indicated that when the school improvement planning process and Performance Agreements are honored with fidelity, there are significant gains in student performance.

Tools and resources for the implementation of the Performance Agreement are provided during years two and three. The resources and expertise are determined on a case-by-case basis for each school, but could include such support as contracting experts to work with diverse student populations (e.g., special education and English language learners), funding professional development to implement research-based practices and programs, and funding time for staff collaboration and training.

Schools and school districts are expected to ensure that existing funds are used effectively and to dedicate school district resources as identified in the jointly developed Performance Agreement. This agreement also includes a timeline for meeting implementation benchmarks and student improvement goals.

Monitor Progress

Since the program's inception in 2001, approximately 130 schools have participated in School Improvement Assistance. These schools represent the diversity of Washington State with respect to size, location, and demographics. They include K-12 schools; primary, intermediate, and middle schools; and alternative and comprehensive high schools. Program components for SIA include: a school improvement facilitator; comprehensive needs assessment/educational audit; school improvement process, tools, and support; funds for staff planning and collaboration; a performance agreement; and professional development. In a recent independent study of the program, it was noted that Cohort I schools (2001-2004) showed greater achievement gains than both their respective comparison groups and the state. To date, 30 schools that have been served by SIA have met AYP.

In addition, 27 districts are currently engaged with the SDE in District Improvement Assistance (DIA). Similar to schools participating in SIA, these districts represent the geographical, size, and demographic diversity across Washington State. Participating districts receive funding and professional development; five districts chosen to participate in "DIA Plus" are provided additional resources and a part-time district improvement facilitator to support their district improvement work.

SDE staff believes this level of participation by both schools and districts in SIA and DIA is remarkable in light of the voluntary nature of the program. As stated earlier, in Washington, unlike most other states, schools and districts identified for improvement have the option to participate in School Improvement Assistance or District Improvement Assistance. Beyond publicly reporting results on the Washington Assessment of Student Learning (WASL) by different student subgroups as required by federal and state laws, there are no provisions in state laws or administrative rules for mandatory state interventions in schools or districts based on student achievement. Hence, if schools or districts not meeting AYP choose not to obtain assistance in spite of continuing poor student performance, they are not required to do so. However, districts in District Improvement (second consecutive year of not meeting AYP) are required to complete and keep on file a Timeline for School System Improvement Stages, along with an Assurances page signed by the district superintendent attesting that phase one of the planning process has been completed within 90 days of receiving their notification of not meeting AYP.

Lessons Learned

Lesson 1—Common, Aligned, Sustained Effort. A statewide system of support requires a common, aligned, and sustained effort by the state board of education, legislature, and department of education. It also requires a constancy of purpose and commitment. An illustration of this is the School System Improvement Resource Guide (SSIRG) jointly written by the SDE and the Washington Association of School Administrators in July 2005. The purpose of this document was to

- Support districts as they analyze existing systems and look at additional district-wide structures they may need to create a culture in which the importance of student achievement is reflected in an on-going, data-driven process.
- Provide a model planning process that fits the parameters defined by the federal government for those districts that must develop a district improvement plan as a result of not meeting AYP in one or more areas over a two-year period.
- Highlight research findings from state and national experiences that provide examples of best practices with proven track records of success in improving student learning.

This document provides a host of forms, templates, and strategies for local educational leaders to use not only for their general program but also for the English language learners and special education pupils.

Lesson 2—District Capacity to Support Schools. SDE staff believes in order to provide success at scale, they must focus on building the capacity of districts to support their schools. As one strategy to build district capacity, the SDE disseminates rubrics, included in the SSIRG, for local leaders to use as they determine their district's current status in each of the Nine Characteristics of High Performing Schools. The rubrics provide consistency for both district staff and state providers of technical assistance to more clearly define each district's evolving strengths and weaknesses over time.

The Nine Characteristics of High Performing Schools are:

- Clear and Shared Focus;
- High Standards and Expectations for All Students;
- Effective Leadership;
- High Levels of Communication and Collaboration;
- Alignment of Curriculum, Instruction, and Assessment with Standards;
- Frequent Monitoring of Teaching and Learning;
- Focused Professional Development;
- Supportive Learning Environment; and
- High Levels of Parent and Community Involvement.

Each of the 9 characteristics is divided into a number of sections, ranging from 4 sections in Effective Leadership to 9 in Focused Professional Development. Each of these sections describes stages of development or sophistication according to four descriptors: Initial Stages, Development, Partial Implementation, and System-wide Coherence. (See Appendix for example.)

An important adjunct to these rubrics in the SSRIG is a list of guiding questions to assist district staff as they gather the data necessary to complete the rubrics. More in-depth rubrics have been developed and will be field-tested during the 2007-08 school year in the schools and districts participating in the state improvement assistance programs. These rubrics will be the foundation of the performance reviews (educational audits) but will be made available in the future for all schools and districts to use in their improvement efforts.

Lesson 3—High Standards for All Students. School improvement assistance has evolved over time, but remains constant in a belief and focus on high standards for all students. It is about changing the hearts and minds of adults. The Washington documents are clear about the intention that districts should hold all adults in the system accountable for student learning.

The Washington school improvement documents are also clear that districts should have comprehensible and consistent expectations for instruction and for improved outcomes for students. Districts should focus intensive attention to classroom practices and provide guidance and oversight for teaching and improvement of learning for all students. Central office staff has the responsibility for defining goals and standards. Schools have latitude in the use of resources and influence over issues important to school staff in the support of high standards and expectations for all students.

FUNCTIONS OF A STATEWIDE SYSTEM OF SUPPORT

This section organizes the information provided by SDE personnel into the evidence-based framework described in the chapter "State Role in Supporting School Improvement."

Provide Incentives for Change

In 2001, the legislature provided seed money to begin the school improvement program and continues to show its commitment by investing $3.2 million per year into the School Improvement Assistance Program. The money is focused on improvement in the schools not receiving Title I dollars, yet are still in need of improvement. Currently, Washington is inviting non-Title I high schools and districts to participate in improvement efforts through grant dollars from the Bill and Melinda Gates Foundation.

Incentives for change are limited. While there is pressure of public accountability in response to a district's or school's assessment scores, the public response is short lived. As mentioned earlier, the State's only leverage for undesirable consequences for persistent low performance is the eventual withholding of federal dollars. There is limited capacity for the State to intercede. There are a few financial rewards available such as the Blue Ribbon and State Capitol budget for those schools that have made improvement, but the subsequent impact on schools is not known.

There are no special rewards for administrators, but there is an additional $5,000 bonus for the 2007–08 school year for National Board Certified Teachers to teach in a school with 70% or higher free and reduced price lunch student body. There are no charter schools in Washington, and competition for students through public school choice is limited to schools identified as missing AYP. However, the SDE does recognize schools for improvement at its summer institute. Along with these public acknowledgments, plaques for meeting reading and math goals are also awarded by the State.

While incentives are limited, Washington does have a process for districts to request waivers from specific state requirements. For example, a district may apply for less than the full instructional year of 180 days after the community approves. The days are often used for professional development. Districts may request waivers from provisions in teacher contracts if a school improvement plan calls for that. When a staff embraces a plan, the local union usually allows the change, but there is at times a "push-pull" experience.

Build Capacity to Change

Build Systemic Capacity

In response to the question about whether there is a systematic review process to determine what state policies hinder effective improvement efforts in districts and schools, the SDE staff replied that a review is now beginning. "It is not just policies that diffuse school improvement issues—the voluntary nature of our improvement system hinders the process."

The SDE staff believes that the department of education could provide assistance to them with information about research-based best practices and what is working across the country in school improvement—what are the good indicators and descriptors.

Create and Disseminate Knowledge. During the 2007 legislative session, Washington legislators provided significant funding for professional development targeted at math and science teachers. Fourth and fifth grade teachers will be provided two additional days of professional development. Secondary math and science teachers will receive three additional professional development days. Funding was also allocated for one lead math and one lead science teacher from each secondary school to be provided five additional days of specialized professional development. The budget included funding to develop a statewide math and science instructional coaching program, including a coach development institute, coaching seminars, and coaching activities within schools.

Enhance Supply of Personnel. Washington state does not require superintendents to hold a superintendent's certificate. Washington state has four primary routes for alternative teacher certification to bring new teachers into education.

Washington does not have a systemic process in place for alliances between higher educational institutions and the SDE. Standards-based instructional pedagogy is taught at teacher training institutions. While no formal alliance exists between higher education institutions and the SDE, doors have always been open, and there are additional emerging opportunities for communication and engagement for universities and the SDE to work together. The Professional Educators Standards Board works closely with state colleges and universities in the development and maintenance of quality pre-service programs for teachers, and alternative certificate programs.

The University of Washington-Tacoma has developed its principal training program to focus on developing leaders with skills to work successfully with low-performing schools. The SIAP has opened an office on the UW-Tacoma campus, and state staff hope that SIAP's physical presence on campus will continue to open more doors for partnerships.

Build Local Capacity

Capacity Building Structures.

Coordinate Structures and Roles. Department staff have a variety of ways to communicate within the SDE and with the field regarding meetings and trainings. Staff continue to make efforts to improve the level and quality of communication including evaluation by the recipients of communications.

State Education Agency. The mission of the SIA program is to help build capacity for schools and districts to improve student achievement through the use of a continuous school improvement model. Staff note that the Washington accountability system does not focus on rewards, punishments, or takeovers, but rather on assisting local educators with strategies for improvement.

Washington has a needs assessment and educational audit system available for schools. It is conducted by the SDE through a team of peer educators and experts. The school's strengths and challenges are identified, and recommendations for improvement are developed. The school's curriculum, leadership, instructional practices and resources, assessment results, allocation of resources, parental involvement, support from the central office, and staff, parent, and student perceptions are examined. Student performance data, indicators from the Nine Characteristics of High Performing Schools, and the results of a review of the school's reading and math instructional practices and programs are used to identify areas to consider for improvement. The assessment and audit includes the administration of survey instruments and an on-site visit. Resources allow for up to 25 audits to be completed annually by the SDE.

Intermediate Agencies. There are nine regional Educational Service Districts (ESDs) across the State. The ESDs funding is through state, local district funds, and grants. The ESDs provide representation at each of the monthly meetings of the school improvement facilitators, as well as facilitating implementation (Year Two) and sustainability (Year Three) training for the School Improvement Leadership Teams. ESDs also support their regional schools and districts by providing professional development tailored to their specific improvement plans.

External Partner Organizations. Some state education alliances exist with the Business Roundtable, but they are not directed specifically to school improvement efforts. Most of the partnerships developed have been with administrator organizations such as Association of Washington School Principals (AWSP) in supporting and training principals in school improvement and the Washington Association of School Administrators' (WASA) work in developing the SSRIG, as well as, supporting and training district improvement facilitators. Working with these organizations provides the State credibility with schools and districts. The State is also supported by the Gates Foundation for high school and district reform.

Distinguished Educators. In Washington, distinguished educators contracted by the State are called school improvement facilitators (SIFs) and district improvement facilitators (DIFs). Currently 61 SIFs are serving 70 schools in 29 districts. SDE personnel have assigned eleven external DIFs to collaborate with district superintendents. The SIFs and DIFs facilitate the improvement process that includes the needs assessment and educational audit and the subsequent revision of a school improvement or district improvement plan at each site. Facilitators support the District/SEA Performance Agreements mentioned earlier. They help and support the leadership team at the school. The facilitators guide crucial conversations, bring issues to the table, and may mentor principals, but a key part of this mentoring is to build capacity and not reliance.

Over the last six years, the role of the SIFs has evolved. Originally, their primary responsibility was to initiate school improvement planning. The SDE is now working with schools that already have a plan in place. Facilitators help local educators build capacity and sustainability of working programs in the schools. The SIFs are not district employees, which allows them to provide an outside voice and perspective. The SIF has no authority but tremendous responsibilities as an external change agent. SIFs are generally not assigned to a district in which they were employed.

SIFs work with the SDE, the school district, and a School Improvement Leadership Team to develop and revise a current plan to address identified needs and to prepare and implement the jointly developed Performance Agreement. During this three year period, the SIF will work approximately 2.0–2.5 days a week with each school, depending on school size. SIFs act as external change agents to facilitate school improvement. SIFs help the school staff identify and eliminate barriers to change and promote necessary school consensus for change.

Funds for planning time related to the development of the school improvement plan are provided by the SDE. Funds may be used to pay staff stipends, substitute teachers, consultants, and other activities, including training supported by the school improvement plan, research, and best practice. A minimum of three days must be devoted to planning time for all staff during the development of the school improvement plan. The annual state grant for these schools for stipends and substitutes ranges from $35,000 to $80,000 based on the size of the school.

DIFs are also contracted by the SDE annually. WASA is a partner in helping to define the pool of potential DIFs, some of whom are retired superintendents. DIFs are contracted directly by the districts with funds provided by the SDE.

The SIF and DIF selection process is a rigorous, competitive process. Potential SIFs and DIFs progress through a series of steps that serve to identify the applicants representing the most highly skilled administrators and educators. Applicants complete an application which includes multiple written response background questions, undergo screening reference checks, and are interviewed by SDE staff. Once selected, potential SIFs/DIFs are placed in a pool and assigned to a school dependent upon geography, school needs, and a match with their skill set and experience.

SIFs attend a required one week training in the summer. Day one includes introduction to the program and operational support. The four following days include differentiated training on how to work with local personnel in each year of program involvement. Year one focuses on the planning process—using data, doing a performance review, allocating resources, working with people, and developing reasonable expectations for growth. Year two training is focused on successful implementation of the revised school improvement plan, and year three is continued development of capacity to sustain the implemented changes. The SDE uses this training week as an opportunity (especially with new facilitators) to identify their strengths to best match the SIF with the needs of the district and school.

In addition, SIFs are required to attend monthly meetings which provide topical professional development and cohort, regional, and grade level breakout sessions to address identified common needs. SIFs also attend SDE and AWSP workshops with their School Leadership Teams up to 12 days per year.

Generally, DIFs attend separate trainings from the SIFs. They attend a total of 15 days which include five three-day trainings throughout the year. Some of the trainings include the superintendents and support administrators. There have been two three-day meetings per year, which SIFs and DIFs jointly attend. SDE staff believe that the variety of backgrounds among the facilitators provides shared expertise that otherwise would not be possible.

Although the SDE assigns the SIFs, superintendents discuss the selection and sign off on the placement. To date, 97% of the initial matches have been successful. While there is no formal evaluation, the SDE does conduct site visits and has ongoing conversations with School Improvement Leadership Teams. State staff also obtain informal feedback from principals and superintendents as well as SIFs and DIFs themselves. This year a "How am I doing?" survey has been added to the informal collection of feedback. A key component of any evaluation review is the successful completion of the Performance Agreement. SIFs are required to submit quarterly reports.

SDE staff believe that their system of using SIFs and DIFs as independent voices of highly skilled educators is very effective. They believe that this approach of using experienced and credible educators to make a significant contribution in struggling schools is critical to the State's school improvement system. Since they are paid as contractors and are flexible in terms of assignment, the approach has also been cost effective for the SDE.

A majority of the school and district facilitators are retired educational professionals, but the availability of qualified retired educators will be significantly reduced due to a change in the Washington State retirement system. The SDE may consider the possibility of building improvement facilitator capacity by incorporating current educators who would be able to remain a part of the K-12 system and retain membership in the K-12 retirement system. The SDE seeks assistance from their Regional Comprehensive Center or the U.S. Department of Education with research about building systemic, sustainable improvement through coach or facilitator models, how best to increase capacity, and how to reduce dependence on external support.

School Support Teams. There are no state supported school level teams as part of the statewide system of support for schools and districts volunteering to be involved in the state school or district improvement process. School improvement support is provided as an embedded model through the SIFs and DIFs and technical assistance specifically addressing school or district identified needs (i.e., cultural competence, mathematics).

The SDE, through the School and District Improvement division, does have a School performance review (Ed Audit) system. School performance reviews are conducted with all schools that have volunteered to receive SIAP services. Ed Audit teams, consisting of six to ten professionals (identified in a similar competitive selection process as SIFs and DIFs), spend four to five days on-site looking at curriculum and instruction through the lens of the Nine Characteristics of High Performing Schools and alignment with the research on high performing districts.

Data sources that support the School Performance Review include classroom visits and observations, interviews, focus groups, and other documentation. The School Performance Review final report is one component of a data portfolio that staff consider and discuss for data-driven decisions and the revision of the school improvement plan. Within two weeks of the visit, the SPR team leader presents the report to the full staff; the school is responsible for sharing the report with their community for input. The final report becomes one part of the school improvement process.

The SDE staff believe their efforts to date have been effective. The Ed Audit process has been successful in gearing up local staff to think and work together and to change their culture. The State will be taking the next step in improving the process by implementing the School Performance Review

Descriptor Rubric reflecting Washington State Standards and Indicators based on the Nine Characteristics of High-Performing Schools and *High Schools We Need: Improving an American Institution* (http://www.k12.wa.us/research/pubdocs/NineCharacteristics.pdf). This continuum provides schools an opportunity to identify where they are in comparison to the standard as a result of their school performance review (Ed Audit). The SIAP is also looking at ways to better engage parents and community members.

Differentiate Support to Local Districts and Schools

Each of the 27 districts that fall into Step 1 of corrective action under NCLB guidelines were encouraged to apply for district improvement assistance (DIA) support. Schools not meeting AYP in multiple cells and in federal improvement status are invited to apply for SIA. The SDE's capacity is to serve approximately 25 new schools annually with 75 schools supported at any one time. Priority is given to Title I designated schools with the most subgroups not meeting standards and schools that have been in improvement status for the longest time. Non-Title I schools can be supported with state dollars, and non-Title I high schools have been supported through a matching grant from the Gates Foundation. Currently there are 343 schools in Year 1 or Steps 1–5. SIA has served approximately 130 schools since 2001. It is estimated that as many as 500 additional schools may be in an improvement step by 2008.

Because of the nature of the volunteer process, high-needs schools with many groups not making AYP were given high priority for full assistance. The school improvement plans in SIA schools are used to identify needs, such as low income, mathematics, ELL. The Ed Audit provides focus on individual schools to help formulate and direct goals and action steps. Those schools with more needs can receive additional technical assistance support. Differentiating services is the common core of the role of both the SIF and DIF. SIFs and DIFs have the latitude to adjust services and assistance to meet the needs of the schools and districts.

Beginning in 2005, the Washington legislature appropriated additional funding dollars (matched by the Gates Foundation) to expand the SDE assistance program to focus specifically on high schools. The High School Improvement Initiative (HSII) focuses on comprehensive high schools in diverse communities across Washington to ensure that students graduate prepared for college, careers, and civic engagement, and the present achievement gap is closed. Schools are chosen through a competitive process; to be eligible schools must have failed to meet AYP for one or more years. Both Title I and non-Title I high schools are eligible to participate. Under current legislation, students in the Class of 2008 and beyond will be required to demonstrate proficiency in reading, and writing (math and science beginning with the Class of 2013) in order to graduate. HSII was developed as a "high octane" model focused on improvement of learning and teaching at the high schools. This initiative is anchored in the present SDE School Improvement Assistance Program including the previously mentioned Nine Characteristics of High Performing Schools.

The SDE is working with two organizations to implement this mandate. During this three-year program, High Schools That Work (HSTW), from the Southeast Regional Education Board, works with six schools to support implementation of ten key practices determined by HSTW to be significant in preparing all students for post-secondary careers and college opportunities. The key practices include: high expectations, intellectually challenging career/technical studies, rigorous and relevant academic studies, challenging program of study, work-based learning, teacher collaboration, actively engaged students, guidance, extra help, and keeping score through use of data.

Working in partnership with the Council of Chief State School Officers (CCSSO), the Successful Practices Network (SPN) is engaged in a multiyear initiative designed to bring effective practices to scale by gathering and sharing information on high schools that have been most successful in providing all students with rigorous and relevant education. The International Center for Leadership in Education developed four learning criteria to help high schools move from "promising" to "proven." Network schools use these criteria to create a personalized action plan to have all students perform at high levels. The four learning criteria are: core academic learning, "stretch" learning beyond minimum requirements, student engagement, and personal skill development. The six Washington high schools selected to participate in this initiative have access to a national "best practice" repository for ongoing improvement of instruction, technical assistance, resources, support, materials, and professional development.

Differentiate by Point of Impact. There are 296 districts and 2,223 schools in Washington. In 2005–2006, 5 of 29 districts that did not make adequate yearly progress were selected to receive additional funding and support (District Assistance Plus) through a competitive application process (14 districts applied). A component of the support package included a third party evaluation of each district's progress on its improvement initiatives.

The baseline report for one of the five districts noted, for example, that: "Topenish School District has not only supported school level change, but district personnel are also attempting to reinvent the function of the district by using data; aligning curriculum, instruction and assessments; targeting interventions; and making decisions that build human, political, and fiscal capital."

Deliver Services to Districts and Schools

Provide Services. In all its guides and planning documents, the State continuously refers to data-based decision making. To facilitate that approach, the SDE has longitudinal data for each district and school available on its website. The SDE's website provides a district improvement link and a web-based planning tool. The Center for Educational Effectiveness, an external partner, provides in-depth data packages, facilitation, and technical assistance to schools and districts participating in SIA and DIA.

Support to districts with schools in need of restructuring includes bringing teams from each district and school together to share common concerns, answer technical questions, review the importance of data in guiding changes, and hear from "experts" from the Educational Service Districts and the Northwest Educational Research Lab on state and national efforts in this area. Clustered trainings also provide teams an opportunity to share resources, professional development, and trainers. The SDE provides financial support to districts so they can more easily support the restructuring efforts in the designated schools.

Allocate Resources for Services. Support has been driven by the financial resources available to the SDE with regard to the intensity and duration of services a district receives. Currently, the State uses a combination of federal, state, and foundation money to support districts and schools. The SIA program commits to three years of support to schools, and limited fourth year funding is provided for a school if they have not exited improvement status. A SIF is assigned for three years, and the funding level to support professional development and implementation of the plan remains in place for each year.

Provide Opportunities for Change

Washington removes barriers to change by providing a flexible approach to both the district/school improvement process and the technical assistance provided through the statewide system of support. What is the process for deciding what services a district receives? Services provided or supported through the SDE are identified through collaborative conversations with the superintendent and local leadership teams. The SDE encourages and provides financial support for superintendents to add a district facilitator (DF) who works directly with the superintendent and leadership team as he or she engages in district improvement.

AYP status and number of the 37 cells below proficiency level determines eligibility to receive SIA services. From this identified group, schools volunteer to participate for state level assistance based on their level of readiness/ willingness. There are some common required program elements and expectations for participating schools. SIFs assist schools in determining their service needs based upon the School Performance Review final report, test data, and needs documented in the school's current improvement plan and specified in the Performance Agreement.

With regard to the common required elements, Washington in its January 2005 *School Improvement Planning Process Guide*, has eight stages in its School Improvement Process:

1. Assess Readiness to Benefit—Focuses on need for staff, in collaboration with students, parents, and community to have a clear picture of what it will take to go through the eight stages of the school improvement process.

2. Collect, Sort, and Select Data—Highlights gathering current data on achievement, demographics, staff/student/parent perceptions, and school programs to help "tell the story" of the school, so the full faculty is prepared to carefully consider the data in the next stage.

3. Build and Analyze the School Portfolio—Utilizes data showing the current status of the school to highlight areas of concern, strengths, and what to celebrate, and generate a prioritized list of challenges for the next step.

4. Set and Prioritize Goals—Uses findings from Step 3 to group challenges/concerns into themes and develop and prioritize goal statements that are student-centered, clear, measurable, and time bound.

5. Research and Select Effective Practices—Focuses on gathering research on school practices related to their school improvement goals, looking deeply into their data, and selecting strategies for each of the goals.

6. Craft Action Plan—Creates specific action plans focused on each goal area, including the specific activities, timelines, persons responsible, and outcome measure for each strategy.

7. Monitor Implementation of the Plan—Uses formative measures, such as classroom based assessments and analysis of student work, to demonstrate progress in each goal and focus attention on the plan.

8. Evaluate Impact on Student Achievement—Utilizes summative measures, such as the WASL, ITBS, and other summative measures specified in the action plans, to determine how much progress has been made toward improving student achievement.

The above template for school improvement provides local educators with a broad outline to frame their reflections in improvement planning. Within this framework, districts have the flexibility to implement significant changes within their systems. The SDE encourages this flexibility and believes it is a strength of the SDE's technical assistance approach.

EVALUATION OF STATE ROLE IN DISTRICT AND SCHOOL IMPROVEMENT

The Northwest Regional Educational Laboratory (NWREL) and another contractor completed independent evaluations of the SDE School Improvement Assistance Program (SIAP) by looking at its effect on the first three cohorts of schools participating in the program. The evaluations examined fidelity and sustainability of the program at the state, district, school, and classroom level; student outcome/achievement data; program management and effectiveness of the state, school district, and facilitator; and impact of the major program components including the educational audits, performance agreements, school improvement plans, and professional development opportunities supporting school improvement. The evaluation methodology included:

- A desktop review of applications, educational audit reports, and annual updates.
- Site visits to each school including interviews aligned with the Nine Characteristics of High Performing Schools that targeted a specific audience and specific aspects of the SIA program.
- Anonymous surveys completed by building staff, administrators, district leadership, parents, and the school improvement facilitator.
- A review of WASL achievement data and performance trends.

Among the findings common to each of the evaluations:

- Fidelity of implementation of school improvement efforts has been strong for each cohort as reported in survey results and interviews. The continuing presence of the SIF has been consistently cited as a key to this fidelity and helped schools make adjustments aimed at meeting their goals.
- 98% of school staffs expressed that they were familiar with the school's improvement plan, and 76% indicated that they were involved in its development and were actively engaged in its implementation.
- The role, support, and responsiveness of the SDE has consistently received high marks. 90% of staff indicated that professional development provided by the state resulted in changes in their classroom instruction.
- The use of data to drive planning and instruction has been evident in all schools.
- Eighty percent of school staff reported that their school had a sustainability plan in place for the year after SIAP involvement,

and that they were confident that their improvement efforts would continue. In a small number of schools, concern was expressed that they had become dependent upon the facilitator to drive their work.

- Sixty-five percent of survey respondents felt that student achievement had increased during the three years of the SIAP program as measured by the percent of students meeting the standard on the WASL reading and mathematics.

- The one indicator that was relatively low (49.5% agreement) was in the area of high levels of community and parent involvement. Interviews indicated that schools had increased the amount of information flowing from the school to the parents and the community, but felt the communication had only been in one direction. School staff expressed a need for additional assistance and work in strategies to engage parents in meaningful ways.

In addition to the independent evaluations, the Center for Educational Effectiveness (CEE) has provided the Educational Effectiveness Survey (EES) annually in SIA schools since 2002. This perception survey, which is administered to parents, school staff, and students, measures performance on the Nine Characteristics of High Performing Schools. In each cohort there is evidence that positive gains have been demonstrated in each of the nine categories with the highest gains noted in: increased communication and collaboration in schools; curriculum, instruction, and assessment; and clear and shared focus. The Center has also noted a high correlation in gains in student performance as evidenced in the WASL and increases in positive responses on the EES.

Student performance data on the WASL, provided by CEE, also notes significant gains in performance in reading and math when compared to the state. For example, annual average percentage gains in reading from 2002 to 2005 for students in grade four in SIA schools was 11.2 compared to 4.5 for the state, and grade 10 gains were 10.6 and 4.4 respectively. Gains in math were also noted. Further analysis of the comparison between SIA participating schools and the state for the same time period shows evidence that the achievement gap for minority students in SIA schools when compared to the state has significantly narrowed particularly in reading performance. African American students showed annual average gains of 13.9 and Hispanic students 12.3 compared to 4.3 at grade four for white students between 2002 and 2005. At grade seven, gains for Hispanic students was 12.6, African American at 8.6, and white students at 8.1. Similar gains were also noted in math at grades 4 and 10.

In addition to conducting program evaluation on the first three cohorts of the School Improvement Assistance Program participating schools, a baseline evaluation of the state's District Improvement Initiative Plus (DIA Plus) was completed. The purpose of the review was to provide baseline information about improvement efforts for school districts participating in DIA Plus and the extent to which school district personnel are making progress towards grant goals and objectives. Evaluators obtained information through evaluation activities that included:

- interviews and focus groups
- site visits
- evaluators attending SDE-sponsored meetings
- conducting classroom observations
- analysis of various documents including course guides, master schedules, graduation requirements, transcripts, SAT/ACT scores, and WASL scores.

The general questions explored during the evaluation of the impact of the DIA Plus were:

1. What is the effect of this initiative on school district practices that support school improvement and student achievement?
2. Has the culture of the school district changed?
3. Where there have been positive changes in the districts around effective practices, what has occurred to cause these changes?
4. Did this initiative assist in developing sustainability over time, and how?

Among the findings:

- These DIA-Plus districts are at the beginning of their district improvement efforts and most of the information available on the impact of the grant outcomes are generated from qualitative information rather than any noted changes in student outcomes data.
- The district improvement facilitator plays a critical role in the DIA Plus initiative. It is critical that the DIF be an external coach who can be objective and cross lines of authority without fear of retribution. The DIF should also have substantial experience at the district level in order to gain the recognition and authority of district personnel.
- The DIA plus program has clearly helped district administrators align and organize their goals.
- The key promising practices demonstrated by the DIA-Plus districts include involving more staff in the decision-making process; using data to help make decisions; improving staff collaboration and

openness; working to improve instructional practices; and improving rigor by investigating data.

VIEWS FROM THE FIELD

The information in this section is a synthesis of interviews with two super-intendents and two principals, who received services from the Washington statewide system of support.

Factors That Contribute to Improvement and Lessons Learned

The administrators interviewed by Center staff credited the following factors as being instrumental in their students' improved achievement:

- Teacher collaboration, shared leadership, team and trust building.
- A clear focus on the school improvement plan.
- Extensive use of data—both formative and summative—for school improvement planning, planning professional development, and for guiding policy at the school board level.
- Purposeful, individualized support of students not achieving at grade level and shared responsibility for assisting those students.
- Educating the school board on best practices that could guide policy-making and allocation of fiscal resources.
- Use of research-based instructional practices.
- Professional development assistance from the state and ESD and state staff development grants that enabled schools and districts to hire consultants and established networks of superintendents of like districts.
- District and school improvement facilitators.
- Audits conducted as part of the state improvement grant program.

Lesson 1—Narrow Focus. Said one superintendent: "Once you have decided what initiatives you're going to undertake to improve a district, you have to fight the temptation to keep adding other initiatives." A principal concurred: "You have to be careful there aren't multiple agendas, and you're not going in multiple directions, or you have this shotgun approach and nothing changes." She also recommends that schools avoid embarking on two major programs in the same year.

Lesson 2—Openness. "Always be open to whatever it may take to improve your district," including having outsiders, such as district improvement facilitators, play a role.

Lesson 3—Common Expectations. District improvement needs to be exactly that—a set of district-wide initiatives and common expectations for everyone, regardless of a school's NCLB status.

Lesson 4—Involvement of the Local School Board. "You have to involve the school board."

Lesson 5—Fun and Freedom. "Fun and freedom have to be elements in staff development. I believed it before, and now I've really seen success...it helped to build a team, and it also helped [the school] to be a place where people wanted to be." One example: "We wanted to have the teachers really understand the Nine Characteristics of Effective Schools...and we had them divide into teams, and they had to teach us that [characteristic] any way they wanted. We had skits, songs, videos, all sorts of fun, silly things, but yet we can point to a person and say 'supportive learning environment' and everyone will laugh because of the way it was presented." The principal felt it made the content of the training more meaningful to those who attended, and they more readily incorporated it into their daily practice. It also modeled good teaching practice, since there was something other than a teacher talking. She also regards this as an important factor in her school's extraordinarily low rate of teacher turnover (last year just 2 of 65 left, one to retire, the other to move out of the country).

Lesson 6—SIP a Working Document. "The school improvement plan we put together as a team is a working document. Every decision we make is based on, goes back to, that school improvement plan we put together based on lots of data, analysis, lots of research, best practices, visiting other schools. My job as a principal is to make sure that this is happening and to continue that momentum...and that we're not going down some side street....You need to make sure that when you have a [school improvement] plan, the plan is followed, that it's not a document that sits on a shelf."

Lesson 7—Communication. "Communicate, communicate, communicate. It's so important...you don't want anybody in the building not to know what's going on, and why a decision has been made, so we really try to make decisions as a team, make decisions based on the plan, the research, and then communicate why. And the first time I don't communicate, it comes back to bite me." She emphasized the importance of patience and the necessity of telling people the same thing more than once. "Make it clear and communicate and repeat to remind each other in a friendly way, in a positive way, in an encouraging way."

Lesson 8—Time. "It takes time. You can't do it in just a year."

State Policies: Incentives and Opportunities

All of the administrators reported that the pressure of public accountability had affected their schools or districts, but they disagreed on whether it affected school and district improvement. One superintendent said, "We don't like it, but it really hasn't changed what we're doing." One of the principals observed, "Teachers are already teaching their hearts out." Another principal, however, said, "It's had a positive effect, I think, because it really holds us accountable."

Several administrators mentioned the stress that the pressure of public accountability engenders among their staff. "It has been very difficult on administrators. Three administrators have been removed or left the district. Is it a positive or a negative thing? Well, somebody would say if they didn't improve scores, then you get somebody new. The negative effect is if you're trying to establish continuity in an administrative team."

One administrator was concerned about possible financial repercussions of low performance, both for her school, which would lose flexibility in how its NCLB funds could be spent, and for the district, which would have to bear the cost of transportation for students participating in public school choice. The administrators will all be following with interest the effects of a new program that will give stipends to National Board Certified Teachers to teach in schools with a large proportion of low-income students. Although there were no special financial rewards for improved performance, the superintendents said that recognition by the state for good work was always appreciated.

Two superintendents received waivers that enabled them to modify their school calendars and praised the state for its willingness to accommodate their needs. One of the superintendents hired several alternatively certified science teachers and felt that the teachers had made a positive impact; the other expressed hopes that alternative certification programs would ease teacher shortages in mathematics, science, special education, and programs for English language learners. Neither principal had experience with alternatively certified teachers. Although there was no special training for administrators to serve as turnaround specialists, a superintendent pointed out that principals in school improvement have received training, and that the results have been positive. The other superintendent was looking forward to superintendents being included in some upcoming training sessions for district improvement facilitators.

Building Local Capacity

A key resource for schools and districts is the SDE website, which they consult for data, professional development materials, grade level expectations, information on the Nine Characteristics of Effective Schools, and the *School System Improvement Resource Guide,* which provides a systematic framework for those embarking upon school and district improvement.

The school report card, accessible through the SDE website, gives disaggregated state assessment results and results by subgroup and content area. Another useful resource is the survey data compiled by an outside agency retained by the SDE. These surveys of parents, students, and staff, provide helpful contextual information. The state's data carousel process has been instrumental in school and district improvement planning. One of the principals described how her school used it: "The data carousel process involved the entire staff. Just the most amazing, beneficial process that we could not have done without. Real clear guidelines and procedural pieces, and [the school improvement facilitator] really helped to facilitate that."

The school report card website has proved similarly helpful, and its graphic capabilities have improved. Staff at one of the schools wanted to see what schools with similar student populations were doing to help their students succeed. They were able to use the data filters on the website to identify schools that they later visited. Their principal also provides hard copies of her school's school report card data for every teacher. "One other way the website has been really useful is that...I can go into math [WASL results] and see how many kids passed measurement or telling time...I can go to my teacher teams and show them...we are so strong in measurement. Whatever you're doing, keep doing. But yet, if we look at telling time, we're pretty weak there. So then we work to strengthen that, and it's really important structural information." The schools and districts supplement the state assessment data with a variety of formative assessments. In the words of one principal: "I think we're pretty rich in our data resources."

Another source of data is the Ed Audit conducted for schools in the improvement assistance program. The process is valuable to the participating schools and districts, as reflected in the fact that one superintendent decided to conduct audits of all schools in his district; the teachers at one school created their own audit instrument and established a thrice-yearly audit process for their school. The data obtained are used to plan professional development.

The school-improvement state grants have benefited schools in a multitude of ways, enabling them to: (a) bring in consultants for professional development; (b) send teachers to conferences, (c) provide financial support for school planning meetings that included non-certificated staff, and (d) provide released time for teachers and reading and math specialists to work on curriculum alignment. The schools and districts appreciated the flexibility afforded them under this program.

The school and district improvement facilitators were praised for the help they provided. A principal described her school improvement facilitator in this way: "One thing that's really nice about having [her] is that we've never felt she's a person from the SDE who's spying on us and going back and reporting to somebody.... She has really been a factor here. She's done a lot of research for us; she helps us find professional development opportunities.... She'll go in and model instruction in the classroom in areas that she is proficient. Facilitating the process has been her main role." The school improvement facilitator also helped them compile and use data in their improvement planning. The superintendent appreciated the fresh perspective the district improvement facilitator brought.

The ESDs were lauded for the training they offered and their assistance in locating people who could provide professional development in areas that schools and districts needed. The SDE also sponsors an annual conference where alignment of curriculum, instruction, and assessment are discussed, and models are presented. One superintendent observed that the conferences are "very helpful if you can send sufficient amounts of people, but again, it comes during student learning time and that causes problems because we have to pull teachers away from kids to get the learning they have to have." One of the principals expressed concern that professional development opportunities are not conveniently located for all districts, particularly those in the eastern part of the state.

Those interviewed singled out curriculum, increasing parental involvement, and assistance in serving English language learners as areas in which the state has provided especially helpful materials and training. Both superintendents especially appreciated the state's convening networks of superintendents with schools in improvement. They meet periodically to discuss common challenges they face, and the state superintendent has met with them to find out how the SDE could help. The state superintendent also visited the schools in the districts, meeting with teachers and the district teams. "I think the state agency's involvement in school and district improvement has been excellent, and the staff is always available to help us."

NCLB Sanctions and Provisions

Neither of the principals' schools has faced corrective action or restructuring under NCLB. One of the districts made AYP last year and the other was a few students short in one cell. Choice and supplemental services were little used and had no discernible impact on school improvement.

Suggestions for Evaluation of Statewide Systems of Support

Suggestions for continuously examining the statewide system of support involved surveys of principals and superintendents and face-to-face meetings with school and district staff. A principal noted, "There are obviously two levels of support—one would be to districts, and one would be to schools." She suggests that the state "survey their districts and find out about the support they're providing, but then have a secondary survey of their principals and make sure that support is trickling down and really getting to their schools."

In the view of one superintendent:

> The [state department has] come out to visit us and asked for that kind of feedback, and we've told them what's going well and what's not going well. They should have a regular survey, but they need to make sure that people give them honest feedback about what's working well and what's not working well and to model becoming a learning organization. The difference for me between a learning organization and a compliance organization is one that asks for that feedback and is not punishing or retaliatory in terms of what the data says.

The administrators recommended the following criteria for evaluating the effectiveness of a state's system of support:

- Assessment results
- The number of schools and district that enter school and district improvement
- Whether schools in improvement that receive state services fare better than those that do not
- What forms of communication [with the state] are available, and how frequently they are accessed
- Fairness and equity of services provided to schools throughout the state.

Since 2001, the state of Washington has implemented a highly successful voluntary program of support for schools in need of improvement. The SIA program has proven to be effective as noted by significant gains in student performance on state assessments, evidence that the achievement gap has narrowed, and by the numbers of SIA schools that have made AYP and exited federal improvement status. Washington has recognized that there still remains large numbers of schools in the state in need of intervention, and that the lessons learned from the School Improvement Assistance and District Improvement Programs can serve to inform the development of a comprehensive state accountability system in order to meet the diverse learning needs of all students.

ACKNOWLEDGEMENTS

We thank the following staff from the Washington Office of the Superintendent of Public Instruction for their time during our interviews and in providing supporting documents:

Janell Newman, Bill Mason, Dan Barkley, Shannon Thompson, Mary Schrouder, Bob Butts, Gayle Pauley, and Sue Cohn.

We would also like to thank the following local educators who gave generously of their time to talk with us:

Richard D. Cole, superintendent, Sunnyside School District, Sunnyside, WA

George Juarez, superintendent, Othello School District, Othello, WA

Karen Leary, principal, Eleanor Roosevelt Elementary School, Vancouver, WA

Lori McCord, principal, and staff members Jean Bowman, Nadine Hanson, Marlene Schueighardt, and Jan Slagle, Amistad Elementary School, Kennewick, WA.

APPENDIX: HIGH STANDARDS AND EXPECTATIONS FOR ALL STUDENTS

Circle the level that most clearly matches you perceptions of the district's current status in each of the subcategories

Initial Stages	Development	Partial Implementation	System-wide Coherence
1. Staff demonstrates belief that some students can learn.	1. Staff demonstrates belief that all students can learn if conditions are right.	1. District supports and teachers believe that they can teach all students to learn to high standards.	1. Everyone in the district demonstrates the belief in and takes responsibility for all students learning to high standards, effectively closing achievement gaps among groups of students.
2. All students receive similar instruction and curriculum based on a single text book.	2. Staff recognizes the need to provide challenging content for all students; they also understand the need to provide additional support for students to learn that content.	2. Professional development supports staff in developing challenging content and trains them in skills and strategies to support students in learning that content.	2. All students engage in challenging relevant and rigorous content and receive support to succeed in learning that content. Counselors and teachers encourage students to participate in rigorous course work.
3. Teaching is isolated and/or textbook dependent; little attention is paid to classroom practice.	3. Attributes of powerful teaching and of learning are identified; expectations of instruction that engages students are communicated.	3. A variety of appropriate strategies to ensure learning are identified and used; standards for classroom practice are implemented.	3. Effective instruction using research-based strategies is implemented system-wide to advance learning of all students.
4. Any level of student work is accepted; grading is based on factors such as attendance, effort and completion, as compared to quality of student work.	4. Definitions of quality student work are developed, grading continues to reflect factors such as attendance, effort, and completion.	4. Clear standards for quality work are consistently applied.	4. Quality work is observable across grade levels and content.
5. Little attention is paid to use of data to monitor teaching and learning.	5. District supports use of data focused on learning and classroom practices to inform instruction.	5. Training is provided to staff on using disaggregated data on learning and teaching to inform classroom practice.	5. Staff district-wide use disaggregated data to inform instruction and to assess teaching and learning.

Note: Used with permission. *School System Improvement Resource Guide Putting It All Together* Revised July 2005

CHAPTER 9

EXEMPLARY EDUCATORS IN TENNESSEE

Thomas Kerins, Susan Hanes, and Carole Perlman

The information included in this profile of Tennessee's statewide system of support is derived from an on-site visit of the Tennessee State Department of Education (SDE), the state's education agency, by two of the authors; telephone interviews with district superintendents and school principals by the third author; and artifacts provided by the SDE.

INTRODUCTION

This section provides background on the state's development of a system of support, the factors SDE personnel have determined to have the greatest impact on school improvement, and the lessons SDE personnel have learned along the way.

Handbook on Statewide Systems of Support, pages 141–166
Copyright © 2008 The Academic Development Institute and Information Age Publishing
All rights of reproduction in any form reserved.

Evolution of the Statewide System of Support in Tennessee

In 1992, the Tennessee Department of Education began to implement the Education Improvement Act. To implement this law, the SDE developed lists of low performing schools. During the 1998-1999 school year, the SDE made the lists of underperforming schools public, using Tennessee's own form of AYP as a yardstick. Tennessee's performance standards were based on the school's scores on state tests in reading, language, mathematics, and writing, in addition to a value-added assessment score (TVAAS). In 2000, using cut scores to determine levels of proficiency, the SDE identified 48 schools in need of improvement. Therefore, the Tennessee Department of Education's accountability system predated NCLB by two years in identifying high priority schools and school systems (Local Education Agencies—LEAs) which were not moving all subgroups of students to proficiency on state assessments.

After the initiation of NCLB, Tennessee embedded state law with federal requirements, beginning a seven-year schedule with sanctions. In 2001, Tennessee combined Title I and non-Title I schools in the set of schools identified as needing assistance. The SDE adopted a single set of criteria for identifying these schools and districts for both assistance and corrective action, at the same time switching from norm-referenced to criterion-referenced tests. Title I schools were held to the same requirements as non-Title I schools and required to implement NCLB-mandated interventions.

To work with these identified schools, Tennessee launched its Exemplary Educators (EE) Program. Exemplary educators, employed by the state, provide assistance to Tennessee's high priority schools by modeling innovative teaching strategies, serving as mentors to principals and teachers, analyzing student performance data, connecting with professional development providers, and building capacity for continuous school improvement.

All schools must be successful in three "cells" to meet Adequate Yearly Progress (AYP) benchmarks. These cells are: math, reading/language arts/writing, and an additional indicator (attendance at the elementary/middle levels and graduation rate at the high school level). A school or district that fails the same cell for two consecutive years is deemed "high priority" in Tennessee (referred to as "schools in improvement" in NCLB). Tennessee also provides assistance to target schools, those that have failed AYP for one year.

Factors That Contribute to Improvement and Services That Address Them

Leadership. The superintendent of each district is the first key to success. Tennessee's SDE learned over the years that working directly with the school and bypassing the district office and superintendent was a failed strategy. To sustain change in a district, working with the superintendent is a key.

Among the services that the state provides is training in understanding and using the state assessment system and school report cards so the superintendent and the district leadership team can use data, especially the value-added component, as they write improvement plans. The state staff also helps these leaders to understand and use the information from the Tennessee school audit program.

Tennessee "value-added" assessment has gained U.S. Department of Education approval as a growth model for AYP based on 2005–2006 data, one of two states to receive this approval. All elementary and middle schools are evaluated based on the traditional AYP model and also through the growth model. The schools may meet AYP through the traditional model, the growth model, or both.

To meet AYP through the growth model, all subgroups must meet the benchmarks in reading/language arts and math using the percentages of students with proficient or advanced scores on the assessment, projected three years into the future. For example, if a 5th grade student scores below proficient in math in 2005–2006, but has made such progress since the 3rd grade that the student has a projected score of proficient on the 8th grade math test, the student will be counted as "proficient" in the growth model. Conversely, if a 5th grade student scores proficient in math 2005–2006 but has made such declines since the 3rd grade that the student has a projected score of below proficient on the 8th grade math test, the student will be counted as "below proficient" in the growth model.

Awareness of Equity and Adequacy. The SDE provides district leaders training on how to expend funds and distribute resources. Superintendents need to build capacity in all the schools based on their unique needs. SDE staff believe that where needs are the greatest, local district leaders must show that they are giving those schools the most help.

The training enables district leaders to evaluate indicators such as whether a school with low scores also has a faculty with a high absentee rate, weak experience, or low productivity. In its March 2007 *Research Brief* (http://www.state.tn.us/education/nclb/doc/TeacherEffectiveness2007_03.pdf), the SDE discusses whether the most effective teachers are assigned to the schools that need them the most. The SDE believes it is essential to study the distribution of teacher effectiveness across schools. In Tennessee, students in poverty and minority students are less likely to meet grade-level standards than other students. "While they make about the same rate of academic progress each year as other students, they are more likely to start out below grade level. They need effective teachers—teachers who have the ability to accelerate their rate of academic progress—to reach grade level expectations and beyond," observed one interviewee. Tennessee is positioned to carry out this analysis since for more than 14 years the state has been harnessing its longitudinal student assessment database, which includes links between students and their teachers, to measure teacher effectiveness.

Alignment of the Curriculum with Instruction and Assessments. Tennessee relies on its February 2007 publication, *What is a Good School Appraisal Guide and Rubric,* as the focus of its work with districts on curriculum, instruction, organization, and assessments (both formative and summative). This document provides a consistent message to local staff that "...teams of educators visit schools across Tennessee to determine if teachers are really teaching and if all students are really learning to the best of their potential," as one interviewee put it. The site visits employ a set of criteria for effective schools and a connected set of standards and measurement statements with matched rubrics. The site visits result in an individual school profile of strengths and areas of planning needs.

Lessons Learned

Lesson 1—Importance of District Central Office. The SDE's direct technical assistance to a school is ineffective if the central office is not included. When the Tennessee EEs left a school, districts generally did not have the capacity to sustain improvement. Also, models or pathways have to be available so that the improvements are not person dependent.

Lesson 2—Comprehensive Planning Process. The Tennessee Comprehensive System-wide Planning Process (TCSPP) infrastructure needed to be in place for sharing and coordinating resources. There were redundancies in programs and requirements that were interfering with improvement efforts. A consolidated application for federal funds, connected to a unified planning template, was a preliminary step. All 136 districts now submit their plans annually to be approved by a cadre of SDE staff. In each plan, local personnel develop priorities for improving schools using the following template, and share the process by which they arrived at their priorities:

- School System Profile Development and Collaborative Process Identification
- Beliefs, Mission, and Shared Vision
- Academic and Non-Academic Data Analysis and Synthesis
- Curricular, Instructional, Assessment, and Organizational Effectiveness
- Comprehensive Systemwide Action Plan Development
- Analysis of the Process/Implementation

Lesson 3—Systemic Audits. The SDE now believes that comprehensive system audits are critical in identifying problems in curriculum, instruction, organization of the school day, and the use of formative and summative assessments. Through the audits, the central office staff develops skills for implementing the recommendations of the visiting teams using the previously mentioned *What is a Good School Appraisal Guide and Rubric.*

FUNCTIONS OF A STATEWIDE SYSTEM OF SUPPORT

This section organizes the information provided by SDE personnel into the evidence-based framework described in the chapter "State Role in Supporting School Improvement."

Provide Incentives for Change

SDE staff believe the pressure of public accountability in response to a district or school's assessment is positive, as are undesirable consequences to a school for persistent low performance. So far, of the 20 schools in re-structuring/alternative governance status, 12 have been successfully reconstituted and are working in partnership with their district.

Tennessee does not provide financial rewards to a district or school for improved results. However, there is a law on the books, but not yet implemented, that would provide a financial loss to a district or school for persistent low performance. Public Law 49-1-602 gives the Commissioner the authority to approve the allocation of discretionary grants to schools/districts beginning with School Improvement 2 ("On Notice" in state law). It also gives the Commissioner authority to approve the district's allocation of funding to schools in Corrective Action ("On Probation" in state law).

Tennessee has used federal School Improvement Funds for Title I districts. For example, Fayette County has two projects. One is with the University of Memphis to work with central office staff to build capacity with intense seminars (including an intensive summer program) and ongoing technical assistance. A full-time consultant from the University is assigned to this county district. In addition, for the 2007-2008 academic year, a special tax will provided funding to districts to improve the achievement of identified subgroups of students.

A new law (http://tennessee.gov/sos/acts/105/pub/pc0376.pdf) just passed in 2007 provides for bonuses and a differentiated salary structure in low performing schools. The SDE will be required to "...develop guidelines for the establishment by LEAs of differentiated pay plans, including plans which offer bonuses, including performance bonuses that are supplemental to the salary schedules...such plans shall address additional pay for teaching subjects or teaching in schools for which LEAs have difficulty hiring and retaining highly qualified teachers." Each LEA is required to have in place an approved differentiated pay plan prior to the beginning of the 2008–2009 school year.

Tennessee has dramatically increased the school aid formula beginning in 2007–2008. This same law requires that LEAs identify their areas of strengths and weaknesses as well as strategies to improve weaknesses. They also specify how additional funds provided through changes made in the Basic Education Program School Funding formula will be used to address their areas of weaknesses and how the LEA will measure the improvements supported by these funds. Up to this point, monies for this purpose were privately raised from such sources as the Benwood Private Foundation in Hamilton County, which funded $10,000 for teachers and leaders to work in specific high priority schools.

A state law requires principal performance contracts based on student performance and other specific indicators. Since 1995, Tennessee has required superintendents to use a "Principal Performance Contract" to evaluate principal performance. Public Law 49-1-602 has required superintendents to implement performance contracts for principals in schools in Corrective Action ("On Probation" in state law).

There are only 12 charter schools in Tennessee, and they can only enroll students from low performing schools. They are located in Davidson County and in Memphis. Also, there is legislation allowing conversion of an existing school to charter school status, but that has not yet been done.

Tennessee has established a systematic review process to determine what state policies and other barriers hinder improvement efforts in districts and schools. Since 2004, the SDE has had a Project Management Oversight Committee (PMOC) that provides the necessary coordination to conduct these reviews. The effort is similar to the Alabama Roundtable approach.

Examples of how PMOC coordinates and tightens internal policies and procedures include: the Statewide Longitudinal Education Data System, State Improvement Grant, Early Childhood Education, Teacher Licensure, Tennessee Comprehensive Systemwide Planning Process, Integrated Technology, High School Redesign, and Building Transitions from High School to Community College and Careers.

PMOC recommendations are exemplified in a March 2006 evaluation of the value of state services to districts, which included a survey of changes recommended by districts. Another PMOC project considered a possible revision of the Tennessee Report Card. Staff from across the SDE worked together under a plan of the Deputy Commissioner to make the system more accurate, complete, and useful for school improvement planning. The project team's organizational structure, value statements, project scope, project risk, project assumptions, deliverables, and timelines are put on the SDE website to serve as an incentive for team members.

Build Capacity to Change

Build Systemic Capacity

Schools do not request waivers, and school districts rarely do. However, Tennessee does provide alternate certification routes. The University of Memphis's alternate route to principal certification (Aspiring Leaders Program) brings new leaders into education from other fields. In addition, there are alternate routes to teacher certification such as the Teach Tennessee program geared toward new mathematics and science teachers. Teach Tennessee (http://www.state.tn.us/education/teachtn/) has recruited and trained mid-career professionals to pursue a new teaching career.

Troops to Teachers (TTT) provides a route for veterans. It is a federally-funded program to assist eligible military personnel begin new careers as public school teachers in "high-need" schools. Counseling, referral, and placement assistance is provided through the SDE. Given availability of funds, financial assistance may be provided to eligible individuals as stipends, up to $5000, to help pay for teacher certification costs or as bonuses up to $10,000. Stipend and bonus recipients must agree to teach for three years in school locations that meet SDE criteria as schools that serve a high percentage of students from low-income families.

The Tennessee Academy for School Leaders (TASL) provides professional development opportunities for educational leaders who shape organizational cultures to promote high student performance and learning. The Academy focuses on replication of effective practice as taught by turn-around experts who are experienced principals. TASL programs are designed to be consistent with the Tennessee Master Plan for schools and the six standards from the Council of Chief State School Officers' Standards for School Leaders.

Create and Disseminate Knowledge. Dr. Connie Smith is in charge of the division of accountability. This division includes school approval, accreditation, school and school system report cards, exemplary educator and high performing schools, school improvement planning, and performance monitoring.

Through consistent communication to districts, exemplary educators, universities, and other activities, she and her staff disseminate information about how to improve the effectiveness of Tennessee's schools and school systems. The division's goals are to:

- Assist educators in understanding the use of student performance data for school improvement;
- Provide an inclusive reporting document for each school and school system which details disaggregated student performance data;

- Provide systematic technical assistance, including a collaborative approach to school improvement;
- Link school improvement teams from regional offices to other SDE initiatives in a service delivery model to high priority schools;
- Identify high priority schools based on student performance data;
- Provide technical assistance through the use of the Exemplary Educator Program and departmental resources for identified high priority schools;
- Develop a systemic process for measuring success in implementing improvement in low performing schools;
- Provide a collaborative approach in distributing/providing federal and state resources for school improvement;
- Provide a variety of grant opportunities for innovation in Tennessee schools;
- Improve student performance in all Tennessee schools; and
- Act as a catalyst in the SDE to bring a focus on school improvement initiatives.

Enhance Supply of Personnel. Tennessee SDE staff realize the importance of forming an alliance with teacher pre-service institutions to emphasize strategies teachers should know as they enter low-performing schools. Over the last year, SDE has begun a teacher quality initiative with the Tennessee Board of Regents to accomplish this goal.

Recent legislation requires the initiative to be evaluated by the State Board of Education with the assistance of the SDE and the Tennessee Higher Education Commission. The State Board must develop a report card or assessment on the effectiveness of teacher training programs. The State Board must annually evaluate performance of each institution of higher education providing an approved program of teacher training. "Such assessment shall focus on the performance of each institution's graduates and shall include, but not be limited to, the following areas:

- Placement and retention rates;
- Performance on PRAXIS examinations or other tests used to identify teacher preparedness; and
- Teacher effect data.

Tennessee also provides incentives and financial support to teachers who seek voluntary national certification evaluation by the National Board for Professional Teaching Standards.

The Tennessee Framework for Evaluation & Professional Growth outlines key result areas, goals, strategies, and measures. The framework ensures that all new and experienced teachers are highly qualified (consistent with state and federal requirements) and that teacher shortages are addressed by promoting the development of a diverse, highly educated workforce. To reduce teacher shortages in specified teaching fields, high poverty schools, and among minority candidates, the following actions are intended to improve teacher recruitment and retention:

- Increase scholarships and forgivable loans to attract the best and brightest to teaching.
- Increase the number of minority teachers by expanding the successful Minority Teaching Education Grant program to universities.
- Provide more opportunities for persons seeking to enter teaching as a second career.
- Promote the use of the state online jobs clearinghouse to facilitate placement of qualified teachers in every school.
- Expand the beginning teacher mentoring program to improve new teacher performance, improve student learning, and reduce teacher attrition. Require mentor programs to be research based. Evaluate the effectiveness of existing teacher mentoring programs.

Build Local Capacity

Coordinate Structures and Roles. Dr. Connie Smith as the Executive Director of the Office of Innovation, School Improvement and Accountability, has the primary responsibility for communicating among SDE personnel, partner organizations, distinguished educators, and support teams. As part of her communication, she sends e-mails to district superintendents and other key Tennessee educators.

Within the SDE, the DACC (Deputy, Assistant Commissioners, Commissioner) is the key internal planning group that meets weekly. The group receives and evaluates the intradepartmental special projects, such as the revision of the Tennessee Report Card. DOE staff believes that this internal process and their user-friendly, customer-oriented communication system are very effective.

State Education Agency. Tennessee's SDE holds weekly planning meetings to assure coordination of support services. The nine Field Service Centers are a part of these meetings, and each Center's staff includes an NCLB staff person to work with local districts in complying with NCLB. The SDE staff believe that the team approach they use in working and communicating with local personnel has made their State management approach very successful.

As mentioned earlier in the Lessons Learned section, the SDE has developed a framework for comprehensive systemwide planning. Within that framework, the staff has a consistent template for district staff to complete with regard to their Action Plan. Each district must describe its annual goals and identify which needs they address and how each goal is linked to the district's Five-Year Plan. Local personnel then list the action steps they plan to take to ensure they can progress toward their goals. Tennessee defines action steps as strategies and interventions, which should be scientifically based where possible, and which include professional development, technology, communication, and parent/community involvement initiatives. For each action step, local staff list the timeline, person(s) responsible, projected costs and required resources, funding sources, and evaluation strategy. This strategy allows SDE reviewers, exemplary educators, and others who provide assistance to have a common understanding of the local planning goals.

Intermediate Agencies. There are nine intermediate or Field Service Centers that assist schools and school systems in the areas of special education, career and technical education, Title I and federal programs, technology, assessment and testing, and school improvement planning. A major task for them is helping the identified target schools to assist with improvement.

The director of the Field Service Centers is based at the SDE and reports to the Assistant Commissioner of Career and Technical Education. The Field Service Centers are funded with a mix of federal funds, such as those associated with NCLB, and state Pre-K monies.

External Partner Organizations. The SDE works with various nonprofit groups, such as the Tennessee Voices for Children, when contracting for work with parent involvement. They also collaborate with Community Impact, an organization that works with high school students and is involved with the annual Urban Summit on Equity. In the future, the SDE hopes to expand its partnerships into community organizations to help in such areas as graduation rates.

The Appalachian Regional Comprehensive Center (ARCC) provided valuable assistance to Tennessee by contacting the Education Trust and the National Center for Teacher Quality to work with the SDE. ARCC also provides professional development based on the latest research in school improvement planning, use of assessment results for improved instruction, and the transfer of effective practice. In addition, ARCC provided meetings for Tennessee and other regional SDE staff on restructuring and corrective action, including presentations by the Center on Innovation & Improvement.

The SDE, in consultation with practitioners, has worked to enhance the existing Tennessee School Improvement Planning Process (TSIPP) to meet federal, regional, and state requirements in one plan. Due to the continuing partnership with the Southern Association of Colleges and Schools (SACS), Tennessee schools may use a single planning process for both school approval and accreditation purposes. The TSIPP is also directly aligned with the State's new Tennessee Comprehensive Systemwide Planning Process (TCSPP). This past year, all elementary schools, with the exception of high priority schools, submitted a complete TSIPP for state review to their Field Service Center.

Distinguished Educators. In Tennessee, the key providers of technical assistance to schools and districts are the exemplary educators (EEs), who are retired educators. In high priority schools and districts, these EEs work four days every week providing support in school improvement planning, use of data, curriculum, and effective instructional and organizational practices. Edvantia has trained more than 150 EEs since 2001 and is serving approximately 300 high schools and 26 districts in need of improvement.

Edvantia (http://www.edvantia.org/index.cfmis) is a nonprofit corporation whose mission is to help clients improve education and meet federal and state mandates. In 2005, Edvantia won two major contracts: a $19 million contract to operate the Appalachia Regional Comprehensive Center which provides research-based technical assistance to education departments in Kentucky, North Carolina, Tennessee, Virginia, and West Virginia; and a three-year contract with the Tennessee Department of Education to administer the state's Exemplary Educators program to help struggling schools.

As the independent contractor that hires the EEs under a contract with the SDE, Edvantia chooses EEs after a rigorous evaluation by their peers in addition to a written and verbal test. The contracts for EEs are annually reviewed for renewal.

The Tennessee Exemplary Educators Program, as a partnership between the SDE and Edvantia, received a Top 50 Innovations in American Government Award from Harvard University. The Ash Institute for Democratic Governance and Innovation at Harvard University's John F. Kennedy School of Government (http://www.innovations.harvard.edu/spotlight.html?id=291&preview=0) in spring of 2007 announced that the EE Program was included in the Top 50 Programs in the 2007 Innovations in American Government Awards competition. "The Top 50 Programs were selected from a pool of nearly 1,000 applicants representing all levels of government. These initiatives are recognized for their novelty and creativity, effectiveness at addressing significant issues, and their potential to be replicated by other jurisdictions. They exemplify government's best efforts across a variety of policy areas, ranging from education to the environment, criminal justice to health care, and management to community development."

The EE applicants must demonstrate the following abilities:

- Understand and use qualitative and quantitative data to develop strategic plans;
- Use good judgment when helping schools identify and solve problems;
- Work collaboratively with peers;
- Mentor and provide leadership;

- Model effective organizational and classroom practices; and
- Use technology.

The EEs are trained during the summer and for five weeks through-out the year to keep them current. They are paid $300 per day plus travel expense. The Edvantia project assigns consultants based on needs of the school or district (based on what federal benchmark they failed) and the expertise of the EE.

School Support Teams. The SDE is just beginning to establish Tennessee Targeted Assistance Teams for the 2007–2008 school year. They will assess local capacity for school improvement. The teams will use a practitioner-based accountability process based on *What is a Good School?* A companion guide entitled *What is a Good System?* is under development. These guides represent Tennessee's answer to assessing effective performance as an inte-gral part of school improvement that SDE staff believe will lead to increased student achievement.

Differentiate Support to Local Districts and Schools

To provide support for districts and schools, EEs are assigned to schools based on the specific needs of the districts and schools. The training provid-ed by Edvantia enables the EEs to provide differentiated services. EEs are able to use the combination of test scores and the profile obtained from the completion of the Tennessee Comprehensive Systemwide Planning Guide (TCSPP) as the foundation for their analysis and planning.

Districts that have been identified as not meeting the required account-ability benchmarks must address the required components in the TCSPP Compliance Matrix. This matrix has several components. The first three components focus on the School System Profile Development; Beliefs, Mis-sion and Shared Vision; and Academic and Non-Academic Data Analysis and Synthesis—Developing Priorities. The next component focuses on Cur-ricular, Instructional, Assessment and Organizational Effectiveness. In this section the district is asked a series of questions, based on their responses in the previous sections, to focus on important issues such as the gap be-tween their present curricular practices and what they believe they should become to increase student learning. This analysis includes reflective ques-tions for staff on how they can better use their time, money, personnel, and other resources to make necessary changes.

Component 5 (Comprehensive Systemwide Action Plan Development) is organized into a list of questions or statements in the left hand column. Across the top of the page is a list of six programs such as Federal Programs, Special Education, and Technology as well as a "Systemwide" column. The cells that define where answers or information are provided are marked so that the entire document reminds districts not meeting standards about what must be done. For example, one statement in the lefthand column in Section 5.1 of the Compliance Matrix under Goal 5—Action Plan Development—asks the district to: "Describe the process and accountability measures that the applicant will use to evaluate the extent to which activities funded are effective in integrating technology into curricula and instruction, increasing the ability of teachers to teach, and enabling students to meet challenging state academic content and student academic achievement standards."

The analysis of the data in the Compliance Matrix provides an opportunity to pinpoint where technical assistance is needed, thus differentiating services provided.

Differentiate by Point of Impact. This is the third year for the current school improvement planning process. The process requires local personnel to collect, disaggregate, analyze, and synthesize the data to focus on improving student achievement. Every goal priority has to be linked to data. Local educators receive the State Report Card including numerous test results (Tennessee Comprehensive Assessment Program, Gateway tests, as well as selected end-of-course tests) in addition to demographic, financial, and perceptual information. In addition, the state staff provides a website to assist with improvement planning, including access to trend results.

The Tennessee School Improvement Planning Process (TSIPP) guide and SIP rubric are used by SDE staff and FSC staff to evaluate local improvement plans every other year unless a school has been listed as high priority, in which case the review is annual. The SDE staff believe that their services for districts are very effective because their technical assistance is targeted and because the constant goal is building the capacity of the district to improve student learning.

Differentiate by Intensity and Duration of Services. The state provides services until the school is off the high priority list. The intensity of the services is determined by the AYP results and the district and school profiles from the Compliance Matrix and their improvement plan. Once a school is placed on high priority status, however, it receives the services of an EE until it leaves the list.

The training provided by Edvantia focuses on differentiation of services by ensuring the EEs can customize their services to targeted needs. Since high schools are becoming a higher priority, an additional focus in Edvantia training will be graduation rates in addition to other high school factors.

In the future, the information generated by the completion of the "What is a Good School Appraisal and Rubric" will determine the quantity and intensity of service schools receive.

Deliver Services to Districts and Schools

Exemplary educators begin work with a school or system (district) by demonstrating data disaggregation and summary. They often teach staff how to examine test data and draw conclusions. Then they facilitate data translation— translating data into usable information. After analyzing data with school staff, the EE helps them draft a strategic improvement plan. EEs work with the schools to implement, monitor, and modify the plan. EEs are organized into regional teams of no more than 10 in order to support both morale and problem solving. One member is assigned as the lead to mentor the other EEs.

The EEs are supervised by Edvantia and evaluated with district input. A formal evaluation includes all constituencies. Districts appreciate the provision of an outside consultant with expertise in their areas of need and refer to them as "an extra pair of hands and an extra brain." Some schools want to keep EEs even when they are "off the list." The major problem is trying to find additional funds to provide more help with this service as the number of schools in need grows.

Provide Services. Tennessee SDE staff do not believe that putting schools and school districts on its high priority list is fair without also providing the technical assistance necessary to help these schools and districts off the list. Several models are available but are not complete in their approach to measuring the total school's effectiveness. The SDE decided to develop an appraisal tool that could be used by teams, individuals, or both to measure the capacity of a school in the provision of equity and adequacy in educating all students. This appraisal guide and accompanying rubrics are research based and focus on answering the question: "Is this a good school, and if so, how do you know?"

The Appraisal Guide is organized into 11 domains: Student Achievement, Personnel Roles and Responsibilities, Curriculum, Instruction, Leadership, Organization of the School, Assessment & Evaluation, Climate & Culture, Communication & Collaboration, Safe & Orderly Environment, Parent & Community Involvement. Each of these domains includes a standard followed by measurement statements. These components are then reorganized as part of the rubric that the Targeted Assistance Teams will use during their appraisal.

In this rubric, each of the 11 domains is represented in a series of indicators. The teams will make judgments about each of the indicators on a four-point scale. The judgments are made according to a series of measurement statements under the scale. This system also guides the team members into what evidence should be examined as the ratings are made.

For example, under the domain of Student Achievement, Indicator A-5 (See Appendix) is: "Structure and Organization Supports Achievement."

There are 14 measurement statements or criteria to be judged for this indicator. They include, for example:

- Faculty meetings focus on student achievement;
- Professional development activities are based on student needs;
- Collaboration around improved student performance occurs among all involved constituencies;
- Formative assessment is available for all students; and
- Diagnostic prescriptive process is in place for below proficient students.

To be rated as having Exemplary Performance (4 points), the team must determine that "The structure and organization of the school supports maximum student performance for a diverse population of students as exhibited by all 14 criteria." In a school rated as having Adequate Performance (3 points), 9 of the 14 criteria are present, while in a school at the Partial Performance (2 points) level only six of the 14 criteria are observed. A school receives 1 point if there is no evidence that the structure and organization of the school supports student performance.

Allocate Resources for Services. As mentioned above, beginning in the 2007–2008 school year, new tax funding will be used specifically for identified subgroups in need.

Provide Opportunities for Change

Tennessee has various templates for district and school improvement planning, but these templates serve as guides rather than sets of prescriptive rules. Each district decides the approach it will use to make improvements. The SDE's main requirement in this effort is that the delineation of both the problems and potential solutions must be based on data—both academic and non-academic. The Field Service Centers and the EEs help the districts through the planning process but avoid planning for them.

For example, there is a rating sheet that SDE staff use to evaluate a district's improvement plan. In the area of Curriculum Process, the TCSPP guide simply asks the district to document that it has listed evidence of current practices, determined alignment of current practices to the principles and practices of high-performing school systems, and completed an evaluation of the effectiveness of current practices based on data.

Tennessee makes it clear that school improvement plans provide a framework for analyzing problems, identifying underlying causes, and addressing instructional issues in a school that has made insufficient progress in student achievement.

With regard to Title I high priority schools that are required to offer supplemental educational services (SES), the SDE provides:

- Technical assistance in the form of meetings and web conference calls to review federal and state choice requirements with the local school systems;
- A blueprint planning document entitled *Public School Choice and Supplemental Education Services District Implementation Blueprint* is disseminated to school systems to help them prepare for and implement SES; and
- Regional State Education consultants are assigned to specific school systems to assist them with implementing and monitoring SES.

Tennessee would like more opportunities to communicate with other states to determine their best practices and develop procedures to better evaluate SES provider hourly rates.

EVALUATION OF STATE ROLE IN DISTRICT AND SCHOOL IMPROVEMENT

Edvantia evaluated the EE program based on document reviews, surveys, and achievement data, finding that Tennessee's statewide initiatives have diminished the number of schools in need of improvement. Although most schools with an EE increased student achievement and met AYP targets, their strategies and outcomes varied. Researchers found, "The key seems to be having an experienced, trained, and supported Exemplary Educator working with a low-performing school to focus on improving student achievement." This report and all evaluations were submitted to the PMOC (http://www.edvantia.org/products/pdf/EE06Summary.pdf).

As part of the evaluation, Tennessee has established a system in which each EE completes an end-of-the-year status report for each school or district assisted. This report contains summaries of activities from previous years and identifies strengths and needs in all areas of the performance indicators. Each need is accompanied by a specific recommendation designed to address the challenges presented by the needs. Edvantia staff examine and evaluate these status reports to determine progress in meeting performance expectations and to identify the broadest areas of need of the high priority schools and districts as well as the actions of the EEs. At the same time, the EEs evaluate the tools and training provided to them.

Another part of the evaluation is the Exemplary Educators Performance Evaluation System. The system was developed to evaluate EEs' performance in five areas: Leading Change, School-wide Planning, Curriculum/Instruction/Assessment, Staff Development, and Administrative Duties. The system is based on the commitment to maintain the highest standards for EE productivity. It is designed to encourage some degree of specialization among EEs, to reward EEs for developing and applying their individual skills, and to ensure satisfactory completion of administrative duties. Each EE submits an Annual Activity Report and self-evaluation to the program director regarding each performance dimension and summarizes the details of his or her efforts and accomplishments in the above five areas.

Tennessee evaluated the use of the audit tool described above in four different districts. The Appalachian Regional Comprehensive Center provided an electronic evaluation tool composed of 20 questions.

The Tennessee SDE obviously is very serious about evaluating the effects of their Exemplary Educators program. While the following website provides more detailed information, descriptions of three of the studies are quoted below.

http://www.edvantia.org/about/index.cfm?&t=about&c=tneeResearch

Tennessee Exemplary Educators Program: 2006 Summary of Findings

By James R. Craig, Aaron C. Butler

Format: PDF | Pages: 43 | Copyright: 2006 | EE06Summary

Researchers looked for a pattern linking individual Exemplary Educator characteristics or activities to increasing student achievement and/or attaining adequate yearly progress. While there is evidence that some factors are predictive of schools producing gains in student achievement and attaining adequate yearly progress, there seems to be no clear, decisive path that always works to produce a positive outcome. The success of the EE program seems to remain a function of who the Exemplary Educators are, the professional development and support they receive, and the things they do to assist High Priority schools.

Preliminary Report of Findings: Gains in Achievement for High Priority Elementary and Middle Schools, School Year 2003-2004

By: Aaron C. Butler, James R. Craig

Format: PDF | Pages: 40 | Copyright: 2005 | EEPrelimReport03-05

Using achievement indicators (e.g., Reading Normal Curve Equivalent) for analysis, researchers compared 40 High Priority schools to comparison groups. They found that schools assisted by Tennessee Exemplary Educators tended to make gains on student achievement.

An Initial Report on the Effects of Tennessee's Exemplary Educator on High Priority Schools

By: James R. Craig, Aaron C. Butler, Steven A. Moats, Kristine L. Chadwick

Format: PDF | Pages: 56 | Copyright: 2004 | EEInitialReport09-04.pdf

This report focuses on changes in student performance at Tennessee schools that were assisted by Exemplary Educators. The researchers gathered achievement indicators (e.g., Reading Normal Curve Equivalent) for analysis. Analyses of these data from schools that had 1, 2, and 3 years of assistance show that, in general, student achievement increased in these schools.

VIEWS FROM THE FIELD

The information in this section is a synthesis of interviews with two superintendents and two principals who received service from the Tennessee statewide system of support.

Factors That Contributed to Improvement and Lessons Learned

The administrators interviewed identified the following factors as helpful in improving student achievement:

- "Having a focus, a strategic plan," and training staff and administrators to understand and work from the data. Maintaining a focus on "goals derived from data" and avoiding anything "peripheral or off-target" and "a constant focusing on the numbers and knowing whether we hit the target."
- Having all staff understand and use data intensively.
- Constant monitoring of progress; formative assessments.
- Very close alignment of curriculum with the state framework and assessment standards.
- Ongoing, in-depth professional development.
- Increased levels of accountability throughout the district to ensure that programs are implemented properly.
- Formation of grade level teams that study best practices and specially targeted staff development.
- "We decided to push to make a positive school environment, to increase school pride, to make the physical facility something you'd be proud of when you walked through the door."
- Improvement of school culture. "Before it started improving, there were behavior problems, low expectations for students and families, and, in turn, for teachers." It was necessary to adopt the belief that theirs could be a high achieving school. "The first step we had

to take was changing the culture. In my opinion, it had to happen before other things could happen."

- Focusing on good instruction and making sure that what goes on in classrooms is meaningful.

Lesson 1—Training in Use of Data. "Most educators make the assumption that all educators are comfortable with data and they understand data. That's simply a very false assumption." Conduct ongoing training that includes both new teachers and veterans, and build data teams at each school. "Learn how to use the data effectively so you can address your needs and match your resources."

Lesson 2—Focused Professional Development. The district has "gotten away from the cafeteria approach [to professional development] and maybe the professional development du jour, but [now provides] a more focused, detailed approach that's tailored to our strategic plan."

Lesson 3—Keeping Good Teachers. It is necessary to find ways to keep good teachers in the district from transferring to other districts where pay is better.

Lesson 4—Communication. Maintain open lines of communication with the state and enter into partnership with them.

Lesson 5—Alignment. Align curriculum with state expectations.

Lesson 6—First Things First. "It is a journey. You may have to live with some things that are uncomfortable while you're concentrating on something else." When this principal arrived at her school, it was necessary to get student behavior under control before achievement issues could be addressed.

Lesson 7—Leadership Tone. The principal sets the tone. "Unless you can turn [the staff] around, [the NCLB sanctions] can be seen as a real negative. And so I think it's the role of the principal to be positive....We went through huge changes when I got here and [the staff] didn't necessarily like them all. I tried to really remain positive. As another principal put it, "It's your first year. You're on the failure list. The blame game starts. Everyone's calling you a failure, so I flipped that, and we began to emphasize our good characteristics. We wrote them down. We highlighted them....Don't forget to celebrate all the stuff along your road...as you make your way toward being successful."

Lesson 8—Goal Focus. "Focus, focus, focus. Set academic goals. Have formative assessments to see if you're meeting those goals....Lots of support for teachers is required and in a positive way....Setting a focus on those goals and allowing teachers to go after them is huge." This principal usually goes into every classroom every day.

Lesson 9—Ownership. "Make sure that your staff members understand that everyone has a role in the achievement of all students....All staff, even counselors and PE teachers, are to contribute to students' learning, even outside their own disciplines."

State Policies—Incentives and Opportunities

The educators interviewed felt the pressure of public accountability in response to assessment scores. The effects were both negative (in terms of effect on staff and parent morale) and positive as a motivator. One principal remarked, "In the past...as long as the building wasn't on fire, [schools like mine] were considered successful. People weren't looking at student achievement. And so to me...that pressure actually ignited the fire that put us on the road to higher student achievement." The threat of undesirable consequences also served to motivate teachers and parents, though there is some anxiety about new legislation that gives the state greater power to take over districts and schools.

Although the state does not offer financial rewards for effective educators, one district is piloting such a program now and is also looking into the possibility of financial or other rewards for administrators to work in low-performing schools. Another is lengthening the school day by 30 minutes in high priority schools, thereby giving teachers the opportunity to earn an extra $3,000–4,000 per year. This necessitated negotiations with the teachers union, but the state was not involved in those negotiations.

The administrators reported negligible effects of competition from charter schools and public school choice. None had requested waivers, though one district is exploring a waiver request to create gender-specific and other innovative schools.

Three of the four administrators had experience with alternatively certified teachers. One principal reported that the alternatively certified teachers did not perform well at first, but that they eventually improved. "I don't think they should be working on permits until they get their education. You could see the growth after they were finished and had a little bit of experience. I really struggled with them, but they turned out to be some of my best teachers after two to three years."

One district is involved in a pilot program in which scientists come into high schools on a part-time basis to teach mostly upper-level science and math classes. Preliminary anecdotal evidence suggests that the program will be successful. The other district had hired alternatively certified teachers in high needs areas. "Many of them come in and are good teachers, but after three years you have to let some good teachers go" because they have not completed their certification requirements.

Building Local Capacity

The districts mainly interacted directly with the SDE, though one reported working with their Regional Center, which helped review their strategic plan and kept them updated on new state legislation and policies. Both districts worked closely with the SDE. "It's a very close working relationship. We feel very comfortable. They are very quick on turnaround as far as getting right back to you, so that's something we've really appreciated."

Because of their large size, the districts have not relied extensively on the SDE for professional development, but consultations with the SDE do inform their internal professional development efforts. They have also collaborated with the SDE in planning school reconstitution. "I don't think we've ever had a need that we haven't gone to the state and received the support," observed one district administrator.

Although one of the principals used an SDE consultant for staff development, their primary contact with the statewide system of support was through the EEs, who provided invaluable assistance. "That person...was someone who truly knew about teaching and learning and school culture....They didn't come in with their own agenda, they came in with knowledge, experience, and training." The EE provided "moral support and helped identify resources." In addition, she did surveys, analyzed results, helped teachers understand and use data, and conducted professional development. "We would identify areas of concern and she modeled lessons and did informal observations." She brought in books and resources and set up visits with nearby schools that were effectively addressing some issues that teachers were finding problematic.

The other principal concurs: "...[The exemplary educators] really helped the teachers out, not telling them what to teach, but pulling together some lesson plans that were best practices." This was particularly important, since many of her teachers were new to the profession. The teachers felt that the EEs were supportive "because they came in saying, 'We're not here to evaluate you....We're here to help you become the best you can become. A very few teachers hit heads [with the exemplary educator]. Mainly they were the seasoned people, the ones resistant to change." But as other teachers' students' scores started to go up, resistance changed to a desire for help.

One of the principals observed that while she and her staff got along very well with their EE, this was not the case in other schools. She recommends a process whereby the state learns about a school's needs and its principal's administrative style and tries to match a principal with a potentially compatible EE.

The district improvement plan is long (it can be 60 pages or more), but "used appropriately, it is a very clear and a very good road map for any district to follow. It's made a difference for this school district, I know that." The state plan is aligned with the plan required by the regional school accreditation body, so a single plan suffices for both.

The state provides a wealth of data at their website that districts and schools can use to develop their improvement plans, including value-added data. One of the principals described the value-added data as "a wonderful, wonderful tool from the state.... They're online, they're easily accessible. The value-added really helps me as a principal to look at individual teacher growth." The data is used extensively.

One of the districts has established data teams at each school and at the central office. This has led to a lot of conversation and sharing of strategies between schools. In addition to using the data for planning, one school has individual conferences with the students about their data to help them set goals for improvement.

The SDE has conducted professional development and provided technical assistance to the districts on the planning process. Targeted schools get substantial support from the EEs as they develop their school improvement plans. Although her school no longer has an EE, one principal stated that "the folks at our state department are very accessible as far as picking up the phone and asking a question... or just e-mail the state board."

One principal likened school improvement planning to the development of an Individualized Education Program (IEP) for a student with disabilities. "The plan is an IEP for a school instead of a student. You describe the current level of performance, set some goals, how you're going to get there, how you're going to monitor."

The state's use of rubrics in improvement plans had possibly unforeseen positive consequences in one school. One principal reports that, "Teachers experienced rubrics with the school improvement plan, and they began using rubrics in the classroom." Rubrics are now posted along with student work on bulletin boards.

When asked what specific services were provided by the statewide system of support, one principal replied, "I'm always going to say the exemplary educator, who has the willingness to do whatever it takes." The other principal also cited the EEs, who helped with planning, modeled instruction for teachers, worked on instructional scheduling and delivery, assisted them in analyzing and understanding data, worked with parents, and helped teachers teach students with disabilities more effectively. Through the school improvement grant, the SDE also provided a family specialist who helped work with parents and dealt with any issues in the home that would cause a student to be late or absent. It also funded an in-school suspension program.

Although one large district primarily relies on its own staff for school improvement efforts, they feel the state has been supportive. The SDE also provides school improvement academies and workshops across the state for teachers and administrators, the data warehouse, curriculum frameworks, alignment of curriculum and assessment, professional development on special education, and standards and training for teachers of English language learners. "I don't know what we would do without the state department, because not only do we have a very knowledgeable state department, but they're very quick to get back to you. They keep us abreast; they keep us in compliance."

NCLB Sanctions and Provisions

All of the schools and districts had been subject to corrective action, which, in the case of the schools, resulted in an exemplary educator being assigned. Both districts had restructured schools using a fresh start model in which new administrative and teaching teams were put in place. One of the districts allowed the principal to hand pick all staff, both teaching and non-certificated.

Restructuring (or reconstitution) has been successful in all cases and the districts are looking to restructure additional schools. The districts worked closely with the state to plan and monitor restructures. Few students have transferred under NCLB choice provisions and the effect has generally been minimal. The quality of supplemental educational services has varied widely.

Suggestions for Evaluation of Statewide Systems of Support

One administrator recommended looking at the relationships between districts and regional offices. "Are you able to contact them? Are they providing you information? Are they doing evaluations? Working with people in the community?" Suggested criteria for evaluating the EEs include improvement of school test data, teacher and administrator surveys and interviews (preferably administered at some time other than the busy end of the school year), and changes in schools' NCLB status.

One district administrator said, "We're very pleased with the service aspect of the state department as opposed to being a very punitive making-sure-that-the-mandates-are-met [agency]. It's very service-oriented.... In the last four or five years there's been a whole different culture established within the state department. " She credits the SDE with being responsive to requests and suggestions.

When asked what process would be most effective in enabling a state to continuously examine and improve its system of support, a principal replied, "To have themselves go through the same process schools are going through for school improvement so that [the state department] is in a continuous cycle of improvement. The student IEP, the school IEP, and the state IEP. That's what would have to happen. I tell our teachers here, 'We will never arrive. We will constantly and always need to be saying what's next, and how do we grow?' And that's what they would need to do as well."

ACKNOWLEDGEMENTS

We thank the following staff from the Tennessee State Department of Education for their time during our interviews and in providing supporting documents: Connie Smith, Cory Curl, Susie Bunch, Janine Whited, Jean Sharp, and Carol Groppel.

We would also like to thank the following local educators who gave generously of their time to talk with us:

Alfred Hall, chief academic officer, Memphis City Schools, Memphis, TN

Lisa B. Light, principal, Lonsdale Elementary School, Knoxville, TN

Janet Robbins, principal, Shady Grove Elementary School, Memphis, TN

Donna L. Wright, assistant superintendent, Knox County Schools, Knoxville, TN.

APPENDIX: STUDENT ACHIEVEMENT

Indicator A.5	Performance Levels				Rating
	4 Exemplary	**3** Adequate	**2** Partial	**1** None	
Structure and Organization Supports Achievement	The structure and organization of the school supports maximum student performance for a diverse population of students as exhibited by **all** of the criteria below:	The structure and organization of the school supports maximum student performance for a diverse population of students as exhibited by **nine** of the criteria below:	The structure and organization of the school supports maximum student performance for a diverse population of students as exhibited by **six** of the criteria below:	The **is no** evidence that the structure and organization of the school supports student performance for a diverse population of students.	4 3 2 1

☐ Faculty meetings focus on student achievement ☐ Special needs are identified and and shared among colleagues
☐ Team planning records address student needs ☐ Lessons plans address student needs ☐ Remedial services available for all students' needs
☐ Enrichment services available for all students' needs ☐ Formative assessment is available for all students
☐ Summative assessment is available for all students ☐ Diagnostic prescriptive process is in place for below proficient students
☐ Professional development activities are based on student needs
☐ Professional development activities are based on innovation in improving the teaching and learning process
☐ Students successes are celebrated ☐ Students successes are rewarded
☐ Collaboration around improved student performance occurs among all involved constituencies
☐ There is a culture of focused improvement among all constituencies working in a partnership

Evidence: Special needs records, Diversity records, ESL records, Accountability records, Meeting minutes and agendas, IEPs, Lesson plans, Assessment data, TSIPP.

continued

Indicator A.6	Performance Levels				Rating
	4 Exemplary	3 Adequate	2 Partial	1 None	
Structure and Organization Supports Achievement	Student achievement is monitored and recorded throughout the learning process for analysis and interventions as exhibited by **all** of the criteria below:	Student achievement is monitored and recorded throughout the learning process for analysis and interventions as exhibited by **six** of the criteria below:	Student achievement is monitored and recorded throughout the learning process for analysis and interventions as exhibited by **three** of the criteria below:	There is **no** evidence that student achievement is monitored and recorded during the learning process for analysis and interventions.	4
					3
					2
					1

☐ Student achievement is monitored ☐ Student achievement is recorded and tracked

☐ Summative assessment is addressed ☐ Instructional decisions are data for all students   driven

☐ Formative assessment is addressed for all students

☐ Interventions address assessed needs

☐ A diagnostic prescriptive process is in place designed to assist students who are below proficient

☐ Immediate feedback and interventions are in place to assist students who are below proficient

☐ A variety of assessment data is used for monitoring student achievement

Evidence: Assessment records and data, Meeting minutes and agendas, Student grouping information, Lesson plans, IEPs, TSIPP.

Source: What is a Good School? © 2007 Tennessee Department of Education; Appraisal Guide & Rubric—Page 20 of 57. (Reprinted with permission)

CHAPTER 10

HIGHLY SKILLED EDUCATORS AND SCHOLASTIC REVIEWS IN KENTUCKY

Thomas Kerins, Susan Hanes, and Carole Perlman

The information included in this profile of Kentucky's statewide system of support is derived from an on-site visit of the Kentucky Department of Education (KDE), the state's education agency, by one of the authors; telephone interviews with district superintendents, their designees, and school principals by a second author; and artifacts provided by the KDE. The Kentucky Department of Education will hereafter be referred to as the State Department of Education (SDE).

INTRODUCTION

This section provides background on the state's development of a system of support, the factors SDE personnel have determined to have the greatest impact on school improvement, and the lessons SDE personnel have learned along the way.

Handbook on Statewide Systems of Support, pages 167–195
Copyright © 2008 The Academic Development Institute and Information Age Publishing
All rights of reproduction in any form reserved.

Evolution of the Statewide System of Support in Kentucky

In 1990, the Kentucky Reform Act (KERA) brought a transformation of education to the state, including among its provisions the creation of a Distinguished Educator (DE) Program. On the heels of KERA, Kentucky created the Commonwealth School Improvement Fund (CSIF) to assist local schools in pursuing new and innovative strategies to meet students' educational needs and raise school performance levels. In addition, the SDE implemented comprehensive Scholastic Audits and Reviews, based on the Kentucky Standards and Indicators for School Improvement (SISI), to develop consistent profiles of information. The distinguished educators' expertise, financial support for local school improvement, and the common currency and objective procedures of the audit and review process have been central to Kentucky's ever-evolving system of support. A major finding in a research study of the Highly Skilled Educator Program, completed in October 2006 for the Legislative Research Commission, revealed that, overall, schools that received assistance through a combination of HSE, Commonwealth School Improvement Funds and a scholastic audit or review showed statistically significant improvements in their accountability index scores.

The Distinguished Educator Program, established under KERA, was the predecessor to the current Highly Skilled Educators (HSE) Program. The purpose of the DE Program (KRS 158.782) was twofold. First, it provided highly skilled, direct assistance to schools and districts whose accountability index declined over a biennium. Second, it was designed as a means to reward the most outstanding teachers and administrators with recognition for excellence, provide a salary incentive, and provide an opportunity to assist other teachers, administrators, and schools. Schools whose scores declined over a pre-determined value were considered to be "in crisis." Schools "in decline" and schools "in crisis" were assigned a Distinguished Educator.

During the years 1994–1996, 53 schools were served by 50 DEs. An improved Academic Index at all 53 schools was reported with 34 of the 53 exceeding their goal. During 1996–1998, 178 schools were served by 49 DEs. Of the 167 schools with improved Academic Index reported, 85 exceeded their goal.

In 1998, the General Assembly changed the name from the Distinguished Educator Program to the Highly Skilled Educators (HSE) Program as the state's assessment system transitioned from KIRIS to Commonwealth Assessment Testing System (CATS). The statute was revised to provide a focus of assistance to low-performing schools.

In 1998–2000, 66 schools were served by 63 HSEs. Reports indicated that 65 schools had an improved Academic Index. All Level 3 schools moved out of the Level 3 classification by meeting or exceeding their goal. In 2000–2002, 53 schools and 2 districts were served by 54 HSEs. The Academic Index improved at 46 schools. Again, all Level 3 schools moved out of the Level 3 classification by meeting or exceeding their goal. In 2002–2004, 84 schools and 4 districts were served by 55 HSEs. Improved Academic Index at 80 schools was reported. All but two Level 3 schools moved out of the Level 3 classification by meeting or exceeding their goal.

HSEs have been able to organize the school and its structures around a common focus of improved student learning. They have assisted teachers in changing classroom practice by coordinating and presenting professional development embedded in school structure and focusing on student needs.

Another school improvement tool the SDE has employed over the years with both the DEs and HSEs is the Scholastic Audit and Review process, which is based on the nationally recognized Kentucky Standards and Indicators for School Improvement (SISI). It is a comprehensive analysis of the learning environment, efficiency, leadership, culture and academic performance of schools and districts. The purposes of the audits and reviews are to analyze strengths and limitations of the instructional and organizational effectiveness of schools and districts and to make specific recommendations to improve teaching and learning.

Kentucky continues its State Accountability Program along with the NCLB requirements. For example, in this case study the terminology of Tier 1, 2, and 3 schools/districts refers to the federal requirements while Level 1, 2, and 3 refer to the historical Kentucky classification system under its unique index system.

Factors That Contribute to Improvement and Services That Address Them

High Stakes Accountability. A statewide network of local District Assessment Coordinators (DACs) continually focuses on achievement gaps and analyzing results. The Division of Assessment Support within the Kentucky Department of Education is charged with supporting the efforts of the DACs and school level personnel as they implement the Commonwealth Accountability Testing System. From the logistics of testing, to the administration code, the interpretation of the Kentucky Performance Reports, and the application of test results to the improvement of instruction, the Division of Assessment Support aids the efforts of all these DACs for all schools to reach proficiency by 2014.

Addressing Achievement Gaps. In 2003 the SDE established the Achievement Gap Coordinators, a group of 5 highly effective administrators/educators assigned to work in selected regions of the state to eliminate the achievement gaps as identified in Senate Bill 168 (KRS 158.649). In 2004 the department hired 8 District Support Facilitators to address the requirements of the federal No Child Left Behind Act (NCLB) on a district level. In 2007 these two groups merged and became the District Achievement Gap Coordinators (DAGC). The field-based DAGCs provide leadership and support to districts across the Commonwealth that have fallen into Tier 3 status under NCLB. The DAGCs collaboratively develop individual work plans for each assigned district based on the results of the district scholastic audit which serves as a blueprint for moving the district out of Tier 3 status.

Leadership. The SDE started the Kentucky Leadership Academy for district and school level administrators in cooperation with the Kentucky Association of School Administrators. At multiple levels throughout the system, both at the SDE and local districts and schools, leadership has improved. Shared and sustained leadership is critical for improvement efforts to be successful over the long term.

The vision of the Kentucky Leadership Academy is for Kentucky's educational leaders, at all levels of leadership skill and development, to receive the necessary support to assist them in positively impacting whole school improvement and advancing student learning. The mission of the Academy is to provide ongoing professional growth opportunities for school and district leaders that will result in building and sustaining leadership capacity for whole school improvement. For 2007–2008, the goal is to provide professional growth opportunities for Kentucky's educators to positively impact student achievement as measured by school improvement data.

The core values of the Leadership Academy include:

- There is a high correlation between district/school leadership and district/school success as defined by improvements in student learning.
- Effective leaders have high expectations for themselves, their staff, and students, and these high expectations are evidenced in the work of the district/school and in student achievement.
- Highly effective leaders must be grounded in core values and have a sense of moral purpose that is visible and communicated.
- Highly effective leaders are change agents.
- Highly effective leaders celebrate success at all levels.
- Highly effective leaders recognize and communicate the district's/ school's deficiencies and collaboratively, with the learning community, work for improvement.
- Highly effective leaders develop positive relationships for the betterment of the school community and the learners of the district/school.
- Highly effective leaders are life-long learners, continuously striving to improve their professional selves.

Instructional Support Network

The purpose of the Instructional Support Network (ISN), initiated by the SDE, is to build the capacity of district administrators to provide leadership in making connections between instructional planning and planning for professional development. It is these connections that provide the foundation for continuous school improvement.

School Administrative Managers (SAMs)

This program was launched in 2006 to help school principals focus their attention on curriculum, instruction, and assessment, and spend less time on daily management issues. The School Administrative Managers (SAMs) are school district employees who assume many of the managerial duties of the principals including budgeting, student behavior management, student supervision, scheduling, cleaning, maintenance, food service, transportation, and supervision of the non-instructional staff. Seven schools participated in the pilot project and, to date, an additional 19 schools have been added. SAMs undergo extensive training provided by the SDE based on material developed for the initial SAM Leadership Academy in cooperation with the Jefferson County public school system. Jefferson County has an additional 27 SAMs within their district. Data collection and time-task analysis are important components of the project and will provide research-based information on the program's effectiveness.

Lessons Learned

Lesson 1—Trust. Building trust and the ability to sustain that trust takes time. A key element in the development of that trust lies in the state's Highly Skilled Educators (HSE) Program. Kentucky's approach provides direct, long-term assistance to schools. The HSE cadre assists schools in the implementation of the Standards and Indictors for School Improvement (SISI). These standards are offered to provide on-site assistance to Level 3 schools—a classification assigned to a school that has an index score that places it in the lowest one-third (1/3) of all schools below the assistance line. Level 3 schools are first priority when determining HSE assignments. Monthly professional development and on-going networking among the HSEs insure that best practices are continually modeled in the schools served, and that shared knowledge is applied throughout the state to improve student learning and build local capacity for school improvement.

Lesson 2—District Capacity. The State has to build local capacity to support efforts since it has not had success in taking over districts. Consequently, the SDE must work to develop capacity at the district level but not assume the tasks for local personnel. To assist in accomplishing that, Kentucky is expanding on its long history of sending skilled educators to the rescue of struggling schools. Furthermore, it is moving that approach to entire school districts. Seven of the 152 districts in Kentucky began working with Voluntary Partnership Assistance Teams (VPAT) during the 2005–2006 school year. Thirteen more districts joined the program during the 2006–2007 school year. Under the initiative, four educators joined the district superintendent on a team with the goal of making changes that will turn around lackluster student performance.

The SDE provides one of its staff members and an HSE; the Kentucky School Board Association picks a school board member from another district in the state; and the Kentucky Association of School Administrators (KASA) assigns a retired superintendent to the VPAT team. All the members are from districts that have succeeded in raising student achievement. The superintendent of the struggling district is the chairman of the group.

According to SDE staff, the involvement of the local school board and the leadership role of the superintendent are important ingredients in this process. And when the voluntary assistance team finishes its work, the hope is that the district will be able to keep up the improvements set in motion by this process.

Lesson 3—Professional Competence. It is not the students who lack capacity. The State has to get adults to change behaviors first, then beliefs about children's learning. The State has to ensure that every child has a highly qualified educator in every school experience. As part of Kentucky's Scholastic Audit process, the following are among questions asked of local educators:

- Explain how your school council uses professional development funds. How do you set priorities? Do you have a long-range plan for continuous improvement in specific areas of need?
- Is professional development primarily to upgrade skills and knowledge or as part of an intentional process to bring about specific changes in professional practice and beliefs? How do you balance the professional development needs of individual staff with school-wide needs?
- Is information on student achievement ever used to determine the short- and long-term needs for professional development?

FUNCTIONS OF A STATEWIDE SYSTEM OF SUPPORT

This section organizes the information provided by SDE personnel into the evidence-based framework described in the chapter "State Role in Supporting School Improvement."

Provide Incentives for Change

The pressure of public accountability in response to district and school assessment scores on Report Cards has been positive. A positive incentive has been the use of award flags that are posted according to different levels of school achievement for top benchmarks.

There are no financial rewards to a district or school for improved results. However, there is a financial loss to a district or school for persistent low performance. The State defers a certain percentage of Title I administrative money and directs how local personnel will spend it. For example, the SDE has directed schools to use funds for partnerships with organizations and service providers that have been established by the State.

The state does not provide financial reward for effective leaders or teachers. However, as part of district contract negotiations, local districts may provide rewards for principals to work in low-performing schools or for teachers to teach in low-performing schools.

Furthermore, districts that qualify based on low school test scores may apply for Commonwealth School Improvement Funds (CSIF) to assist with school improvement efforts. This fund (CSIF) was created to assist local schools in pursuing new and innovative strategies to meet the educational needs of the school's students and raise the school's performance level.

Eligible schools are provided grants for the following purposes:

- To support teachers and administrators in the development of sound and innovative approaches to improve instruction or management;
- To assist in replicating successful programs developed in other districts including those calculated to reduce achievement gaps;
- To encourage cooperative instructional or management approaches to specific school educational issues, for example, teacher leadership teams); and
- To encourage teachers and administrators to conduct experimental programs to test concepts and applications being advanced as solutions to specific educational problems.

Though perhaps viewed as a negative incentive by some, restructuring is just now occurring in Kentucky for the first time. As mandated by law, Kentucky has school-based decision-making councils in all schools. Recently, two middle schools' councils have been relieved of their duties. Authority has been returned to the superintendents in the districts because the schools were not meeting certain academic goals for a defined period of time.

Build Capacity to Change

Build Systemic Capacity

There are no charter schools in Kentucky, and subsequently, the only public school choice available is through NCLB requirements. Also, the waiver from districts or schools to the State is rarely used.

Create and Disseminate Knowledge. Kentucky has a Bureau Leadership Planning Team (formerly known as the Associates Clearinghouse) composed of the commissioner, the deputy, and all associates. They meet at least monthly to discuss, review, and evaluate the statewide system of support. Additionally, two key associate commissioners share the responsibility for day-to-day activities around statewide support. One is in charge of Leadership and School Improvement and the other associate is in charge of NCLB and Title I Programs. While the associate commissioners are not located in the same division, the Kentucky system is organized so that they work together for improvement in both the state program and with the federal NCLB initiatives.

The SDE relies heavily on its approach of cross-agency decision making, maximizing limited resources and shared ownership of initiatives and responsibilities. SDE staff report that no grants, major initiatives, or major work is undertaken without prior Leadership Planning Team discussion, review, and approval—including financial commitments. However, staff also say that the system can always be improved with fewer silos in the agency.

SDE staff believe that their current organizational structure is very effective in managing the statewide system of support. Feedback from low performing districts that are receiving services provides a primary source for this judgement. Improved scores are emerging from previously identified low performing schools and districts that have been served.

Kentucky's various intervention initiatives to support schools and districts rely on accurate and robust data to help pinpoint the needs and determine the best intervention strategies for struggling schools and districts. In 2005, Kentucky was one of 14 states awarded funding from the Institute for Education Sciences (National Center for Education Statistics) to establish a Statewide Longitudinal Data System (SLDS). The purpose of the $5.8 million grant is to:

- enable states to manage, analyze, disaggregate, and use individual student data;
- increase the number of states that maintain statewide longitudinal data systems;
- support decision-making at state, district, school, and classroom levels; and
- help states meet reporting requirements of NCLB.

In addition to and in support of the federal goals, The Kentucky Instructional Data System (KIDS) will ultimately:

- add longitudinal student tracking with both enrollment and assessment data;
- enable interoperability of data systems across district and state databases;
- create a data warehouse that combines demographic, assessment, and financial data;
- create a foundation that will allow other sources of data to be added and searched/queried, such as data from the Council on Postsecondary Education and the Education Professional Standards Board; and
- be the foundation for a more robust Knowledge Management Portal that will serve up a wealth of targeted instructional resources, including standards-based units of study, lesson plans, curriculum maps, assessments, and other educational resources. The portal will offer a collaborative workspace that teachers can use to share best practices, develop test items, and expand their professional skills.

Enhance Supply of Personnel. Kentucky has an agreement with the University of Kentucky to provide leadership certification for HSEs through the completion of three courses. There is no alternate route for principals from other fields. The State is presently working with the Wallace Foundation, nationally recognized for its involvement in educational and cultural programs, to revamp principal certification.

In 2006, House Joint Resolution 14 established the Education Leadership Redesign Task Force. Its mission is to develop recommendations to redesign the preparation and professional development programs of district/school educational leaders. Their report will be presented to the legislature in October.

With the goal of bringing new teachers into education from other fields, Kentucky implemented the Transition to Teaching program. The SDE recruits mid-career professionals, recent college graduates, and highly qualified paraprofessionals who have not completed a teacher preparation program. The program strives to retain these highly qualified individuals to meet the needs of high-need, high-poverty Kentucky school districts in specific subject areas.

The eligibility requirements include:

- A desire to teach in one of the subjects identified as high need (math, science, language arts, social studies/government, arts and humanities, special education, English as a second language (ESL), or foreign language); and

- Status as a mid-career professional, paraprofessional, or recent college graduate who has not completed a teacher preparation program.

Participants receive a $5,000 stipend ($3,000 first year, $2,000 second year), a one-on-one coaching experience, provisions for professional development, and teacher certification upon the satisfactory completion of all requirements.

The commitments of the participants include:

- completion of an interview process;
- successfully applying into the alternative Master of Arts in teaching (M.A.T.) program with one of the State's partner universities;
- securing employment with one of the State's partner schools;
- making a three-year commitment to teach in a school district;
- completion of coursework;
- completion of the Kentucky Internship Program (KTIP); and
- successful completion of the specialty test.

The SDE maintains strong alliances with all Kentucky universities that have teacher pre-service programs that emphasize strategies for low-performing schools and high need students. Through its Future Educators of America (FEA) program, the agency funds summer camps for future educators at the 8 state universities and Campbellsville University, a comprehensive, Christian institution that offers undergraduate and graduate programs. A statewide annual FEA conference, which attracts over 600 would-be teachers from middle and high schools across the Commonwealth, is also hosted by the SDE.

Build Local Capacity

Coordinate Structures and Roles.

State Education Agency. The SDE is a leading member of the Educational Leadership Development Collaborative, a unique association of educational organizations in Kentucky working together to improve student learning through leadership. The group's mission is "to advance student learning through a collaborative focus on leadership development." Members of the collaborative include:

- Education Professional Standards Board;
- The Prichard Committee for Academic Excellence;
- Kentucky School Boards Association;
- The Partnership for Successful Schools;
- Kentucky Association of School Councils;
- Kentucky Association of School Administrators;

- Kentucky Association of Educational Cooperatives;
- Collaborative Center for Literacy Development: Early Childhood through Adulthood;
- P–16 Councils;
- Southern Association of Colleges and Schools – Council on Accreditation and School Improvement; and
- Commonwealth Consortium for Leadership Preparation Programs; and the Colleges of Education at Kentucky Public Universities.

The group meets monthly to discuss current issues in education and address programs and strategies being used by their respective organizations to improve student learning in the Commonwealth. They also listen to presentations concerning education programs and initiatives, relevant issues, and legislation affecting education in the Commonwealth.

Intermediate Agencies. Kentucky has 16 State Regional Educational Cooperatives (RECs) that provide assistance and expertise for the benefit of their member school districts. The cooperatives provide comprehensive educational services and programs that support the member districts and their schools in school improvement efforts. While funded by local school districts, the RECs offer professional development in partnership with the SDE. The District Achievement Gap Coordinators are assigned to work with the cooperatives that service their assigned districts and serve as agency liaisons with the co-ops. Also, there are 11 Special Education Cooperatives funded by the SDE that also provide services with SDE.

External Partner Organizations. One can go to the site below and find over 60 agencies that the SDE works with: http://education.ky.gov/KDE/ HomePageRepository/Partners+Page/Partners+Page.htm. One example is the Partnership for Successful Schools. This Partnership is a coalition of Kentucky businesses, educational groups, and government officials which believes that business has both a stake and a role to play in helping children learn. In one initiative, the Partnership developed a One-to-One Practicing Reading with Students Program. One-to-One is more than a reading program. It provides a business with the support and resources it needs to start a volunteer program in a local elementary school, train its employees to work one-on-one helping children with their reading, keep informed on the most recent reading test data, and use that data to make decisions in local communities. Reading practice sessions are presented in focused 35-minute slots. Coaches receive step-by-step instructions on how to maximize every minute of that time to help students practice vital reading skills. Businesses and their volunteer coaches receive continuing support through a website that provides updated testing data and coaching tips. The One-to-One project includes 79 reading coaches from 12 companies and organizations. These coaches serve 10 Kentucky schools.

In another example, the Partnership developed the Kentucky Scholars Program, a new initiative that encourages middle and high school students to take the types of courses that will best prepare them for the changing expectations of today's higher education and work environments. The Kentucky Scholars Initiative is made possible by federal funding that comes to the Partnership for Successful Schools from the Center for State Scholars in Austin, Texas. The Scholars Program is typically introduced in the classroom by the very business and community representatives who will be making tomorrow's hiring decisions. By joining business and education in the classroom, staff believes that students will have the best chance to know what is expected of them after graduation.

In spring 2005, the Kentucky Legislature passed legislation that provided for the establishment of the Kentucky Center for Mathematics at Northern Kentucky University. In collaboration with the Committee for Mathematics Achievement, the SDE, the Council on Postsecondary Education, all Kentucky public universities, and other institutions, the Kentucky Center for Mathematics (KCM) is responsible for developing and executing an implementation, research, and evaluation plan to put into action the goals outlined by the Committee for Mathematics Achievement. Two statewide initiatives launched in the summer of 2006 are: (1) Diagnostic and Intervention Programs, and (2) Coaching and Mentoring Programs.

The Center provides extensive training to prepare local math teachers to serve as math coaches in their local schools. Key goals for the Center are: to enhance Pre-K-16 teachers' mathematics knowledge and ability to differentiate instruction to meet the needs of all students; enhance the awareness and knowledge of Pre-K-12 teachers, adult educators, and postsecondary faculty regarding effective mathematics resources, including curriculum materials, intervention and remediation programs, and technology; provide them the support necessary to use the resources effectively at the school level; and finally, increase the number of Kentucky teachers with expertise in mathematics and mathematics teaching through aggressive recruitment programs and support-based retention strategies.

Distinguished Educators. One of the provisions of the original KERA was the Distinguished Educator (DE) program, which was the predecessor to the current Highly Skilled Educators (HSE) program. In 1998, the General Assembly changed the name from the Distinguished Educator program to the Highly Skilled Educators program as the state's assessment system transitioned from KIRIS to CATS. The statute was revised to provide a focus of assistance to low-performing schools.

Highly skilled educators provide assistance to schools with a growth accountability index that falls below the assistance point. Level 1, Level 2, and Level 3, all within assistance parameters, are differentiated according to the following:

Level 1—classification assigned to a school that has an index that places it in the highest one-third (1/3) of all schools below the assistance line.

Level 2—classification assigned to a school that has an index score that places it in the middle one-third (1/3) of all schools below the assistance line.

Level 3—classification assigned to a school that has an index score that places it in the lowest one-third (1/3) of all schools below the assistance line. Level 3 schools are first priority when determining HSE assignments.

HSE educational and professional experiences are matched with the needs of the schools in need of assistance. Geographical information is also a consideration when making placement decisions.

HSEs remain employees of their home district. The SDE signs a Memorandum of Agreement (MOA) with the HSEs' home districts on an annual basis. MOAs are renewable for a second year and may be renewable for a third year. Three years is the maximum tenure for a HSE. Then they return to their district and become a resource to build internal district capacity. Some states use only (or mainly) retired educators as their key consultants to districts. However, in Kentucky that is not the case. In order to be eligible to apply for a position as a HSE the following criteria must be met:

- Kentucky certification as an educator;
- A minimum of five years of successful experience as a teacher or educational administrator; and
- Involvement in teaching or administration within the last three years.

The selection process is rigorous, and applicants are held to the highest standards. Candidates progress through a series of steps that serve to continuously narrow the pool of applicants from which the next cadre will be selected. The application process covers a period of five months and consists of the following steps:

- Written Assessment. Open response questions, designed by a team of SDE experts, are administered to applicants. Then, responses are double-blind scored by SDE personnel.
- Performance Events. Based on the written assessment scores, candidates are selected to move to the second phase of the selection process. Selected candidates participate in a full-day assessment that includes a simulated HSE experience, delivery of a professional development session, a technology assessment, and submission of a video presentation of a classroom lesson.

- Reference Checks. SDE personnel conduct in-depth reference checks for the applicants who successfully complete the performance events evaluation. (Background checks by the Kentucky State Police Agency are also completed.)
- Site Visits. SDE representatives make visits to work sites of all applicants who advance to the final step. The site visit includes shadowing the applicant and interviews with applicants, colleagues, students, and supervisors.

Once applicants are selected as HSEs, they are required to participate in three to four weeks of training during the months of July and August. The specialized training assures that these educators have the skills and resources necessary to deliver exceptional service to schools under a variety of diverse and unique circumstances.

Additionally, trainings continue throughout the school year through monthly regional team meetings and HSE cadre training sessions that are scheduled every 6 to 8 weeks. Training topics are selected based on the needs of the schools in assistance and the HSEs' Individual Growth Plans. There are also weekly online chats called Cadre Online. SDE has an agreement with the University of Kentucky for alternative certification for highly skilled educators to qualify for leadership certification.

SDE staff report that one of the strengths of the HSEs is their ability to build relationships with the teachers and administrators in a school. Their previous experiences and knowledge base, working knowledge of a school, and knowledge of best practices and current research all add to the strength of the program. Although HSEs have no authority or power to mandate change, 95.7% of the Level 3 schools served by them since 1998 have moved out of Level 3 classification by meeting or exceeding their goals.

HSEs work with all 9 SDE Standards and Indicators for School Improvement: Curriculum; Instruction; Assessment; Culture; Student, Family, and Community Support; Professional Growth; Development and Evaluation; Leadership; Organizational Structure; and Resources. The nine standards are organized within three sections: Academic Performance, Learning Environment, and Efficiency (http://education.ky.gov/KDE/Administrative+Resources/School+Improvement/Standards+and+Indicat ors+for+School+Improvement/).

As a practical matter, the HSEs receive 135% of the daily salary they were making at the position they held prior to coming into the program. They have a 240-day contract and their salary is capped at $90,000. HSEs are funded by the State and 100% of the salary counts toward retirement. They remain an employee of their local district and maintain the same benefits.

Of the 105 HSEs who entered the program as teachers, 81 accepted leadership positions beyond that of classroom teacher after exiting the program.

In fact, of the 251 HSEs who have exited the program, many have gone on to leadership positions as follows: 52 principals or assistant principals, 19 superintendents or assistant superintendents, 75 central office administrators, 22 SDE staff leaders, 23 national and state consultants, 8 university faculty, 3 cooperative directors, and 2 federal government administrators.

School Support Teams. In Kentucky, the Voluntary Partnership Assistance Teams (VPAT) are one of three options the state made available to districts who had reached the Tier 3 level of consequences under NCLB. Tier 3 districts have failed to meet adequate yearly progress (AYP) for four years. The other two options are State Assistance Teams (SAT) and Network Assistance Teams (NAT). These three options make up the Kentucky system of support as required by NCLB for districts falling into this level of consequence.

In the fall of 2005, the SDE, Kentucky School Boards Association (KSBA), and the Kentucky Association of School Superintendents (KASS) developed the VPAT intervention model with the intention of piloting it with several districts before the Tier 3 consequences took effect. The model is called "voluntary" because the district volunteers accept the extensive involvement and scrutiny as well as support of a team of people who will engage with the district leader, school board, community, and schools within the district. The intervention provides the local district with an intensive, collaborative assistance process designed to build capacity at the district and school levels. It also provides essential support and oversight for immediate and sustained student achievement improvement.

As mentioned earlier in the Lessons Learned section, VPAT membership is comprised of a five-person team that assists the district in reviewing its needs and developing an improvement plan to address those needs. Each team consists of the district superintendent (who acts as team leader), a KASS mentor for the superintendent, a KSBA local school board mentor, a HSE, and a SDE staff member. More specifically, members of the first two types of teams may include HSEs, Achievement Gap Coordinators, District Support Facilitators, and Targeted Assistance Coaches as well as consultants from the SDE's Division of Federal Programs.

Members of the support teams are chosen based on district need and geographic location. Training for these support teams is conducted at the beginning of the year. While the district chooses its representatives, the SDE chooses its staff, and the other organizations choose their representatives. Team leaders send in monthly reports and have regular follow-up meetings with SDE leadership. The associate commissioner meets with representatives from the Kentucky School Board Association and Association of School Superintendents on an ongoing basis to evaluate the process. SDE has finished its first full year with these teams. In some places the approach has been embraced and is very effective, especially with building capacity. In other districts, headway is slower.

As of June 2007, there are 44 districts in Kentucky in Tier 3. Of those 44 districts, 24 districts are in the VPAT program and 13 in the SAT program. In addition, 7 districts are in the NAT program where local personnel work outside the purview of the SDE. These teams collaborate to provide technical assistance to schools and districts that are not meeting state and federal requirements.

SDE staff would like to see their Regional Comprehensive Center provide opportunities to network directly with other states on how they are approaching statewide systems of support for schools, i.e., the roadblocks, what has worked well, how they are staffed, and how they are holding districts accountable.

Differentiated Support to Local Districts and Schools

The Standards and Indicators for School Improvement define the elements of whole school improvement that schools can put into effect at the elementary, middle, and high school levels to produce desired learning results. The SDE is required to conduct audits/reviews of schools that fail to meet their achievement goals for each biennium; that is, only schools in Level 3 based on student achievement and Tier 3 for NCLB are required to have audits. Level 2 and Level 1 schools may have a review, and while the process is identical, it is not mandatory. The SDE is also required to conduct scholastic audits in a percentage of successful schools each biennium, and the Office of Leadership and School Improvement produces a biennial report that highlights the variance points between successful and low-performing schools. Leadership and school culture consistently emerge as the top factors affecting student achievement.

In addition, in Tier 3 districts the agency conducts district audits that serve as blueprints for action to move these districts out of Tier 3 status. In order for a Tier 3 district to be eligible for participation in a VPAT, they must receive a district audit.

The scholastic audit process uses the Standards and Indicators for School Improvement document as the measure of a school's preparedness for improvement. The nine indicators cover the following:

Academic Performance
- Standard 1: Curriculum—The school develops and implements a curriculum that is rigorous, intentional, and aligned to state and local standards.
- Standard 2: Assessment—The school utilizes multiple evaluation and assessment strategies to continuously monitor and modify instruction to meet student needs and support proficient student work.
- Standard 3: Instruction—The school's instructional program actively engages all students by using effective, varied, and research-based practices to improve student academic performance.

Learning Environment
- Standard 4: School Culture—The district/school functions as an effective learning community and supports a climate conducive to performance excellence.
- Standard 5: Student, Family, and Community Support—The district/school works with families and community groups to remove barriers to learning in an effort to meet the intellectual, social, career, and developmental needs of students.
- Standard 6: Professional Growth, Development, and Evaluation—The district/school provides research-based, results driven professional development opportunities for staff and implements performance evaluation procedures in order to improve teaching and learning.

Organizational Efficiency
- Standard 7: Leadership—District/school instructional decisions focus on support for teaching and learning, organizational direction, high performance expectations, creating a learning culture, and developing leadership capacity.
- Standard 8: Organizational Structure and Resources—The organization of the district/school maximizes use of time, all available space and other resources to maximize teaching and learning and support high student and staff performances.
- Standard 9: Comprehensive and Effective Planning—The district/school develops, implements, and evaluates a comprehensive school improvement plan that communicates a clear purpose, direction, and action plan focused on teaching and learning.

Team members use these Standards and Indicators to judge how effective a school has been in the performance levels observed under each indicator of the nine standards. The indicators show the degree to which a standard is in place. Implementation is viewed in terms of degrees since every school may be in a different place along each continuum.

For example, under Standard 1 Indicator 1.1f is: "There is in place a systematic process for monitoring, evaluating, and reviewing the curriculum." There are examples of supporting evidence for the team members as they decide whether to rate this indicator as:

1—Little or no development and implementation;
2—Limited development or partial implementation;
3—Fully functioning and operational level of development and implementation; or
4—Exemplary level of development and implementation.

A school or district would receive a rating of "1" if there were no local board of education curriculum policy; district leadership did not ensure each school had a curriculum policy and procedures to implement it; district leadership did not assist schools in the revision and updating of their curriculum; or district leadership did not have collaborative discussion of curriculum issues at the district level.

However, a district/school receives a "4" if the district leadership helps school councils analyze student performance data and reviews their policies and procedures to make data-informed curricular improvement decisions; district leadership initiates and facilitates collaboration among schools within the district to ensure implementation, monitoring, evaluation and revision of the aligned curriculum and to ensure that school staff members are cognizant of the most up-to-date curricular trends.

The SDE staff believes the scholastic audit visit helps local school leaders and teachers to identify changes needed to improve the academic performance of all students. The chairperson makes team assignments based on team members' expertise and experience as related to the Standards and Indicators for School Improvement.

All team members are responsible for reviewing the data in the school portfolio, which is compiled by the school. In preparation for the audit, team members are strongly encouraged to research and become familiar with the school portfolio, e.g., CATS (Commonwealth Accountability Testing System) results, school report card, comprehensive school improvement plan, etc. During the audit, team member responsibilities include visiting classrooms; engaging in classroom observations; and interviewing administrators, counselors, teachers, teacher assistants, council members, parents, and students.

Team members also conduct surveys of a random number of parents, teachers, staff administrators, students, and community members. For example, under the Academic Performance Standard, respondents are asked to reply to a series of statements and asked to judge whether they Strongly Agree, Agree, Don't Know, Disagree, or Strongly Disagree. Two sample statements are:

- "Students understand what qualifies a performance to be considered novice, apprentice, proficient, or distinguished. Parents also understand these differences."
- "Teachers use a variety of assessments that are standards-based, rigorous, developmentally appropriate, authentic, and which accommodate different learning styles."

The SDE staff believes 11 states are using this process or some modification of this process. While they do not believe they need any federal assistance to strengthen their review process, they would like to see research based strategies for districts that are struggling with how to help certain subgroups improve achievement, such as students with disabilities and English language learners.

Differentiate Support to Local Districts and Schools

Differentiate by Point of Impact. In deciding who receives district-level assistance, the SDE starts with Tier 3 schools, that is, schools that have not made AYP for four consecutive years. Districts must choose one of three options: (1) VPAT teams; (2) State Assistance Teams; or (3) Network Assistance (central office has capacity to implement strategies as part of a network). They can work with universities to customize their plans in this latter approach. Districts in Tier 3 receive information on the three types of services, and they indicate their order of choice which in most cases has been honored. SDE staff have found that working with a district is a better option than concentrating on schools.

Differentiate by Intensity and Duration of Services. Once a district is identified as in Tier 3 status, it remains in this category for two years and will receive services for this time. Intensity is determined by need and AYP status. The VPATs deliver the most intense services. SDE staff believe that their approach allows for customization of services, and that indeed is a strength of their approach.

Delivery of State Systems of Support Services

Provide Services. In 1996, in an effort to improve the planning process, the SDE developed a computer application to consolidate planning. Districts develop both plans and funding requests simultaneously to the SDE. During 1999–2000, Kentucky created a Comprehensive Improvement Planning system that streamlined district funding requests. While the system addresses compliance requirements, the planning document is more about strategies that the district will use to address its documented needs.

SDE provides annual performance reports by subgroups and content areas tested and by teacher and student to help guide the district and school planning process. In addition, its website (http://education.ky.gov/KDE/) provides multiple tools such as sample plans, the role of a school council, etc.

Kentucky's District Improvement Planning Roles & Responsibilities document begins by noting that the process is designed to include all stakeholders (parents, staff, and administrators) in creating a plan that promotes and supports school improvement efforts by:

- Creating and sustaining a vision for improved student achievement;
- Establishing a district needs assessment process to determine what the district must do to help schools increase student performance; and

- Building upon the policy role of the local board of education and school-based decision making councils to provide systemic methods for improvement planning.

The document goes on to outline the 8 critical steps for improvement planning in Kentucky:

- Needs Assessment—What does the data tell us our needs are?
- Prioritizing Needs—Which of these identified needs are of greatest concern (2-3 needs)?
- Cause Analysis—What factors caused these needs of greatest concern to occur?
- Setting Goals—What is our goal in addressing each of these needs, and when will we reach these goals?
- A Plan to Achieve the Goals—What steps will we take to reach our goals, and who will oversee each step?
- Resources for Achieving Goals—What resources will we need to reach our goal?
- Monitoring the Plan—What method(s) will we use to ensure each step is completed, and how often will we check for implementation?
- Evaluating the Impact on Student Performance—What method(s) will we use to measure the effectiveness of our actions, and how often will we check?

With regard to supplemental educational services, SDE has developed and disseminated a handbook that describes, in detail, information about SES. In addition there is a statewide media campaign to share information about eligibility and services available through SES. The SDE has collected baseline information about providers and is working with an outside evaluator to complete a comprehensive evaluation.

Allocate Resources for Services. For Tier 3 districts, deferred District Title I funds are used to implement the strategies that the VPATs develop. Additional Commonwealth School Improvement funds are based on the State Accountability System and are state funds used for the schools that did not make their state goals.

Provide Opportunities for Change

Districts decide their own planning cycles. Each district reviews and updates their district and school improvement planning policies to include a section related to the Annual Planning Cycle. The district improvement plan will be posted on the district website and updated at least annually, based on the district planning cycle.

There are no specific program requirements for the district improvement plans. The SDE website provides multiple tools that provide options districts may utilize.

However, there is more structure for districts in Tier 3. Tier 3 districts have seven requirements for inclusion in their comprehensive district improvement plan (CDIP) which they must post to their district website in November:

- The CDIP for Tier 3 districts must include a determination of why the district's previous plan did not bring about increased student achievement;
- Tier 3 district improvement plans must incorporate, as appropriate, activities before school, after school, during summer, or during an extension of the school year;
- Tier 3 district plans must include strategies to promote effective parental involvement in the schools;
- CDIP must connect high-quality professional development with high-quality teacher and student learning in a systemic way;
- The CDIP should include research-based best practices to support each activity;
- The CDIP must include measurable goals and targets for each of the subpopulations identified in NCLB; and
- The CDIP must show how the district is addressing the teaching and learning needs and academic problems of each of its low-achieving students as shown in its needs assessment.

EVALUATION OF STATE ROLE IN DISTRICT AND SCHOOL IMPROVEMENT

Program Facts regarding the evaluation of HSEs:

In 1998–2000, 66 schools were served by 63 HSEs. Reports indicated that 65 schools had an improved Academic Index. All Level 3 schools moved out of the Level 3 classification by meeting or exceeding their goal.

In 2000–2002, 53 schools and two districts were served by 54 HSEs. The Academic Index improved at 46 schools. Again, all Level 3 schools moved out of the Level 3 classification by meeting or exceeding their goal.

In 2002–2004, 84 schools and four districts were served by 55 HSEs. Improved Academic Index for 80 schools was reported. All Level 3 schools, with the exception of two, moved out of the Level 3 classification by meeting or exceeding their goal.

HSEs remain as employees of their home district while serving in the program; therefore, traditional personnel evaluations are not conducted by SDE. Informal evaluations are used to assess the work of the HSEs on a continuing basis using the following tools:

- HSE monthly reports;
- HSE mentor visits;
- HSE cadre participation;
- Development and presentation of HSE cadre training tools, resources, and documents;
- Anecdotal information shared by HSEs;
- Feedback from HSE Team Leaders;
- Conversations with HSEs and district/school administrators;
- HSE end of the year and/or exit reports;
- CATS accountability reports for assisted schools; and
- NCLB reports for assisted schools.

A study by the Partnership for Kentucky Schools entitled *Improving Low-Performing Schools: A Study of Kentucky's Highly Skilled Educators Program* drew several conclusions about the impact and effectiveness of the Highly Skilled Educators Program. Their data found impact in four critical areas. The areas and some of the findings are below:

Curriculum and Instruction

- Teachers attributed improvement in their teaching to HSEs.
- Teachers reported that HSEs contributed to improvement in teacher knowledge of effective teaching.
- Teachers credited HSEs with helping to improve curriculum and instructional coordination in the school.
- Teachers credited HSEs with enhancing attention to state test data.

Professional Development

- Teachers found professional development to be more focused on curriculum and instruction and the critical needs of the school.

Leadership, School Organization, and Morale

- Teachers believed that school leadership had improved as a result of the HSE.
- Teachers believed that the presence of an HSE improved morale and contributed to a shared school-wide focus and a culture of collaboration that had not previously existed.

Test Scores

- Overall, HSE schools outperformed the rest of the schools in the state.
- A higher proportion of HSE schools (56%) met their accountability index goal than did non-HSE schools (46%).
- Thirteen percent fewer HSE schools than non-HSE schools had scores that were lower than the previous biennium.
- No HSE school remained in need of assistance while 8% of non-HSE schools fell into that category.
- Overall, HSE schools gained twice as much as the non-HSE schools.

The scope and quality of the HSE intervention turns what would otherwise be a punitive set of sanctions into assistance that is appreciated and has a positive impact on low-performing schools.

A major finding in a research study of the Highly Skilled Educator Program, completed in October 2006 for the Legislative Research Commission, revealed that, overall, schools that received assistance through a combination of HSE, Commonwealth School Improvement Funds and a scholastic audit or review showed statistically significant improvements in their accountability index scores.

VIEWS FROM THE FIELD

The information is this section is a synthesis of interviews with two superintendents (or their designees) and two principals who received service from the Kentucky statewide system of support.

Factors That Contributed to Improvement and Lessons Learned

The administrators interviewed attributed their students' improved achievement to the following factors:

- Distributed leadership both at the district and school levels;
- High expectations for students that motivate them to achieve;
- Establishment of grade-level teacher teams where student performance is the focus of discussions;
- Professional development targeted on improving pedagogy;
- A restructured organizational chart to ensure that principals were truly instructional leaders;

- Use of formative assessment tied to state standards to guide instruction;
- A commitment to "support, monitor, and evaluate programs and teachers, trying hard to let people know what's expected," and establish professional growth plans;
- Linking instruction to state standards; and
- A change from a teacher-focused school culture to a student-focused culture, thereby getting critical student engagement and buy-in.

Lesson 1—Meeting Rigorous Standards. "You have to not only say you're going to reach every child, but you have to act to reach every child." When the staff realized that they were not holding all students to rigorous standards, "that was a very eye-opening and humbling experience for us."

Lesson 2—Hard Work. "It's hard work." Teaching at-risk students can be challenging, but "... there are ways to do it, and we have to do what we know works, not what we hope will work. Hope is not really a plan."

Lesson 3—Principal Leadership. "Schools need great principals for their students to be successful, and principals need to work to make all their teachers great." Principals must have high expectations for teachers and provide the tools that teachers need.

Lesson 4—Communication. Leadership "from the central office all the way down" must keep everyone informed.

Lesson 5—Data-Based Decision Making. Decision making must be driven by data, and research-based practices should be employed.

The following lessons came from principals:

Lesson 6—Curriculum. There must be a focus on curriculum.

Lesson 7—Positive Culture. Maintaining a positive school culture is essential. "We understand that everybody's going to have different points of view, but they need to offer only positive solutions."

State Policies—Incentives and Opportunities

All the administrators interviewed felt the impact of the pressure of public accountability in response to assessment scores ultimately had a positive effect on achievement. Said one superintendent, "Your whole community— everyone's looking at you for success." There were costs associated with that pressure, too. One principal said that it had a negative effect for the first two years, and another acknowledged that it "makes for an environment that is a little more on edge." All but one said they were affected positively by the possibility of undesirable consequences for low performance, though again, one principal said the initial effect was negative. "We turned it into a positive." Financial rewards or loss were a factor only in one district which had a local program that provided financial rewards for administrators and teacher leaders. One superintendent added, "What [the State] provided was a commitment to us that they knew we could get it done."

Charter schools were not a factor for any of the administrators, and the superintendents reported being unaffected by competition from public school choice. Not so for the principals, who did encounter some positive fallout from that competition, though one said the effect was slight. One principal said that his superintendent prominently displayed graphs showing each school's scores in the district office meeting room. This fostered competition among the principals, and he was anxious to improve his school's scores, which were the lowest of the five schools in the district that served the same grade levels.

The only administrator affected by a waiver was one principal who received permission to offer supplemental educational services during the school day. None had experience with alternate routes to administrative certification, and feelings about alternatively certified teachers were decidedly mixed. One superintendent, whose district received a federal Transition to Teaching grant, said, "It's had a huge positive effect for us. We've brought in seven teachers in the last three years [in a variety of subjects]. Most of them have been excellent."

The other superintendent, who had hired recipients of MAT degrees, demurred: "Some of these people were making decent teachers…it's not all around been a totally positive experience because these people have never had education courses. It depends on the person.…They just don't have the education philosophy and experience with how to deal with students." While acknowledging that other districts have had better results, he planned to retain few of his district's alternatively certified teachers. One of the two principals, who had also hired seven alternatively certified teachers, concurred: "I was not overly pleased with them." Of the seven who were initially hired, only two remain. "They knew the subject matter, but they did not have adequate training or experience in classrooms."

None of the administrators had participated in explicitly designated training for turnaround leaders, but one principal spoke highly of his experience with the Kentucky Leadership Academy, which convinced him that "failure is not an option. It totally turned my thinking around."

Building Local Capacity

The schools and districts make extensive use of state assessment and demographic data. Additional data are available to schools that request culture or safety audits from the state. Data are used to identify achievement gaps, evaluate programs, determine where professional development is needed, and monitor the NCLB status of subgroups and students. One district and one school each devote an entire day of professional development each year to analyzing student data.

In the words of one principal, "The SDE web page is great. You can find anything you need there." One superintendent frequently uses information on the teacher leadership program and references to research on best practices. Also mentioned were free online professional development, the improvement planning toolkit, and a variety of curriculum materials, including templates for curriculum alignment, lesson plans, unit plans, and useful sample plans. The website is also used to locate contact people at the SDE and keep informed about upcoming staff development opportunities.

Help in school and district planning came from Achievement Gap coordinators, highly skilled educators, and improvement teams. While SDE staff did not generally get directly involved in constructing district and school improvement plans, the superintendents explained that the SDE did provide training, and that they were comfortable calling the SDE if they had questions. In one instance, a state Title I consultant visited a district to speak with them about budgeting and learning goals for the coming year. A principal said that the Regional Cooperative was "really good [at providing assistance] if you request [it]," but that he had not felt the need to do so.

Commonwealth School Improvement funds have been used for professional development, work on school culture, and curriculum mapping. One of the districts partnered with the state to obtain a grant to expand high school Advanced Placement programs.

The state's scholastic review process has proved extremely valuable. One superintendent described it in this way: "The scholastic review was a very good experience for us," bringing up issues they had not previously confronted and "giving us suggestions and information on how to do it. The assistance team here gives me a group of professionals that I consult with regularly and routinely, and I receive assistance and guidance in the decision-making process." The scholastic review provided them with suggestions for next steps to take in moving forward with student achievement. For example, it revealed some ways in which instructional time was being lost to non-instructional activities. It also showed that differentiation of instruction was another area that needed improvement. Through subsequent work with a HSE and Gap coordinator, the school has improved its use of instructional time, instructional delivery, and monitoring.

Although the principals interviewed often turn first to their districts for help, state-provided professional development plays a crucial role and is delivered through a number of different means. The state provides funds that enable school and district staff to attend workshops and conferences. In addition to workshops on such topics as curriculum, data systems, instructional delivery and planning, free online courses for teachers are also offered. The administrators interviewed feel free to request additional training as needed. For example, the state provided one district with a consultant to advise them on middle school and high school schedules. HSEs are also instrumental in providing professional development. Said one superintendent: "Our highly skilled educator has helped us significantly by delivering professional development, but more importantly, I think, by helping me and us reach a point where we now do most of our professional development internally." In addition, the state provides training to district central office staff who in turn train members of the site-based councils responsible for making decisions at the school level.

When asked about state services related to information and data systems, the superintendents were complimentary. "They are always very responsive when I call them and ask for rankings or historical data. Kentucky does have a very thorough data system." The other superintendent regards the SDE as a helpful resource when they experience difficulties: "We have a point of contact with them to correct any problem."

Curriculum, instruction, and assessment are three areas in which the administrators reported particularly fruitful collaborations with the state. In addition to the professional development opportunities mentioned above, one superintendent related how a highly skilled educator and math coordinator helped redesign his district's curriculum maps and better connect the lesson planning process to the curriculum. The state helped one district find appropriate materials and set up a formal system of monthly student assessments. The district had previously used some assessments sporadically, but "they did make us aware of how to move to the next level by making sporadic assessments systematic. It helped us know and understand that [the assessments] could be so much more powerful." The state also provided professional development on classroom assessment and how to write and use scoring rubrics.

Parental involvement and special education were two other areas in which the administrators received especially beneficial assistance. "[The state has] helped us quite a bit with [parental involvement]. In the development of our district improvement plan, they were very picky about our parent involvement activity, and they have provided us support to structure communication with parents about holding high expectations for all students." The other superintendent spoke favorably of the state's willingness to come out to help districts and schools train volunteers and find ways to increase parental involvement in the schools.

The administrators interviewed had few, if any, English language learners, but they did receive professional development and consulting services to help them better serve students with disabilities. One superintendent declared that the state "helped us significantly there by making us aware that many of our special education students have no cognitive barriers to reaching proficiency and then by helping them know how to more effectively instruct those students."

NCLB Sanctions and Provisions

Neither of the schools interviewed had been subject to corrective action, but one of the districts had. That district's superintendent remarked: "The corrective action is the Voluntary Partnership Assistance team. What distinguishes it here in Kentucky is that its corrective action is in a support mode, not a 'we're going to get you.' Again they're honest, and they share brutal facts, but they also say we're here to support. It's a great process."

None of the respondents had been involved with school restructuring and choice, either within or outside of NCLB. Both districts offered supplemental educational services, as did one of the schools. Results were mixed.

Suggestions for Evaluation of Statewide Systems of Support

The following were mentioned as measures of the effectiveness of the statewide system of support:

- Growth in student performance;
- Decrease in dropout rates;
- Decrease in districts subject to NCLB sanctions;
- Amount of state assistance to districts;
- How the state determines support is needed and making sure support is provided;
- The extent to which the state is proactive, rather than reactive; and
- The amount of communication between districts and the state department.

Apart from assessment results, the states could obtain the necessary information by surveying or interviewing local educators. As one superintendent put it, "Stakeholder input is a major piece of the puzzle because [the state is] providing services, and you need to know how the services you're providing are working." In the opinion of one principal, "The first thing is to call and talk to [local educators, and ask] what the schools need, and are the needs being met? Can the state department do other things to meet those needs?"

Clearly, much has already been accomplished. One of the principals remarked on the transformation seen in the SDE since he was a new principal. "There was a tremendous change in the state. [At that time] they were the police." Now they are "much more supportive." He saw "a change from 'there's a problem—go fix it' to 'here are the needs you have, and here are the resources we have for you.' And the resources are there."

ACKNOWLEDGEMENTS

We would like to sincerely thank the following staff from the Kentucky Department of Education for their time during our interviews and for their efforts in providing us with important supporting documents: Steve Schenck, Dotty Raley, Barb Kennedy, David Cook, Johnnie Grissom, Pauline Carr, Rina Gratz, Connie Lester, Pat Trotter and Ginger Mason. Also thanks to David Baird who is the Executive Director of the Kentucky School Boards Association.

We would also like to thank the following local educators who gave generously of their time to talk with us:

Andy Dotson, retired principal, Phelps High School, Phelps, KY
Paul Green, principal, Southside Elementary School, Beattyville, KY
Chuck Holliday, superintendent, Fulton County Schools, Hickman, KY
Roger Johnson, assistant superintendent, Brenda Maynard, Director of Curriculum and Instruction, and supervisors Teresa Lockhart and Tonia Hopson, Pike County Schools, Pikeville, KY.

PART D

THE ROLE OF COMPREHENSIVE CENTERS

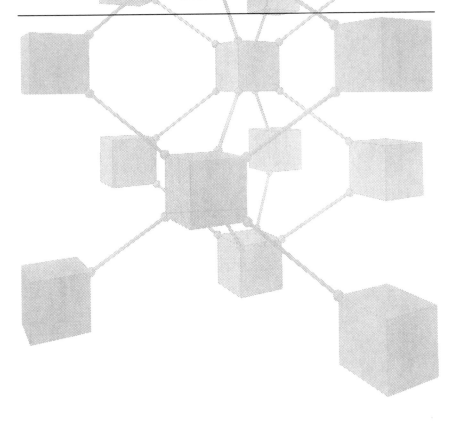

CHAPTER 11

CII AND THE COMPREHENSIVE CENTERS' WORK WITH THE STATES

Marilyn Murphy

OVERVIEW

The Center on Innovation & Improvement (CII) is one of five federally funded Content Centers that directly serve the national network of 16 Regional Comprehensive Centers. Each Content Center has specific, assigned areas of priority, and statewide systems of support (SSOS) is one of several priority areas assigned to CII under the broad topic of innovation and improvement. Additional CII priorities include supplemental educational services and restructuring. The other four Content Centers focus on teacher quality, assessment and accountability, instruction, and high schools. The Regional Comprehensive Centers work alongside the Content Centers to provide responsive service to the 50 states and three U.S. territories. As a Content Center, CII operates as a designated field agent for the U.S. Department of Education, with the explicit task of supporting and advancing the mandates of the No Child Left Behind (NCLB) Act of 2001. The mission of CII and all Content Centers is clear—help the Regional Centers by

Handbook on Statewide Systems of Support, pages 199–204
Copyright © 2008 The Academic Development Institute and Information Age Publishing
199

providing content to support the needs of the states to improve the nation's schools. While CII has 16 direct clients, the potential extended client list reaches beyond the Regional Comprehensive Centers, into the state departments of education and ultimately to the districts they serve and the schools that are struggling to improve. What are the procedures and protocols CII uses to manage effectively this broad network of clients?

A Center-Wide System of Communication and Technical Assistance

Responding to 16 Regional Centers, who themselves serve the entire nation, requires a methodical and reliable communication system. CII corresponds regularly with all 16 centers, beginning with monthly, scheduled telephone contact with a liaison appointed for that purpose within each of the Regional Centers. The liaisons in turn communicate with their own centers and state education agencies (SEAs). Thus an efficient and collaborative communication network is regularly accessed, creating responsive communication between the Content Center and its primary client, the Regional Comprehensive Centers. This communication has engendered a sense of familiarity and reliability that has gone a long way in negotiating requests and efficiently brokering services. Regular communication often results in providing technical assistance, and CII works closely and often side-by-side with the comprehensive centers to produce informational events and retreats on NCLB-related topics; research-based reports, briefs, and tools; and web-based access to an extensive and regularly-updated database of state policies and programs and a search engine of research, reports, and tools.

ASSISTING SEAs IN THEIR WORK WITH THE DISTRICTS

The requirements for states under NCLB are clearly delineated in the July 2006 LEA and School Improvement: Non-Regulatory Guidance (www. ed.gov/policy/elsec/guid/schoolimprovementguid.doc). SEAs have specific duties to fulfill for the local education agencies (LEAs) including those paraphrased here:

- Establish school support teams to work in schools in corrective action.
- Designate and use distinguished principals and teachers with knowledge in how to improve academic achievement.
- Provide technical assistance by drawing on the expertise of other entities...including Regional Comprehensive Assistance Centers.

However, while the language is unequivocal, the "how to" of actually meeting the requirements is much less clear. State departments of education find themselves in a pivotal position, serving both as a conduit between districts and schools in need of improvement and as the vehicle for delivery of the resources provided by the Regional Comprehensive Center system and other entities. How does the state manage to transfer technical assistance, services, and information to the districts and schools it must serve? The challenge for the SEAs is to negotiate efficiently what is available within their system and what is needed by schools—particularly those in improvement status—and somehow deliver it all in a timely fashion and within budget. Responding to this challenge and the problems encountered to move information and resources through an already strained and under-funded pipeline are a major concern of most SEAs. Indeed, according to a recent study from the Center on Education Policy (CEP, 2006), "State education agencies have been stymied by a lack of adequate funding, manpower, and technology." The same report notes what states know is all too true: "The issue of state capacity is fundamental to the implementation of state and federal reform strategies, because if state education agencies are ineffective, the policies will fail."

Failure is not an acceptable option, and the onus is clearly on the responsiveness and capacity of the state. Most state departments are themselves challenged to respond quickly and efficiently—often relying heavily on entrenched systems that are inflexible and under-resourced—to the needs of districts and schools. The yeoman's task has been likened to a battleship being asked to function like a schooner. Burdened by dwindling funds and escalating compliance issues, states must look for ways to improve their own system of support and guide it down a path that is rarely clear from the SEA to the school; rather, the tendency is for numerous twists and turns that slow progress and impede improvement. The window of opportunity for students to improve learning is narrow at best and will not survive bureaucratic delays if achievement is to be raised.

What options remain for a state? The most obvious is to work with what resources are available, streamlining where possible and using additional resources judiciously. The comprehensive center network is poised to work directly with states on NCLB-related issues. Many states have turned to the comprehensive center system for assistance in reviewing and aligning their statewide system of support.

DEVELOPING THE *HANDBOOK* ## ON *STATEWIDE SYSTEMS OF SUPPORT*

In response to the need for a comprehensive document on statewide systems of support, CII developed this *Handbook on Statewide Systems of Sup-*

port. The chapters that follow this "Introduction" were written by representatives of Regional Comprehensive Centers who have been working on SSOS with their own SEAs and were invited by CII to contribute to this volume. Eight Regional Comprehensive Centers spread geographically from New England to Oregon accepted CII's invitation to contribute the stories of their center's work with one of their assigned states. Narratives from the Appalachia Comprehensive Center (ARCC), Great Lakes East Comprehensive Center (GLECC), Mid-Atlantic Comprehensive Center (MACC), Mid-continent Comprehensive Center (MCCC), New England Comprehensive Center (NECC), Northwest Comprehensive Center (NWCC), Texas Comprehensive Center (TXCC), and the Southwest Comprehensive Center (SWCC) are included. Each of the contributing centers was asked to provide information on the background of how the center is organized in its relationship with the state. The centers were also encouraged to include information on the process of working with the SEA, potentially including how need was assessed, and some of the nuts and bolts of setting up a system for responding to requests. Finally, they were asked to reflect on progress since the process began, including any lessons learned that would be helpful for other Regional Centers and states who may be embarking on, or fully immersed in, a similar process. Not unexpectedly, their stories differ in as much as states, comprehensive centers, and state structures differ; yet commonalities exist, particularly in the universality of many of the lessons learned.

COMMON ELEMENTS AND LESSONS LEARNED

State Liaisons. All of the contributing center narratives described a structure for interacting with the SEA. Most of the centers have assigned individual staff to serve as a discrete point of contact for the states; this individual is generally a senior staff member who, ideally, has a prior relationship with the state. In SWCC, the staff member must be a resident of the state or fully versed in the state's context. The NECC, for instance, employs a similar system, and the New Hampshire story notes the importance of the prior relationship between the SEA and senior personnel within the center. In its strong support of New Jersey, MACC likewise cites as critical that state's prior work with the George Washington University Center for Equity and Excellence in Education, where MACC is housed. Other center structures include state liaisons embedded within the state departments, a relationship which seems ideal from a communication perspective, as noted in the narratives of both MCCC and ARCC, both of which detail an embedded structure. A number of centers have formed hybrid organizations that include SEA and center staff in cooperating structures, such as the MCCC State Coordinating Council and the MACC–SEA state committee. Still others, such as GLECC, maintain a single point of contact with each state to facilitate communication and call on staff with demonstrated expertise on an as-needed basis. Whatever the system described, all report that consistency and responsiveness is critical to a successful, ongoing relationship.

Knowledge Building. All of the centers reported the importance of providing reliable, research-based information to help build the knowledge base for planning and developing statewide systems of support. Needs sensing, whether by facilitated discussion, surveys, or other means, was noted as a critical component in planning and maximizing available resources. A number of the centers reported engaging CII in their capacity-building efforts, responding to the U.S. Department of Education's guidelines by approaching the Content Center for technical assistance to be delivered by the Regional Center. For instance, a meeting in February 2007 with the SEAs of two, large, one-state centers, negotiated by CII, brought together state department representatives from New York and Texas for a 2-day CII, TXCC, and NYCC event on restructuring. Texas scheduled a follow-up annual forum with their state in June 2007, again working alongside CII to develop content. Recently, MCCC and CII worked with a number of SEA staff from Missouri for the specific purpose of looking closely at that state's system of support in order to create a direct and efficient service pathway to districts in need of support. Others, such as ARCC, MACC, and NECC, have accessed CII resources, including several panels and expert presentations to use in their work with the SEAs.

Lessons Learned. There is also commonality experienced by the centers in lessons learned. Thinking systemically is important, as is identifying resources from within rather than looking outside of the department in aligning a statewide system of support, particularly since all state budgets are experiencing overload. A number of centers remarked on the importance of patience and resilience, particularly when circumstances such as personnel changes and unanticipated events, including hurricanes, intervene to impede progress.

There is something positive to be learned from each of the center stories. The clear message in all of the narratives that follow is that CII, the Regional Comprehensive Centers, and their partner SEAs are working diligently to build and sustain a network of relationships that will provide resources for a seamless statewide system of support to assist schools in need of improvement, and provide students of those schools with the educational success they deserve.

REFERENCE

Center on Education Policy. (2007, May). *Educational architects: Do state agencies have the tools necessary to implement NCLB?* Retrieved August 3, 2007, from http://www.cep-dc.org/index.cfm

---

Marilyn Murphy *is Communication Director at the Center on Innovation & Improvement.*

CHAPTER 12

APPRAISING INSTRUCTIONAL PRACTICES IN WEST VIRGINIA

Caitlin Howley

BACKGROUND

The Appalachia Regional Comprehensive Center (ARCC) at Edvantia provides differentiated, evidence-based technical assistance to state education agencies (SEAs) in Kentucky, North Carolina, Tennessee, Virginia, and West Virginia. Each state in the region served by ARCC is assigned a dedicated ARCC staff member who acts as the primary contact between the SEA and the ARCC. Imbedded in the SEA, each of these state liaisons conducts regular needs assessments and leads the development, implementation, and monitoring of technical assistance.

The state liaison also leads a specially composed technical assistance design team, a three to five member group that works closely with SEA staff to plan technical assistance in each state. Members of the design team include ARCC staff and/or collaborating organizations, depending on the expertise that is needed to design each state's technical assistance plan. The composition of the team may change as SEA needs evolve over time. Design team members purvey information about research- and evidence-based programs, models, and practices, as well as broker proven services

Handbook on Statewide Systems of Support, pages 205–208
Copyright © 2008 The Academic Development Institute and Information Age Publishing

and programs to SEAs, to enhance their capacity to meet NCLB requirements and student achievement goals.

PROCESS

In the spring of 2006, the state liaison in West Virginia met with key West Virginia Department of Education (WVDE) staff to plan the following year's work. During this meeting, the state's system of support for struggling schools was discussed. This system includes the provision of technical assistance by comprehensively trained specialists assigned to schools in need of improvement. Despite this support and despite the implementation of other improvement efforts (such as the Enhanced High Schools That Work program and the statewide 21st Century Learning Initiative), schools were not making needed achievement gains, particularly in mathematics and science.

Several WVDE staff suggested that the state's system of support for struggling schools needed an additional component—a process for appraising the instructional programs in such schools. An appraisal system would allow WVDE staff to collect data systematically and objectively about schools' instructional programs and practices. Instructional inadequacies associated with stagnant achievement patterns could thereby be identified, and technical assistance could then be aligned more closely to each school's particular instructional issues.

The resultant West Virginia Instruction and Learning Appraisal (ILA) project was a joint venture of ARCC and WVDE as part of the 2006–07 ARCC project plan. To design and conduct ILAs in 2006–07, ARCC staff members worked "shoulder to shoulder" with WVDE school support specialists and staff from WVDE's Office of Career and Technical Instruction responsible for the Enhanced High Schools That Work program. Sixteen high schools participating in the Enhanced High Schools That Work program were selected to receive an ILA appraisal.

The ILA provides an objective, external review of the quality of instruction and learning, including the continuous improvement efforts, in a school or district. The appraisal also enables a school or district to monitor its own academic standards and to determine the effectiveness of its teaching and support for student learning. The appraisal is an on-site review that examines the nature of student academic experiences, the types of instructional support provided, the interventions used to strengthen identified learning deficits, and the extent to which student achievement corresponds with expected levels of learning. A pilot test of the process indicated that all data collection components of the ILA were sufficiently reliable, with reliability coefficients ranging from .72 to .96 (Hughes & Mittapalli, 2005).

Using a qualitative model for analyzing validity, reviewers found the process to possess adequate construct and external validity.

The ILA includes a number of data collection and analysis components. Structured interviews are conducted with school or district leaders to clarify concerns and priorities, and structured interviews are also conducted with teachers and students to document perceptions of current practice. ILA team members conduct classroom observations, using systematic and reliable procedures, to obtain "snapshots" of instructional practices and interventions and review relevant documents (e.g., policies, curriculum frameworks). Analyses of data to identify the relationships among educational inputs (e.g., instructional interventions, policies) and student achievement indicators (e.g., grades, test scores) are made, resulting in a report of findings, including recommendations and resources, that can guide schools or districts in improvement planning and assessing continuous improvement. Team members also hold a debriefing session with school or district leaders about the report and findings.

THE PROGRESS

The ILA was conducted with the 16 identified high schools. To customize the process for WVDE, ARCC staff examined the criteria established in the WVDE Framework for 21st Century High Schools, key practices from the Enhanced High Schools That Work program, and recommendations from current educational literature and research. Using this information, staff prepared a series of implementation rubrics based on educational practices that align with Edvantia's Framework for Research-Based School Improvement. Staff members developed rubrics for the subjects of most concern to WVDE (mathematics and science), as well as for other areas in which WVDE sought data (literacy, special education, and English language learners). All of the rubrics included research-based practices as well as the instructional practices recommended by the Partnership for 21st Century Skills. During the appraisal, the rubrics were used to determine the extent to which activities in each area were evident in the instructional program.

As a result of ARCC technical assistance, WVDE has a process for appraising instructional practices and identifying challenges to practice in struggling schools. The capacity of WVDE staff members has been enhanced; they are now able to conduct ILAs themselves. WVDE has requested a collaboration with ARCC to develop an online appraisal to facilitate scaling up the process across the state. But the most meaningful outcome of the ARCC technical assistance to WVDE is that schools in need of improvement now receive support from two WVDE staff, the trained specialist, and the representative of the Career and Technical Education division responsible for the Enhanced High Schools That Work program. These WVDE staff use ILA findings to provide technical assistance and support that are better aligned with individual school needs.

Asked about the utility and effectiveness of the ILA, WVDE staff report that the process has increased their capacity to assess schools' instructional programs. Said one WVDE staff member, "The [ILAs] provide [a] research-based framework to identify school needs and develop recommendations for state and county and school to address deficiencies. Our capacity has been increased, and we can now better assist schools in knowing what high-yield structures and strategies to implement and which to abandon." Another reported that the ILA provided "a rubric to follow for strategic planning for improvement" and produced "invaluable information." The effect of resultant improvement work remains to be seen; ARCC staff will continue to evaluate the impact of WVDE assistance to participating schools.

LESSONS LEARNED

The process of collaborating with WVDE to customize an appraisal system and build SEA capacity to conduct appraisals without ARCC assistance proved the value of differentiated state assistance. WVDE needed a unique appraisal process, one aligned with state needs and priorities. Discerning, honoring, and acting upon SEA needs played an important role in encouraging SEA staff to learn and use the appraisal process as their own, and ultimately extend its use across the state.

REFERENCE

Hughes, G.K., & Mittapalli, K. (2005). *Instruction and Learning Appraisal (ILA): Studying the Reliability and Validity of the ILA Process Pilot Test,* Manassas (Virginia) City Schools. April 18–22, 2005. Charleston, WV: Edvantia.

Caitlin Howley *is Associate Director, Appalachia Regional Comprehensive Center (ARCC), Edvantia, Inc.*

CHAPTER 13

FROM COMPLIANCE TO ASSISTANCE

Building Statewide Systems of Support

Barbara Youngren, Jayne Sowers, Gary Appel, and Mark Mitchell

Take three Midwestern states (Indiana, Michigan, and Ohio), each with its own organizational structure for overseeing public education. Charge the state education agencies (SEAs) with implementing provisions of the No Child Left Behind (NCLB) Act so that all districts and schools comply with the requirements. Add a new service provider—Great Lakes East Comprehensive Assistance Center—funded by the U.S. Department of Education. Mix in some educational service agencies that are authorized differently in each state. What do you have?

If you answered "confusion," you would be partially right—but only initially. The better answer is that you have the potential for building a system of support for districts and schools in corrective action and those in need of improvement—a system that moves from a focus on compliance to a focus on assistance. Key is finding a foothold in the existing structure of the SEA

Handbook on Statewide Systems of Support, pages 209–214
Copyright © 2008 The Academic Development Institute and Information Age Publishing
All rights of reproduction in any form reserved.

that enables important work to move forward. Here is the story of how the work of Great Lakes East is unfolding in the state of Indiana.

BACKGROUND AND PROCESS

At Great Lakes East, we determined early on that selecting a single senior staff member to be the "manager" for Great Lakes East work with each one of the states would be the most effective approach. It is through this single point of contact that all work and communication between the state and the center have occurred—an approach that has proven to be invaluable as the work expands and the technical assistance becomes more complex.

In our initial meeting with the state superintendent of public instruction and other key staff members from the various divisions in the Indiana Department of Education (IDOE), we determined that the center's role of assisting IDOE in implementing NCLB would be best realized through the Division of Compensatory Education/Title I. Since this was the division responsible for assisting schools and districts in improvement, "housing" our work here seemed most practical at the time.

However, it soon became apparent that the Division of Compensatory Education/Title I alone could not serve as a "system" of support to districts and schools. The increasing number of schools and districts in need of improvement and the complexity of the NCLB requirements made us realize that we needed to bring other divisions at the SEA into the work. As a result, an underlying informal goal began to emerge in Year 2 of the Great Lakes East work with Indiana: to find, to encourage, and to build participation from other IDOE divisions to work in conjunction with the Division of Compensatory Education/Title I in providing assistance to schools and districts in need of improvement.

This change in emphasis from one based on a division of labor through federal "Title" programs was not going to be easy. It could occur from the top, down—with a complete overhaul of the organizational structure—or it could be nurtured from and through the Title I division with partners from other divisions joining in the work. We are pursuing the latter, hoping eventually to grow the system outward from the SEA to include other potential partners.

As many educational scholars have noted, the roles and responsibilities of state education staff have changed dramatically over the past several years under NCLB, often requiring a reshuffling of workloads, hiring of new staff (which few state budgets allow), and training of current staff in new knowledge and skills. The major focus of our work is the building of new knowledge and skills through a team-based process that emphasizes co-development. Together, IDOE and Great Lakes East staff members brainstorm ideas, set policies and procedures, develop materials, and deliver presentations at district workshops. With each event, Title I staff assume more and more responsibility for assisting those districts in the improvement process.

When our relationship began, IDOE's priority was to provide assistance first to its school districts in corrective action, followed by those in need of improvement. The first year started with nine districts in corrective action—a manageable number. In the second year, an additional eight were added to the list. In an effort to be proactive and provide assistance earlier, the 35 districts in need of improvement were also added—for a total of 52 in 2006–07.

As the workload increased, so did the involvement of Great Lakes East. From working in Indiana a couple of days a month during Year 1, the Great Lakes East manager will spend 8–12 days a month, approaching 50% of her time, in the state during Year 3. The remainder of her time is spent working on technical assistance goals, corresponding several times a day with the SEA, engaged in conference calls with various stakeholders, researching and gathering information, and drafting processes and materials.

Developing policies and processes concerning schools and districts in improvement under NCLB is one of our two major technical assistance goals in Indiana. NCLB's requirements are specific in many ways, and the SEA needed to establish its own set of corresponding policies and, at times, more clearly delineate the processes for the schools and districts to adhere to the policies. A first step often included the Great Lakes East manager surveying other states' processes regarding a specific topic, such as the NCLB sanction selected for districts in corrective action.

In Year 1, gaining information from other states was more difficult than it is today—just 2 years later. In the beginning, personal e-mails to state personnel served as the major means of obtaining information. The responses were limited, however, with most states reporting that they had not yet addressed the issue in question. Now, fortunately, more information about state policies and processes is available each day. The Regional Centers and the Content Centers are beginning to provide summaries of state-developed policies on various NCLB-related requirements. For example, the Center on Innovation & Improvement website is a particularly rich resource for data that is available in a number of downloadable formats. The summaries allow Indiana and all states to benefit from one another's experiences, lessons learned, and challenges faced as all undergo this change in SEA roles and responsibilities.

The second Great Lakes East technical assistance goal in Indiana is to assist in developing and providing technical assistance to the districts. Although pursuing this goal may seem to follow logically after achieving the first goal of developing policies and procedures, we often found the situation reversed—that the need for specific policies and procedures emerged from the technical assistance provided and the responses from the districts. For example, the initial template for writing district improvement plans seemed adequate in that it listed the NCLB-required sections and topics. As the districts submitted their plans, however, it became clear to reviewers that a more rigorous template was needed that would assist the districts in analyzing their student subgroup data, finding and applying research-based practices for each section, and aligning their practices with the student subgroups not making adequate yearly progress.

In reading and evaluating the ever increasing number of improvement plans, the Division of Compensatory Education/Title I is reaching a saturation point and will be actively seeking ways to develop a system of support that extends beyond the state department of education. Districts in corrective action, too, are confronting a similar threshold of capacity as they are required to develop and implement a new curriculum. Realizing the districts' need for assistance in curriculum development, IDOE—with Great Lakes East support—is providing first-time workshops for districts regarding mapping and aligning their curricula. As the numbers of districts in corrective action grows, Great Lakes East will assist IDOE in processes for identifying qualified partners who can provide technical assistance in writing and implementing effective curricula and improvement plans.

In accepting the responsibility to develop a system that focuses on assistance rather than compliance, Indiana has taken steps in building the foundation of such a system. In many states, an additional entity that supports the SEA in serving schools and districts is the educational service agency. In Indiana, there are nine educational service agencies, which are called education service centers (ESCs) and are regionally operated. In addition to the educational service agencies, IDOE will seek other potential partners—at universities, from among retired teachers and administrators, through other providers, and of course, from within its own agency. Great Lakes East and IDOE are focusing on these potential partners in Year 3 of the work, knowing that engaging their assistance will be a process of several years. The work goes beyond simply identifying those educators who have the knowledge and experience to provide assistance to schools and districts. The work must include developing an effective, research-based, and team-based approach of improvement and then training the providers in implementing the approach with fidelity. These providers will become a critical component of Indiana's statewide system of support.

LESSONS LEARNED

As mentioned earlier, finding a foothold in the existing structure of the SEA is key to building systems of support for districts in corrective action and those in need of improvement. From our work in the Midwest, Great Lakes East can offer the following tips for achieving such a foothold:

- Develop and maintain strong, trusting relationships;
- Understand the system's view of the SEA organization and structure, recognizing the advantages and challenges within that system;
- Develop an understanding of the internal and external supports available to the SEA;
- Serve as a critical friend to the SEA.

Develop and Maintain Strong, Trusting Relationships: Outside forces, even when promising to be of assistance, must demonstrate their worth before being accepted. Promises of "I'm here to help" are not enough. It has taken time to demonstrate Great Lakes East's ability to assist its states and as importantly, its trustworthiness. Great Lakes East has learned that allowing time for relationships to develop, and thereby trust to grow is crucial to the continual evolution of the work with the SEA.

Understand the System's view of the SEA organization and structure, recognizing the advantages and challenges within that system: Like school districts, SEAs are complex structures with divisions or departments, systems, procedures, and policies that at the same time promote and impede their ability to get their work done. Most SEAs built a compliance-driven structure in response to the federal and state government funds they received. Just as each state's name for the department that oversees education varies (e.g., Department of Education, Office of Public Instruction, State Board of Education), so does its organizational structure. Understanding and working within that system or structure is a variable in the way a comprehensive center conducts and completes its work.

In Indiana, IDOE's structure is one of multiple divisions that often correspond to a federal funding stream, such as Title I or Title III. Traditionally, the divisions have operated individually with unique requirements, policies, and procedures for schools and districts. Understanding the internal workings of SEAs has been essential to work productively, and also to recognize opportunities for building capacity. A systems view of each SEA builds over time, as each of the state managers develops working relationships with SEA staff and as the work expands and deepens.

Understanding the Internal and External Supports Available to SEAs: For Great Lakes East, our capacity-building mission includes helping SEAs organize and build coherence from existing capacities of their systems. The first step is to determine those supports, both internally and externally. Within SEAs, divisions and departments are often unaware of each others' purposes, funding sources, and services provided to districts and schools. Increasing conversations among SEA divisions to share such information sounds like a simple, initial step. However, it is a complex step that requires persistence and time to delve into deeper questions such as: How can we help states connect the dots in developing systems of support? How do we help SEAs work across divisions and departments to develop more robust and focused systems of support? What changes in organizational structure and culture will enable SEAs to build and sustain strong systems of support?

As to the external supports, the educational service agencies in Indiana—the ESCs—are defined by state statute as extended agencies of the local public school districts—not extensions of the state department of education, as in some states. Without state oversight responsibilities, the ESCs are not collectively available as a means of support, particularly in the absence of SEA authority to dedicate sufficient school improvement set-aside funds to the ESCs. One of the Great Lakes East goals for Year 3 is to help IDOE build a foundation of assistance tapping into the resources available through the ESCs and other partners.

Approaching the Work as a Critical Friend: As SEAs rethink how to move from a traditional compliance orientation and work culture to one that is able to focus resources and support to all districts—especially to those most in need—established boundaries and lines of communication both within the SEAs and with external entities begin to shift. We believe that Great Lakes East adds value to these efforts by working closely with SEA staff without getting caught up in the internal operations. It is by having a systemic understanding of the organization while retaining our role as an external agent that we are able to facilitate building and organizing capacity to address the growing needs of districts and ultimately the students they serve.

More lessons will continue to be learned as we fulfill the remaining years in the original 5-year agreement. The SEAs and Great Lakes East together can do more for students who are struggling than either group can do alone—a noble lesson in itself.

Barbara Youngren *is Director of Great Lakes East Comprehensive Center at Learning Point Associates.*

Jayne Sowers, Gary Appel, *and* **Mark Mitchell** *are Senior Associates at Great Lakes East Comprehensive Center at Learning Point Associates.*

Thanks to **Marianne Kroeger** *at Learning Point Associates for editorial assistance.*

CHAPTER 14

CREATING A VISION
IN NEW JERSEY

Marilyn Muirhead and Ryan Tyler

BACKGROUND

The Mid-Atlantic Comprehensive Center (MACC)—operated by the George Washington University Center for Equity and Excellence in Education, in Washington, DC—provides technical assistance to state educational agencies (SEAs) of Delaware, Maryland, New Jersey, Pennsylvania, and to the District of Columbia Public Schools, which operates as an SEA. In pursuing its mission to build the capacity of these agencies to develop statewide systems of support for districts and schools in need of improvement, MACC, in its work within the SEA, addresses both organizational and individual capabilities. If SEAs are going to shift their focus from making sure districts and schools comply with regulations to providing them assistance that supports needed changes to practice, the capacity of both the SEA organization and the individuals within it will need to be addressed. To help facilitate this shift, MACC focuses on providing assistance to SEAs in three areas: (a) the cultivation of collaborations across SEA programs and divisions; (b) the analysis of data to identify specific district and school needs; and (c) the design of a service delivery system that promotes ongoing, job-embedded professional development; monitors implementation; and evaluates the satisfaction and impact of services

Handbook on Statewide Systems of Support, pages 215–221
Copyright © 2008 The Academic Development Institute and Information Age Publishing
All rights of reproduction in any form reserved.

provided. MACC believes that capacity building in these areas will help SEAs operationalize a system of support that is focused on assisting districts and schools in making needed changes to organizational and individual practices that support high student achievement.

In an effort to provide services that meet the individual needs of its states, MACC has organized its staff into state teams, each lead by a state team coordinator. Each state coordinator is responsible for an ongoing assessment of state needs and meets regularly with the SEA to identify those needs and refine responses to them. State team members provide support and assistance to state coordinators for services provided to the state.

In New Jersey, the MACC–SEA collaboration was accomplished by the formation of a state committee consisting of key SEA staff who are charged with developing and implementing state policies, staff such as the director of the Title I Office for Program Planning and Accountability and the director of the Abbott Division of Student Services, the office formed in order to address the needs of "Abbott districts," the 30 special needs districts designated in the famous 1997 *Abbott v. Burke* case. The strategy of forming a state committee of key SEA staff is aligned with MACC's focus on facilitating collaboration across SEA programs and divisions. This committee meets once a month to discuss how the SEA can support implementation of policy at the district and school levels.

The George Washington University Center for Equity and Excellence in Education has worked with the New Jersey Department of Education (NJDOE) for over 10 years and has built a trusting and collaborative partnership with state committee members. Because of this pre-existing relationship— particularly with middle managers in key policy-making positions—MACC work has progressed, despite changes in senior-level leadership during the 2006–07 school year.

As MACC began work with its states in October 2005, NJDOE was in a state of transition. The interim commissioner of education was conducting an assessment of NJDOE in an effort to determine the mission, roles, capacity, and responsibilities of the agency. The Title I Office was charged with implementing the federal requirements for high-poverty schools and districts, which included the development and implementation of the Title I accountability system. The Abbott Division was responsible for monitoring and providing support to the high-need districts. Since the fall of 2006, the Abbott Division has been slowly integrated into Title I and other NJDOE offices. There have also been changes at the assistant commissioner level as the now-confirmed commissioner continues to refine her organizational vision of NJDOE.

PROCESS AND PROGRESS: THE NJ MACC INITIATIVES

Much of the work of the MACC and its New Jersey team has revolved around issues concerning schools in restructuring and the state's district-level continuous improvement system.

Restructuring Schools. In 2005, the NJDOE was delivering support to schools identified for improvement from two offices—the Title I Office and the Abbott Division. As a collaborative effort, these two offices were deploying school support teams to schools in corrective action and restructuring in order to (a) conduct Collaborative Assessment for Planning and Achievement (CAPA) school reviews; (b) develop a report based on CAPA findings; (c) prioritize needs; and (d) conduct benchmark visits to determine implementation of strategies that address priority needs. These activities coincide with MACC's goal of using data to identify the needs of districts and schools in need of improvement.

The most recent work with NJDOE began in fall 2005 with a request from the Title I Office to assist with reviewing the restructuring plans for the 56 schools that were entering Year 5 of school improvement status. In response, MACC's New Jersey team, Ryan Tyler and Mary Catherine Moran, developed a rubric that described the required components of the restructuring plans, along with explanations of four different performance levels of practice. The Title I staff revised the rubric and used the tool to assess the quality of all 56 plans and provide feedback on approval or revisions.

In addition, the Title I Office and Abbott Division requested that the NJ MACC team provide feedback on the guidance these offices were developing for future restructuring schools. Drawing upon research studies and reports concerned with restructuring schools (including the restructuring documents developed by the Center on Innovation & Improvement), the NJ MACC team assisted with the completion of the restructuring guidance as well with the development of training for the 20 districts where the restructuring schools were located.

Continued discussions with the staffs of the Title I Office and Abbott Division led to the conclusion that while the schools had developed relatively comprehensive and focused improvement plans, the schools would require support in fully implementing the restructuring strategies identified in their plans. To plan for providing the support to these schools, the Title I Office and Abbott Division needed more in-depth information on the practices of the schools. There was also a need to develop a continuous improvement framework to guide the work with the schools. The NJ MACC team assisted the Title I Office in creating a framework based upon the research of Victoria Bernhardt (*Using Data to Improve Student Learning in*

School District, 2006). Therefore, the NJ MACC team partnered with staff of Title I and Abbott Offices in December 2006 to analyze the data from the 2004–05 CAPA reviews for the schools in restructuring, while the schools were completing the follow-up CAPA reviews during the 2006–07 school year. The data from the analysis revealed that many of the schools had established proficient practice in aligning curriculum to state standards, evaluating teachers, using state resources, and developing school leadership plans. However, fewer schools had established proficient practice in those areas more directly connected to instruction, such as collaborating to review student work, using varied instructional strategies, and using multiple and frequent assessments. These results led NJDOE and the NJ MACC team to conclude that the schools needed assistance in integrating specific instructional strategies into teachers' planning and delivery of lessons.

The Title I Office and the NJ MACC team then reviewed the areas of need to identify the priorities for follow-up support to the schools in implementing their restructuring plans. One challenge in proceeding with providing support was to focus on those areas of school practice that were most critical to improving student achievement. The NJ MACC team suggested that the follow-up support to schools be connected to the research on school improvement. Consequently, in February 2007, MACC guided NJDOE through an alignment of the CAPA indicators with the school practices identified in Robert Marzano's *What Works in Schools: Translating Research Into Action*, a literature review of the research on school improvement over the past few decades (Association for Supervision and Curriculum Development, February 2003). The exercise helped to identify what the Title I Office referred to as "power indicators," which are school practices that are most closely correlated with student achievement. The power indicators were identified and grouped into Marzano's five areas of school practice, in order of the impact on student achievement:

- guaranteed and viable curriculum
- challenging goals and effective feedback
- parental and community involvement
- safe and orderly environment
- collegiality and professionalism.

After the power indicators were identified, the NJ MACC team began development of an electronic library of effective practices for each of the power indicators. The Promising Practices library will provide concrete descriptions, tools and resources to guide the development and provision of technical assistance to restructuring schools. The Title I Office believes that, ultimately, all schools and district will benefit from this resource.

District Reform and The New Jersey Quality Single Accountability Continuum.
During the spring of 2007, a new deputy commissioner of education was
hired at NJDOE. This individual was charged with guiding the work with
the restructuring schools and quickly became engaged with Title I Office
and Abbott Division in planning for these schools. The deputy commissioner was also charged with the administration of the New Jersey Quality
Single Accountability Continuum (NJ QSAC), a district-level continuous
improvement system that is based upon a comprehensive review of practice
in five areas:

- program and instruction,
- personnel,
- operations,
- fiscal management, and
- governance.

One of the concerns of the deputy commissioner is that the school improvement efforts of NJDOE may be hindered by the capacity of districts
to internalize and sustain the reforms. Based upon the NJ MACC team's efforts with the restructuring schools, the deputy commissioner has engaged
the NJ MACC team in the planning process to develop a state technical
assistance plan based on the NJ QSAC findings. Initially, NJDOE will train
facilitators to guide districts reviewing the NJ QSAC reports to identify priority areas and action plans with strategies to address the priority areas. The
NJ MACC team is currently assisting NJDOE with developing the content
for training the NJ QSAC team members (facilitators/coaches, content experts, etc.) who will partner with the districts.

RECENT CHANGES AT THE NJDOE

As a result of reorganization under the new commissioner, NJDOE is moving towards a consolidated organizational approach to support districts
and schools. Specifically, three changes have occurred within the NJDOE
in regard to the support provided to districts and schools identified for
improvement. The first affects the organizational structure of NJDOE.
These changes include: (a) the elimination of the Abbott Division and
the formation of a new Division of District and School Improvement, (b)
the renaming of the Office of Strategic Initiatives and Accountability to
the Office of Strategic Planning and Improvement Services, which is now
placed in the Division of District and School Improvement, and (c) the
creation of a new Office of District and School Improvement Services.
Therefore, the deputy commissioner, the Division of District and School

Improvement and the Title I Office will be the main partners of the NJ MACC team as the work proceeds.

Along with these structural changes, NJDOE is making shifts in its outlook on educational policy. One policy shift includes the principle that building district capacity should be the vehicle for providing technical assistance to schools. Previous NJDOE policy on school reform focused more on schools and less on the roles and responsibilities of the districts in supporting schools in the improvement of teaching and learning. The NJ MACC team has provided research and assisted with developing policy for utilizing the district as the unit of change for schools. The NJ MACC team is also a critical supporter of providing districts with support for assessing their needs and developing and implementing district improvement plans that also address the needs of schools.

Through the analysis of the CAPA data, NJ MACC also provided NJDOE with examples of how to use data from school or district needs assessment to identify overall needs and plan for technical assistance. The example of the Promising Practices library shows how the NJDOE can identify effective strategies in critical areas of school and district practice. These strategies will assist state technical assistance providers as they facilitate the development of districts' action plans and allow them to focus on the important activities that will influence the quality of instruction.

MACC believes that these changes are indicators of progress towards operationalizing a statewide system of support for districts and schools identified by NCLB and will facilitate a more consolidated approach.

LESSONS LEARNED

One of the lessons MACC learned from the work with NJDOE is that SEAs need a vision to drive a statewide system of support. In order to do this, MACC often engages DOE staff in discussions about content that will be used to support districts and schools and then assists in the development of tools for SEA technical assistance providers to use as they apply continuous improvement principles. The NJ MACC team has focused on providing practical and concrete application of the theory and research on school and district improvement for SEA staff, which is vital for building their understanding as well as modeling the support they must provide to schools and districts.

In the case of NJDOE, the vision for the work of a statewide system of support was articulated around a continuous improvement framework which includes (a) key steps in the process and (b) specific examples and tools that explain the process for SEA staff. The ultimate goal of the framework is to build the SEA's capacity in each of the steps in the continuous improvement framework.

Another important lesson learned is that an SEA must build the capacity of individual staff—knowledge and skills—around a continuous improvement framework to support the organizational capacity to operationalize a statewide system of support. The one-on-one efforts with the directors of the Title I Office and Abbott Division have helped to build the capacity of the staff throughout both entities to support the overall SEA initiatives. To build organizational capacity to support schools and districts, changes to roles, responsibilities, and the SEA infrastructure also need to occur. In New Jersey, MACC learned that the level of stability at the SEA leadership level affects the SEA's ability to provide aligned and coherent support to districts and schools. Therefore, we must continually build the individual and organizational capacity to sustain the statewide system of support over time.

Marilyn Muirhead *is Associate Director of Field Services at Mid-Atlantic Comprehensive Center, George Washington University Center for Equity and Excellence in Education.*

Ryan Tyler, *is a Senior Research Scientist at George Washington University Center for Equity and Excellence in Education.*

CHAPTER 15

TELLING THE STORY OF IMPROVEMENT IN MISSOURI

Belinda Biscoe, Stan Johnson, Donna Richardson, Ellen Balkenbush, and Patricia Fleming

The story that follows focuses on the Missouri Department of Elementary and Secondary Education (DESE) and its journey in developing its current system of support and making a bold decision during 2006 to redesign dramatically its existing system. DESE wanted to achieve a more seamless delivery system across programs and organizations within and outside the department. In making these changes, DESE also wanted districts to receive quality services and an intensity of support for school improvement across all partners that reflected appropriate communication, coordination, cooperation, and collaboration, resulting in improved student achievement.

How did this journey and the conversation begin? Who joined hands with DESE to guide the visioning, planning, and implementation of the redesign of the statewide system of support? Where is DESE in the process today? Who are the key players in the redesign? What progress have the partners made? What are the anticipated benefits of this bold redesign? What are the lessons learned?

Handbook on Statewide Systems of Support, pages 223–234
Copyright © 2008 The Academic Development Institute and Information Age Publishing
All rights of reproduction in any form reserved.

BACKGROUND

Mid-Continent Comprehensive Center (MC3), operated by the University of Oklahoma College of Continuing Education, supports the state departments of education in Arkansas, Kansas, Missouri, and Oklahoma.

MC3's Service Delivery System: MC3 has an innovative and technologically advanced approach to technical assistance (TA). Its interactive service delivery system is grounded in evidence-based principles of high-quality TA. Key to the success of the model is a seamless TA network that coordinates services across federal, state, and local providers and other partners in education. Its service delivery system is a three-tiered approach that provides differentiated levels of service to states based on their needs: Tier 1 (universal needs), Tier 2 (targeted needs), and Tier 3 (intensive needs). One of the Center's expected outcomes, through its services, is that states in the region will have an expanded, coordinated, and seamless statewide system of support.

MC3's Organizational Structure: MC3's unique staffing arrangements and organizational structure positively impact the Center's ability to engage continually its state departments in ongoing interactions and dialogue. As a result, MC3 works efficiently and effectively with its state education agencies (SEAs) to develop initiatives and other TA services that meet their needs in implementing the requirements of the No Child Left Behind Act (NCLB). In fact, MC3's staffing and organizational structure created the opportunities for conversations between MC3 and DESE that resulted in the ongoing, high-impact initiative on redesigning DESE's state system of support.

In initiating its work with the states, MC3 worked with each commissioner or state superintendent in the region to support the creation of an MC3 State Coordinating Council (SCC) within the SEA. This council works with MC3 to identify needs and to coordinate the center's TA with the SEA. Members of the council include top-level SEA staffs who work to support district and school improvement across divisions and departments. In addition to the SCCs in each state, MC3 has two TA providers dedicated to its state departments, an MC3 TA coordinator and an MC3 TA liaison. The MC3 TA liaison is housed in the state education agency's office and serves as an on-site technical assistance provider who helps to provide or leverage resources through MC3, its partners, consultants, or the Content Centers. The MC3 TA coordinators are housed in Norman at the University of Oklahoma. Technical assistance coordinators in Norman work closely with the embedded TA liaisons to coordinate services, provide outreach that is proactive, and ensure that services reflect needs related to implementing NCLB. This arrangement provides a unique opportunity for MC3 to maintain open lines of communication, have on-site assistance readily available, and to coordinate planning meetings for continually reviewing, evaluating, and adapting, as needed, the TA work plan developed between the SEA and MC3. Each SCC meets with key MC3 staff at least quarterly and as needed with the embedded TA liaison to address emerging needs and to ensure that services have depth, coherence, and timely delivery.

Missouri's Evolution of State Support: The Missouri Department of Elementary and Secondary Education has a comprehensive system of monitoring and accrediting school districts. The requirements of Missouri's accreditation process are stringent and comprehensive, with standards and indicators that meet and exceed those identified by NCLB. Fifteen years ago, the Missouri School Improvement Program (MSIP) was developed. MSIP consists of standards and indicators in three categories: resources, processes, and performance. These three categories are used to measure the quality of a school district. There are 524 school districts operating in Missouri, and in the first three 5-year cycles of MSIP, each district was visited by an on-site review team. The team, usually 10–15 members, consisted primarily of representatives from DESE and practitioners from neighboring districts who reviewed documentation—including questionnaires previously completed by faculty, staff, students, and parents of the visited district—and conducted interviews with the school board, selected faculty, and staff.

In the first three cycles of MSIP, on-site visits were scheduled every 5 years, except for a few exceptionally high-performing districts in the 3rd cycle. Typically, the site visit lasted 2–3 days, and by the end of the 2nd day, the team members reached consensus on their findings and a report was written. That report was submitted to DESE personnel who reviewed it for consistency and accuracy before it was submitted to the Missouri State Board of Education for approval. School districts were awarded accreditation with distinction, full accreditation, provisional accreditation, or unaccredited status based upon the number of standards met.

Federal programs, such as special education, Title I, Title II, Title IV, and vocational education, were reviewed in conjunction with the MSIP on-site review; and state standards and indicators aligned to the federal requirements were integrated into the MSIP review process and final report. Once accreditation status was awarded, DESE assisted district personnel in their development of a Comprehensive School Improvement Plan (CSIP).

Affordable, easily accessed professional development and technical assistance (TA) are provided to districts and schools through the nine Regional Professional Development Centers (RPDCs) located across the state on university and college campuses. The RPDCs house experts in several fields including, but not limited to, the following: special education, migrant English language learners, Reading First, Missouri Assessment Program (MAP, Missouri's standardized test) Regional Instructional Facilitators (MAP RIFs), mathematics instructional specialists, and Select Teachers as Regional Resources (STARRs).

With the onset of the fourth MSIP cycle, and the new NCLB requirements, DESE school improvement staff began to redesign their school review process, shifting from a mostly compliance-oriented system to one of providing technical assistance not only to all districts and schools with a desire for improvement, but also intensely focused technical assistance and support to those districts and schools most in need of improvement. This major paradigm shift has had a domino effect. Fourth cycle accreditation is based solely on performance scores. Accreditation is already established when the on-site review team visits a district or school. Districts are not automatically placed on the 5-year schedule for on-site review but selected for review based on their performance. Reviews are tailored to the needs of districts. If the performance data, for example, shows a weakness in the middle grades, elementary schools and high schools in that district may not be visited. In addition, the way services are delivered after the review teams' visitation reports are completed has also required significant change. Located all over the state, RPDCs are staffed with generally equal resources and distribute their services fairly equally across the region. Schools in greatest need, however, tend to be concentrated in the two urban areas of the state. As 2014 approaches and more schools are identified for intensive services, Missouri recognizes that a more effective and efficient delivery of services and allocation of resources will be critical to meeting the growing demands of districts and schools as they work towards achieving the goals of NCLB.

PROCESS

Opportunity Knocks and the Conversation Begins: According to Paul Reville, president of the Rennie Center for Education Research and Policy, an independent policy organization dedicated to the improvement of Pre-K–12 public education, and a scientific advisor for the Center on Innovation & Improvement (CII), one of the key components of a well crafted system of support is professional development that supports development of communities of practice and ongoing embedded professional development focused on student achievement. At a conference sponsored by the New England Comprehensive Center, January 24, 2007, Reville, in his presentation, cited DESE's Regional Professional Development Centers as an example of an SEA offering professional development to local teachers and other school staffs by partnering with Regional Centers.

Despite what appeared to be an ideal state system of support, staffs in both DESE and the RPDCs were frustrated with the workings of the existing system. In the fall of 2005, MC3's initial planning meeting with the SCC provided an environment for reflection on professional development and school improvement initiatives within DESE. Although the SEA did not specifically ask for assistance with this challenge, it was clear through the needs sensing process that MC3 conducted with DESE that most of the discussion found its way back to the need for more consistency between professional development and improvement initiatives. It was also clear that although the core components of a state system of support existed, it was apparent that players within the system, for example, SEA and RPDC staffs, consultants, and support teams, were all operating autonomously. Everyone was voicing the need to attend better to the four levels of networking—the "4 Cs," communication, coordination, cooperation, and collaboration—between and among the partners about their school improvement efforts. Creating this kind of integrated and seamless system of support could avoid duplication of effort, maximize limited resources, and net improved student outcomes.

Joining Hands With DESE: During this part of the discussion at the initial SCC meeting, the director of MC3 offered to convene all the partners for an initial "Taking Stock Retreat" to provide a forum for DESE's leadership team to begin a dialogue about how to foster collaboration and align efforts across state school improvement initiatives. As MC3 and DESE designed the work plan for the 1st year of technical assistance services, a major focus would be in supporting DESE to create a climate for change, with the result being a stronger collaborative network across the state in the delivery of school improvement initiatives. MC3 conducted numerous planning meetings with Missouri's SCC—meetings which included the state's director of federal programs, a representative from one of the RPDCs, and the director of school improvement support—to identify participants for the first retreat and to garner support and approval from the commissioner.

MC3 and Its Regional Content Center Partner: The national Content Center on Innovation & Improvement was invited by MC3 to be involved in this journey. The center director, Sam Redding, participated in the planning of the first 2-day retreat and offered input on effective systems of support to help guide the discussion during the retreat, which was facilitated by the director of MC3. The Mid-Continent Comprehensive Center became the partner that began working with DESE to create a vision, a plan, and strategies to guide the redesigning of its state system of support.

Retreat 1 on Taking Stock: The first 2-day retreat was held in Jefferson City in July of 2006. The retreat opened with a report from the DESE director of school improvement support. Her presentation of the data on school improvement initiatives in each school highlighted some of the issues related to potential gaps, overlaps, and duplication among providers in school improvement efforts. During the course of the 2 days, the 15 participating stakeholders explored challenges and solutions to collaboration, completed a "vision walk" that included an analysis of relationships, processes, resources, practices, accountability, and mechanisms needed to bolster the ideal state system of support. Participants identified strengths and weaknesses in DESE's current TA efforts and developed strategies to address perceived weaknesses and to build on strengths of the existing system. As a culminating activity, participants synthesized outcomes from the 2 days to draft recommendations to the commissioner.

Retreat participants selected three of their peers to represent them in a meeting to share recommendations with the commissioner. This conversation occurred in early fall of 2006. Two key recommendations were (a) to create a cross-divisional team that refines and strengthens DESE's system of support to assist all districts, proactive/general support and information (e.g., on effective practices) for districts meeting state and federal mandates, targeted support for program improvement districts, and intensive support for provisionally accredited and unaccredited districts; and (b) to include a networking goal within DESE's strategic plan that includes the 4 Cs in the action steps.

Within the first recommendation were several action steps. One advised creating a "case management" model for provisional or unaccredited districts at different stages of improvement, a model that stipulated representation from the district, from all DESE divisions, the RPDCs, and other representative partners, all of whom would work together to develop the district improvement plan. Another action step sought to establish a unit within DESE to serve as a clearinghouse for proposed school improvement initiatives; this unit would assess the relevance and "fit" of initiatives with other school improvement efforts in a district.

Although the commissioner supported the recommendations, retirements and other changes in DESE delayed implementation. MC3 continued to provide other services delineated in the work plan, but at every turn the conversation would return to the need for a seamless more collaborative statewide system of support. During a professional development session for the RPDCs and DESE on scientifically based research, this issue once again surfaced. Therefore, the last 2 hours during this professional development event were devoted to identifying strategies for moving the recommendations from the first retreat forward. After facilitated dialogue with participants, it was evident that the first retreat did not include a sufficient number of stakeholders involved in the school improvement process who represented diverse perspectives and who had the authority to enact a course of action. Based on the need to have more stakeholders represented, MC3 proposed a Taking Stock Retreat 2 to widen the circle of participants and ownership for the needed redesign of the state system of support. Recommendations were made to involve over 50 educational stakeholders from DESE, the RPDCs, including regional supervisors, and others in the second retreat. The second retreat was held in May of 2007 in Columbia, Missouri, and was attended by approximately 50 stakeholders.

Immediately following the training in the use of scientifically based research, DESE and RPDC leaders began planning collaboratively with MC3 and the Center on Innovation & Improvement to create a framework for the next retreat. The first meeting for the Taking Stock 2 Planning Committee began in February of 2007 to continue work started in July of 2006. An intensive 3 months of planning through teleconferencing and a few face-to-face meetings were devoted to designing the second 2-day retreat. In addition, the planning committee expected, during this retreat, that stakeholders and partners would clarify their roles and responsibilities within this system of support. It is important to note that the deputy commissioner and all the assistant commissioners attended the retreat, and that the commissioner participated in aspects of the retreat, offering both his encouragement and endorsement for redesigning the system.

Retreat 2 on Taking Stock: This retreat was hosted and facilitated by MC3 with significant participation and involvement from the Center on Innovation & Improvement. The second retreat was convened to provide a forum to develop a common understanding of how DESE's statewide system of support needs to function to fulfill better its intended purpose and recommend changes to realize the identified needs. Several intended outcomes were proposed:

1. creation of a common understanding of the components of the current state system of support and how these function;
2. clarification of roles and responsibilities of service providers, both what is and what needs to be;
3. identification of barriers impeding the operation of a seamless system, with recommendations for overcoming these hindrances;
4. identification of consistent processes for determining commonly agreed upon effective, evidence-based practices, programs, and strategies; determination of who is responsible for delivery and providing support roles;
5. development of mechanisms that ensure commitment to the 4 Cs between and among all service providers; and
6. articulation of next steps to (a) invite feedback from end users regarding retreat outcomes, and (b) implement recommended new directions.

The retreat opened with the DESE director of school improvement support providing a brief review of activities over the past year that resulted in this second retreat, including the July 2006 retreat and subsequent steps to encourage collaboration. Several presenters from DESE and MC3 made comments to provide context for the 2-day retreat. In particular, the MC3 TA coordinator reviewed the four levels of networking, mentioned above, which MC3 proposed in its original grant application. She stressed the importance of using this framework during the 2-day retreat to help guide the discussion and to frame the recommendations.

The director of the Center on Innovation & Improvement, Sam Redding, played a critical role in setting the stage and general context for understanding the national impetus for building the capacity of state systems of support. He delivered a PowerPoint presentation to establish a common base of understanding among the retreat attendees concerning research on state systems of support and to prepare these stakeholders for a critical analysis of their own system. Participants then worked in small groups to identify barriers to creating a seamless system of support and to develop recommendations for achieving such a system. Among their recommendations are the following:

1. Restructure scope of work/priorities for DESE programs within RPDCs to allow more regional decision-making authority by the RPDCs in their work with districts and schools.
2. Figure out ways to reallocate and combine funding streams and create flexibility in how funds can be applied to school improvement priorities.
3. Leave days open on calendar for work with priority schools.
4. Align meeting schedules to facilitate the 4 Cs.
5. Align the nine RPDC regions with Missouri's 10 area supervisor regions. RPDCs and area supervisors would have common regions, thereby reducing scheduling and coordination conflicts for school districts working with RPDCs and area supervisors.
6. Continue periodic meetings of the MC3 group (from the second retreat) to foster the 4 Cs.
7. Change the focus of the educational support system from a focus on low-performing schools to a focus on students.
8. Develop a responsibility chart for school support teams to include benchmarks, accountability measures, and resources provided for program improvement for districts and schools.
9. Use FTEs more efficiently by focusing greater effort on districts with the greatest needs.
10. Recognize the value of different perspectives.
11. Provide common professional learning opportunities.
12. Train all DESE and RPDC staff on the same strategies and topics to create broad expertise, common mental models, and a collaborative environment.
13. Use MSIP needs and evidenced-based best practices to shape the professional development agenda.
14. Ensure setting aside fiscal resources for this to occur.

15. Work toward equitable salaries for the DESE to recruit and maintain highly qualified staff.

In addition to these recommendations, the participants at the retreat identified several barriers to establishing a seamless system of support. Two examples of barriers were (a) uncertainty about who has ultimate responsibility for the statewide system of support and (b) program boundaries that create silos that hinder collaboration between DESE and within and across the RPDCs. To address these barriers, participants reached consensus on important short-term and long-term action steps:

1. Create a statewide leadership team and clarify its roles, internal operations, communication mechanisms, and governance, and ensure that the right people are at the table.
2. Evaluate and fine-tune programs and services, including the elimination of programs that are not effective and appropriate.
3. Work with the RPDC director and DESE staff to ensure that RPDC directors are designated as the regional authority for making decisions about committing resources contracted through the RPDCs (funds, personnel, etc.) to serve schools at the district level for districts determined as priority districts.
4. Designate the Division of School Improvement as the coordinator of all DESE's school improvement initiatives that are part of the Missouri statewide system of support to all schools.

On the final day of the retreat, the deputy commissioner appointed the initial members of the newly constituted leadership team, and a memorandum affirming this and the other action steps was to be forthcoming from the commissioner. The other recommendations to further enhance Missouri's statewide system of support were to be considered by the then newly appointed leadership team and, potentially, by the commissioner.

PROGRESS

To date, action steps one, three, and four generated at the second retreat have been accomplished.

The commissioner sent a letter of support to the appropriate individuals announcing the creation of the leadership team and other outcomes from the retreat. The leadership team has been charged with the responsibility for coordinating all services provided to schools in need of improvement and enhancing communication between DESE, the RPDCs, and the area supervisors. The team convened its first meeting on July 17, 2007, and is generating recommendations for the process of evaluating and eliminating ineffective programs (action step number two, above). A calendar for leadership team meetings has been published with protocols for communicating and coordinating events and meetings. The summary report from the Missouri Taking Stock Retreat 2 has been used as a priority guide for the team to address short-term and long-term goals. This report, prepared by the leadership team in July to document its progress, was submitted by the assistant commissioner of the Division for School Improvement and presented to stakeholders who attended the Taking Stock 2 Retreat at a meeting following the annual back-to-school conference convened by the commissioner on August 7, 2007. The assistant commissioner of the Division for School Improvement has been appointed as the official contact for the leadership team and the stakeholders.

The process for evaluating programs will be studied, and the catalog of school improvement and professional development programs will be revised by DESE leadership. Because MSIP provides some type of support to all of Missouri's schools according to their needs, the RPDCs are now collectively focusing on the issues of school improvement and professional development. A unified contract is being developed for the RPDCs, and direct jurisdiction over the operations and functions of the nine RPDC will fall under the Division of School Improvement, a systemic change to be fully implemented by FY 2009. These changes represent a dramatic shift in the way future business will be conducted.

On July 30, 2007, following its first meeting earlier in July, the leadership team provided retreat participants a summary of the team's first meeting via e-mail. The leadership team also began exploring the second retreat's recommendations as a preliminary step to advancing them to them to the assistant commissioner of school improvement.

In general, the retreats organized by MC3 and the resulting recommendations and action steps, in particular the timely establishment of the leadership team, have initiated and continued to move forward Missouri's redesign effort. In looking at what has been accomplished and what is now possible in enhancing the operation of the statewide system of support, MC3 expects that:

- DESE will obtain a better return on its investment for school improvement dollars, as evidenced by improved teaching and learning as well as fewer unaccredited program improvement districts.
- DESE will take stock of what is needed and avoid "activity traps." (Needs will be aligned with proposed programs, services, resources, and outcomes.)

- DESE will be able to allocate resources more strategically, effectively, and efficiently.
- The resulting collaboration will generate synergy that results in a cross-fertilization of ideas, new approaches, and out-of-the-box thinking.

LESSONS LEARNED

DESE's road to school improvement is affording opportunities for both the SEA and TA providers to learn valuable lessons about how multiple, complex, systems come together to create strategies and opportunities to impact teaching and learning. Some of the lessons learned follow.

1. In planning services for state departments of education, TA providers should use all of their senses to determine needs, both spoken and unspoken. Often SEAs are experiencing challenges but may be uncertain about how to translate these into services a comprehensive center might provide. It is through both formal and informal meetings and conversations that opportunities emerge for TA providers to design and provide creative approaches to problem solving. It is important to be proactive.
2. Significant change can occur within a relatively short period of time if efforts have been made to garner involvement and commitment from a critical mass of stakeholders, in particular those who are decision makers. Although DESE's redesign effort appeared to lose momentum, once all the key players were at the table, progress and change began to occur with rapidity. The current redesign effort for DESE should continue gaining momentum with the buy-in garnered from diverse systems and key leaders.
3. Overcoming barriers is a normal part of the process. The question that TA providers must always ask is, "Are there legitimate ways to help the SEAs remove the barriers by looking inwardly for solutions and by having them think creatively and outside of the box?"
4. Involving the expertise of a Content Center where there is depth of knowledge on a particular topic can move the work more quickly because the critical issues can be readily identified, and the best research and evidence-based practices can be shared with the SEA in a timely manner.
5. Factors that supported collaboration included recognition of a common goal; identification of common benefits, strong leadership

for the collaboration effort; key players who share beliefs; characteristics, and commitment to the process; an openness to problem solving; and broad-based representation.

Belinda Biscoe *is assistant vice president, College of Continuing Education, and director, Mid-Continent Comprehensive Center, at the University of Oklahoma.*
Stan Johnson, *is assistant commissioner, Missouri Department of Elementary and Secondary Education, Division for School Improvement.*
Donna Richardson *is associate director, Mid-Continent Comprehensive Center, at the University of Oklahoma.*
Ellen Balkenbush, *is the Missouri embedded technical assistance liaison, Mid-Continent Comprehensive Center, at the University of Oklahoma.*
Patricia Fleming, *is the Missouri technical assistance coordinator, Mid-Continent Comprehensive Center, at the University of Oklahoma.*

CHAPTER 16

WORKING SMA-TAH, NOT HA-DAH IN NEW HAMPSHIRE

Adam E. Tanney

Could the New England Comprehensive Center (NECC) help the New Hampshire Department of Education (NHDOE) improve its statewide system of support (SSOS) for schools? That was the question Carol Keirstead, director of the New England Comprehensive Center, had just been asked by a NHDOE leader on the phone one morning in late January 2006.

In March of 2006, the U.S. Department of Education would make a Title I monitoring visit to New Hampshire, and certain NHDOE leaders believed the state's SSOS would fall below full compliance. If it did, it would not be from a lack of effort. A host of industrious state activities related to SSOS could be found. New Hampshire was intent on fully complying with federal requirements, but it wasn't just federal compliance pressure compelling New Hampshire to seek help. The department was struggling to articulate a theory of action behind its efforts and a strategy that connected its many individual activities. With a growing cadre of schools identified for improvement, districts struggling with influxes of English language learners, and a national mood urging state education agencies (SEAs) to add support to

Handbook on Statewide Systems of Support, pages 235–243

their monitoring role, New Hampshire recognized the need to improve and coordinate its system.

Over the next 18 months, four themes would emerge and guide NECC's work with New Hampshire's SSOS: (a) using research-based models to organize thought and action, (b) thinking systemically about all elements to create coherence and improve efficiency of action, (c) enhancing communication practices, and (d) leveraging institutional authority to generate necessary resources.

BACKGROUND

NECC's work is comprised of regional initiatives that serve all six New England states as a whole as well as several state-specific initiatives. Since its funding award in 2005, NECC—operated by RMC Research Corporation, in partnership with The Education Alliance at Brown University; Education Development Center, Inc.; and Learning Innovations at WestEd—has worked with none of its six states more intensively and collegially than it has worked with New Hampshire. The close connection between the two organizations can be attributed to a good relationship between the NHDOE commissioner, Lyonel Tracy, and NECC, as well as a long-term collaboration between the staff members from both organizations, established well before 2005.

One of NECC's state-specific initiatives in New Hampshire seeks "to collaborate with NHDOE...to define a school support system that is comprehensive, coherent, builds on existing systems, and integrates federal programs and state initiatives." Several factors have carved a NHDOE structure that has contributed to New Hampshire's SSOS needs. Like other SEAs, NHDOE's structure came to its current configuration before NHDOE had taken on augmented expectations to support, not just monitor, school improvement. The NHDOE structure, therefore, tends to reflect a dedication to ensuring accountability to various federal and state funding streams. A tradition of local control in New Hampshire has also kept the total resource allocation to NHDOE low.

The NHDOE is currently organized into three major divisions: the Division of Instruction, the Division of Program Support, and the Division of Career Technology and Adult Learning. Each division is subdivided into bureaus and offices providing specific services. Bureaus with functions pertaining to a statewide system of support, however, lie within each, not just one, of the three divisions. For instance, the Office of Educational Technology, which helps schools integrate technology into teaching and learning, lies under the Division of Instruction. Meanwhile, the Bureau of Information Services, which manages and analyzes educational data, rests within the Division of Program Support. Nonetheless, at the outset of NECC's work, the department had solely tasked its School Improvement Team with supporting districts and schools in need of improvement. In other words, despite other bureaus performing work that an ideal SSOS relies on, only the School Improvement Team was considered responsible for SSOS.

PROCESS

On February 1, 2006, when NECC convened its first formal meeting with the NHDOE school improvement group to address SSOS, it wasn't the first time New Hampshire had attempted to systematize its support to schools. In response to the 1994 re-authorization of Elementary and Secondary Education Act, NHDOE had tried to improve coordination of its field providers. But the commissioner's unexpected resignation brought a halt to the incipient redesign effort. Gary Guzouskas, NHDOE school improvement administrator, summarized the situation: "We've done a variety of things over the years...but we've never had a formalized structure."

Accordingly, NECC observed that supports to districts and schools in need of improvement were not coordinated across bureaus and divisions, resulting in a fragmented approach to school improvement. The state offers an array of professional development opportunities, but not, however, aligned systematically to the improvement needs of districts and schools. In preparation for the March 2006 monitoring visit, NHDOE asked NECC to explain the NCLB compliance requirements and articulate what New Hampshire had in place. But NECC wanted to do more than that, "We offered them ways to meet compliance and go beyond merely listing activities to begin building a comprehensive plan," says Keirstead.

Initially, though, an accounting of school support efforts was a key to getting NHDOE to think systemically. At the February 2006 meeting, NECC and NHDOE brainstormed a list of all the services available to all New Hampshire schools, not just those identified by the department and not just for schools in need of improvement. The result was an assembly of 16 programs and services, which, upon analysis, revealed uncertain purposes and interconnections. State participants took away from this activity a heightened awareness that (a) New Hampshire is expending tremendous effort to support schools, (b) that a SSOS should leverage existing efforts that fall outside strict in-need-of-improvement boundaries, and (c) that "there is a lot of redundancy in the system," as one participant flatly stated.

As the SSOS work got underway, NECC was involved in a separate but integrally related initiative with NHDOE. The New Hampshire Alignment and Coordination Project had the goal of collaborating with department leaders to coordinate and align department activities, particularly with respect to monitoring, professional development, financial oversight, and account-ability. Deputy Commissioner Mary Heath recognized that NHDOE needed to open up communication between divisions and knew that improving communication would bolster achievement of the department's entire mission, including support to struggling schools and districts. Consequently, as NECC moved forward assisting NHDOE with technical aspects of SSOS, it attended to modeling effective communication skills in its interactions. NECC ensured meetings always had agendas, facilitated them to enhance time on task and to ensure time to assess what did and did not work before participants dispersed. At a meeting's beginning, someone was explicitly identified to record follow-up tasks, while assurance was made that notes and tasks were recorded in one place and would be e-mailed to all participants later. Moreover, NECC tried to be explicit about these practices and their importance, sharing NECC's internal codified communications "norms" when they became available.

Work devoted to SSOS began with the head of each of the NHDOE divisions, along with other staff members, joining in cross-divisional conversations. For one meeting, NECC project principals, Karen Laba and Joe Trunk, invited 35 NHDOE staff members to share their monitoring tools. Laba and Trunk then organized the tools on a large matrix, providing staff a visual sense of the overlapping responsibilities within the department. Although staff members were visiting the same places, they were often looking at different things—school plumbing and insulation versus school textbooks and curricula. Reluctantly, the group concurred that little consolidation of monitoring visits was possible. While the effort didn't merge many activities, it did bear fruit. Before the NECC meeting, NHDOE staff stored their monitoring tools in disassociated places. Laba, Trunk, and the NHDOE team took action to warehouse the different tools in a centralized database on the state website.

January 2007 Regional Meeting and Follow-Up

While NECC was working intensively with New Hampshire, it was also supporting a regional SSOS effort for all New England states. On January 24, 2007, NECC convened a 1-day regional meeting on SSOS in Framingham, MA. Representatives from across New England assembled to examine research, hear from experts and peers, and confront problems of practice. A number of researchers and experts presented current information on SSOS, including resources and expertise provided by the Center on Innovation & Improvement (CII). NECC strives to anchor its technical assistance in research, yet employ frameworks that busy policymakers can apply. NECC found a framework with the right blend of robustness and utility when it asked NECC Advisory Board member Paul Reville to create an evidence-based model on the components of an effective statewide system of support.[1] Reville also entreated participants to found their SSOS efforts on theories of action (collective beliefs about why certain actions will lead to a desired outcome) and coherent strategies to service their theories of action. NECC would draw upon this entreaty many times in the upcoming months.

New Hampshire was well represented by roughly a dozen staff members across all divisions at the meeting. After hearing presentations from experts and dialoguing with peers across states, participants met in state-specific teams. With Reville's petitions about establishing a theory of action fresh in mind, the New Hampshire team went to work, discussing actions needed to develop its SSOS. Keirstead facilitated the meeting to ensure avid discussion was not the only outcome, but also that the conversation followed communications norms and the group delineated follow-up commitments. The group's commitments included:

- the development of a theory of action on which to found a state system of support driven by purpose and focus,
- the continued efforts to integrate NHDOE activities in support of school improvement,
- the use of New Hampshire's existing tools and practices as part of the system of support, and
- the comparison of the framework provided by Paul Reville with New Hampshire's conceptual framework to identify alignment and gaps.

The meeting had two other key outcomes. First, the presenters' exhortations to systematize supports resonated with New Hampshire and reinforced for NHDOE participants, in view of the earlier technical assistance provided by NECC, that they already had a lot in place. They also recognized that much work remained to be done. Second, the cross-state conversations enabled the New Hampshire group to see it wasn't alone in its struggles; it didn't have to shy away from public conversations for fear of exposing weaknesses.

The follow-up to the January 24th meeting didn't progress as smoothly as NECC had hoped. Twice in March, NECC staff visited the department and twice had "off-focus meetings," fueled by individual frustrations. At the second meeting, some participants stated that unless top department authority gave a clear signal of commitment, they were not continuing. The resistance was understandable. With plenty of responsibilities imposing immediate deadlines, it was hard for NHDOE staff to invest in work sure to consume time but uncertain to secure value from supervisors, let alone improve policy. As one NECC staff member put it, "They've tried with the best efforts to systematize before and it never got to implementation, so people are rightfully a little cynical."

Emotional swells brought the group to an impasse during the second March meeting. Keirstead, who was co-facilitating, called for a break and found deputy commissioner Heath in her office. Heath confirmed she would make SSOS a department-wide initiative, and Keirstead carried the message back to the group. The disquiet abated, and NHDOE and NECC scheduled a meeting that would join top department authorities alongside staff members from across divisions in a working session on SSOS.

Commitment Realized, May 2007

Fifteen NHDOE staff, including the commissioner and Mary Heath, joined four NECC staff at RMC Research's Portsmouth, NH, office on May 25, 2007, for an all-day meeting that would see all four of NECC's technical assistance themes play out.

The meeting intentionally embodied the communication protocols NECC had been modeling throughout the SSOS engagement, including a pre-circulated agenda and goals for the day sent to all participants. Nick Hardy, the NECC's project co-leader, led a discussion on the proffered goals, with NHDOE staff offering refining comments. Joe Trunk led NHDOE staff in generating meeting norms for which participants agreed to hold each other accountable. NECC structured the remainder of the meeting to address six essential questions that NHDOE would discuss:

1. Why does New Hampshire need a coherent statewide system of support?
2. What is New Hampshire's theory of action for a statewide system of support?
3. What are the components of a well-crafted comprehensive statewide system of support?
4. What is in place in New Hampshire?
5. What capacities need to be developed?
6. What are the gaps?

One NECC staff member kept public notes at all times on chart paper while another facilitated the discussion.

For question four, NECC led a 4-step activity that mirrored the activity from February 2006, when NECC had invited state education officials to list all the activities in operation that relate to SSOS. This would be May 25th's defining event. First, NECC asked all participants to brainstorm programs New Hampshire once had in place, currently had in place, or planned to have in place. Second, NECC isolated the "current activities" and clustered those according to their correspondence to Reville's seven components. Third, participants formed small groups and used a 4-point scale to rate how the state was implementing each component. Fourth, NECC charted the ratings and solicited objective observations, not normative judgments, about the data.

The activity achieved a small breakthrough, representing the first time that this group had met at once on SSOS issues. NECC credits the success to crafting the meeting in a way that recognized the ardent work New Hampshire was performing, rather than approaching state efforts from a deficit model. The emphasis on observable facts, not on normative judgments, also paid dividends. "It empowered everyone to be more open by taking the personalization of 'that's my program' out of the discussion," said Nick Hardy.

Participants went on to craft a theory of action—fashioning a collective belief about why doing the work they planned would cause schools to improve. Though they didn't finish their theory and didn't resolve technical changes to their SSOS, NECC witnessed the NHDOE's disposition shift. Designed to create momentum for a follow-up, the meeting demonstrated to participants that a SSOS presents problems too complex to be solved by any single person in any single meeting.

PROGRESS AND LESSONS LEARNED

A few highlights from what NECC and NHDOE have learned and the progress NHDOE has made warrant attention.

Using models. "We keep bringing people back to what research and models have to say," says Keirstead. "Because improving districts and schools is difficult and urgent, if we're going to make an impact, we have to rely on what works." Organizing New Hampshire's activities according to Reville's components and endeavoring to codify a theory of action represent progress in putting models in the service of action.

Improving communication. Although NECC has been didactic in presenting some SSOS strategies, such as taking a tiered approach to school intervention, its emphasis has been on capacity building, modeling an approach New Hampshire needed to get started and to sustain itself. Nick Hardy explains that by engaging NHDOE in work it didn't feel it could do, but now is doing, it has a greater sense of self-efficacy and will be able to do more on its own. Deb Wiswell, NHDOE administrator for accountability, concurs, "The facilitation and planned meetings NECC has brought have gotten people together to raise the discussion to another level." Mary Heath believes the way NHDOE does business is changing, which, she says, is a bigger issue than SSOS.

The alignment work led NHDOE staff to commit to quarterly cross-divisional meetings. The May meeting established that NHDOE would regularly place SSOS on its own meeting agendas.

Leveraging institutional authority. The fact that deputy commissioner Heath and the commissioner committed to and then attended the May 25th meeting gave great impetus to and sanctioned the SSOS effort. Nick Hardy credited the deputy commissioner and commissioner, "They were there for the entire day. The commissioner did a good job accepting the fact that all voices are heard in the room and bringing people back to task. The collaboration of key figures—the commissioner, deputy commissioner, division directors—with program administrators and consultants and other staff not only achieved a consensus on what to do but also the sanction to do it," according to Deb Wiswell. Gary Guzouskas believes that the idea of a coordinated system has now achieved buy-in further up the organizational ladder.

Thinking systemically. NHDOE has come to understand that discrete parcels of support given directly to individual schools are no longer adequate. Furthermore, the department is gaining the ability to see issues more systemically and address them more strategically. "We're a small organization with limited resources," Heath explains. "The funds given to us have not been adequate to meet the demands brought by federal legislation. Thus, we have to think smarter. We're not all the way there yet, but we are thinking differently. There's been a paradigm shift." New Hampshire is beginning to look for the existing resources that may lie outside the department. "What has caused us to miss in the past is that everyone is working feverishly, and you sometimes forget to make connections," explains Guzouskas. Keirstead points to the January regional meeting as a catalyst for reflective, systemic thinking. "Instead of just being focused on individual tools and techniques, they were focused on a statewide system of support," she says. In fact, New Hampshire has made discernible inroads of late.

As NHDOE tries to integrate SSOS efforts, it has brought the Title I and Special Education Offices to work with the School Improvement and Accountability Offices. This has created a "little better system" thus far says Deb Wiswell. The NHDOE admits that it still has three types of state-sponsored school improvement coaches, "But now we talk to each other about the particular roles and how districts can access them," says Wiswell. An effort is underway to join school approval with school improvement, examining how to avoid separate school visits and align work. Aligning program funding streams has been another recent endeavor. Follow the Child Leadership Institute in July 2007, co-funded by special education and school improvement funds, saw both a review of participant applications and agenda planning accomplished by collaboration across the department.

NHDOE is thinking beyond mere compliance to envision an integrated departmental approach that leverages a spectrum of existing resources within and outside of the department. Acknowledging that such an approach will require new skills and ways of thinking which aren't "package deliverable," the NHDOE personnel know they will have to learn. The staff at NECC hopes to keep enabling that learning.

NOTE

1. To hear an audio transcript of Reville's presentation, view his slides, and view the slides of the other presenters visit http://www.necomprehensivecenter. org/events/SSSforum1_07

Adam E. Tanney *is a research associate at RMC Research Corporation, New England Comprehensive Center.*

CHAPTER 17

BUILDING RELATIONSHIPS IN TEXAS

K. Victoria Dimock

BACKGROUND

The Texas Comprehensive Center (TXCC) is organized to provide technical assistance and support to the Texas Education Agency (TEA) and the Texas statewide system of support to assure Texas has an education system with the capacity and commitment to eliminate achievement gaps and enable all students to achieve at high levels. Housed in Austin, Texas, at SEDL, a non-profit corporation focused on education research, development, and dissemination, the TXCC provides technical assistance and professional development to build capacity at two levels of the Texas system of support: the state level and the regional level. In initiating its work, TXCC staff met with the leadership of the TEA to present a plan of work and negotiate an agreement. The center staff also met with the executive directors of the Regional Education Service Centers (ECSs), with which TXCC had proposed to partner.

Texas Education Agency: The work of the TXCC with TEA is led by a state liaison, who collaborates closely with the staff of the TEA's Division of No Child Left Behind (NCLB) Program Coordination. This TXCC staff member, who has a long history of working with TEA and serving on statewide

Handbook on Statewide Systems of Support, pages 245–251

committees and boards, builds on those past relationships in her work with TEA staff. In monthly meetings with TEA staff, the director of the TXCC and the state liaison discuss needs identified by the TXCC and by TEA. The state liaison facilitates these discussions and helps the state focus on potential activities that the TXCC staff can conduct to support TEA in meeting those needs. She then identifies particular staff members and resources available to work on the activities agreed upon during these meetings. At times, she serves as a sounding board for ideas. At other times, she arranges for technical assistance from other agencies, such as the national Content Centers.

Statewide System of Support: The Texas statewide system of support is comprised of four entities: TEA, the School Improvement Resource Center (SIRC), the Statewide School Support/Parent Involvement Initiative (SSS/PII), and the 20 regional ESCs. The TXCC works with all of these entities to build capacity to meet the purposes and goals of NCLB. Each entity serves a distinct function in working with districts and schools across the state. The TEA provides technical assistance directly to each of the other three agencies. Figure 1, developed by TEA in collaboration with the TXCC, illustrates what each entity does and with which schools. The SSS/PII works primarily with "potential schools," schools that fail to achieve adequate yearly progress (AYP) under NCLB for the first time. The SIRC works with those schools that are in the various stages of school improvement. The ESCs work with all schools within their respective regions of the state. The work of each of these entities is organized to build the capacity of schools by improving leadership, instruction, and, ultimately, student outcomes.

In the prelude to the TXCC initiating its work, the Texas Education Agency (TEA) requested that the center also work with "potential schools." As subsequently constituted, the Regional Comprehensive Centers do not work directly with schools, and the TXCC therefore focused its work to increase the capacity of staff of the ESCs, who then work directly with potential schools to assist them in school improvement efforts.

Starting school improvement work before a school enters NCLB school improvement status is an example of the proactive approach Texas designed for providing technical assistance to schools and districts through the statewide system of support. Beginning the first year a school does not make AYP, SSS/PII provides information resources and professional development for these potential schools. Once a school enters stage one of school improvement, the Texas School Improvement Resource Center selects a technical assistance provider to work with the school to develop an improvement plan. In addition, the ESCs provide professional development to all the schools in their regions, with targeted assistance provided to Title I schools in improvement.

PROCESS

As the TXCC began its operations, two hurricanes, Katrina and Rita, struck the Gulf Coast. The work of the TXCC was immediately focused on the issues raised by these disasters. Thousands of students from Louisiana enrolled in Texas schools, and numerous schools and communities on the upper Texas coast were devastated. In meetings with TEA staff, a comparison of Texas and Louisiana standards and regulations was identified as a major need. In collaboration with the U.S. Department of Education's regional educational laboratory, then housed at SEDL, the TXCC staff assumed the task of conducting a comparative analysis of the state standards for Texas and Louisiana in every content area and at every grade level. The standards were presented in parallel columns that allowed educators in both states to search for a specific grade level standard and find the related standard for the other state. Quick Guides were created that highlighted the key similarities and differences. Training sessions were then provided for ESC staff to provide them with these tools that could be used to assist schools in understanding what Louisiana students were to have learned at each grade level. In addition, tools to support the work of the ESCs to help schools, parents, and families provide for the emotional needs of students were adapted from materials of the UCLA Center for Mental Health. The TXCC presented these tools, called Tools for Transition, to the ESCs in December 2005. These materials remain on the SEDL website (http://www.sedl.org/pubs/catalog/items/change104.html).

Development of these materials and the provision of professional development helped TXCC build its relationship with both the ESCs and TEA. Urgent needs were met quickly with high-quality services and products, establishing the center's credibility and demonstrating its ability to provide technical assistance and support to state agencies in their work in improving schools.

After this challenge was met, the TXCC met again with the leadership at the TEA to discuss its scope of work. The Texas commissioner of education assigned the senior division director for the NCLB Division as her designee for working with the TXCC. In addition, the executive directors of the ESCs met with the leadership of the TXCC at TEA offices. In this meeting, plans for the partnership between the TXCC and the ESCs were finalized.

Once the plans were established, the TXCC director and the TXCC state liaison scheduled meetings with TEA staff. Initially, meetings included the NCLB Division director and his program assistant. At each meeting, a day and time for the next meeting was set. Additional meetings were set up to include the Title I director and the directors of SIRC and SSS/PII. Meetings are now regularly scheduled for a specific day and time each month.

Meeting regularly was key to building the required relationships needed for providing technical assistance to the statewide system of support. A second necessary ingredient in building this relationship was finding a place to add value to the work that was already in progress in the state when the TXCC came into existence.

Staff working on the SSS/PII were developing two guides related to NCLB requirements on parental notification and involvement, one for administrators and another for professional development. The TXCC gladly volunteered to assist with this project. The center hosted meetings, reviewed documents, and provided feedback, and supported printing costs for one of the documents developed, the Administrator's Abbreviated Checklist for NCLB—Parental Involvement. These documents have since been distributed to every administrator in Texas and shared with other states.

The TEA began to request more information and assistance from the TXCC. One example of such a request was for feedback from the National Comprehensive Center for Teacher Quality (NCCTQ) on the state's highly qualified teacher plan. The TXCC forwarded the request to NCCTQ, which provided feedback on an extremely short timeline. The TEA was able to use the feedback to revise its plan prior to submitting it to the U.S. Department of Education.

The TXCC also supported TEA staff participation in events hosted by the national Content Centers. TXCC staff comprised part of the Texas teams at these events and worked closely with the TEA participants. One such event, organized by the Center on Innovation & Improvement (CII), provided an opportunity for the TXCC to offer a menu of five options, focused on school improvement issues. These options were modules developed by CII and presented at its annual Institute for School Improvement and Educational Options in September 2006. Following that institute, in its next monthly meeting with TEA, the TXCC staff discussed these options, and TEA selected restructuring as the focus for our work together. The TXCC then contacted CII to begin a planning process for delivery of professional development and technical assistance to TEA on this topic.

The Center on Innovation & Improvement agreed to tailor a retreat to meet the needs expressed by Texas. One of those requests was to meet with education officials of another large state, as TEA perceived that those states would have more in common with Texas, and consequently CII solicited participation by other Regional Comprehensive Centers serving large states. In February of 2007, the TXCC, the New York Comprehensive Center, and CII co-hosted a joint retreat for key members of the Texas and New York statewide systems of support. Participants included staff of TEA and both the New York City Department of Education and the New York State Education Department. The teams met in New York to learn together and develop plans for providing technical assistance to schools in restructuring.

All the entities involved in the Texas statewide system of support (TEA, SIRC, SSS/PII, and ESCs) were represented in the 12-member Texas team at the retreat. An initial plan was developed, and dates were set for follow-up sessions in April and June, facilitated by the TXCC, to continue the work on this plan.

The resulting plan for schools entering restructuring builds on Texas' previously established statewide system of support. Using the materials and information provided by CII during the retreat and reflecting on the insight gained from CII's technical consultants and another state's leaders, the Texas team used this sheltered time to work on the development of its plan for restructuring. The plan closely follows the recommendations of the resources provided at the retreat: *School Restructuring Under No Child Left Behind: What Works When?* and the *Handbook on Restructuring and Substantial School Improvement.* They are now ready to implement that plan.

In addition to the work on the restructuring plan, the restructuring retreat laid the foundation for additional meetings among all parts of the statewide system of support. The retreat was one of the first times representatives of the four components of Texas' support system had met as a group to work together to meet a need of the state. Subsequent meetings, hosted by the TXCC, have helped to improve understanding among all of entities engaged in the statewide system of support regarding what each of the entities does individually to support school improvement. These retreats provide an opportunity for the TXCC to stimulate discussions about how all the entities might better align their work and collaborate with one another and the TXCC. Quarterly retreats are scheduled throughout the 2007–08 school year. These retreats have proven valuable in supporting collaboration. For example, a discussion at the last retreat focused on alignment of the tools used by SIRC with the professional development that the TXCC is providing to the ESCs on the topic of systemic school improvement. In addition, modifications to the technical assistance database maintained by the TXCC were discussed so that the database may be used by SIRC's technical assistance providers to document their work in school improvement.

Another outcome of these retreats has been the collaborative development of Figure 17.1, referred to above, that illustrates the entire Texas infrastructure for school support. The TXCC initiated this process by asking each entity to describe the strategies and activities it used to support school improvement. Three common strategies, professional development, data collection and analysis, and information dissemination, were found to be in common across all entities. From this common foundation, each entity outlined the schools they served, the services they provided, and found the linkages between their individual work, the work of the other entities, and the work of the TXCC. Figure 17.1 is the result of these conversations over time.

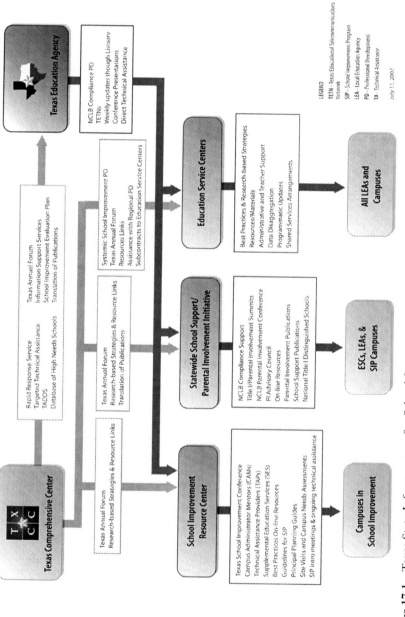

Figure 17.1 Texas State Infrastructure for School Support.

Over time, relationships between the TXCC, TEA, and the Texas statewide system of support have become stronger. TEA personnel have increased their understanding of what the TXCC can do for them and how the center can play a role in increasing the capacity of the state's infrastructure to assist schools and districts in meeting the goals of NCLB.

LESSONS LEARNED

Over the course of our work, we have learned that relationship building is key to working with a state agency and the statewide system of support. Finding a niche and a need that we could fill quickly and expertly helped us build credibility and trust. Maintaining an ongoing dialogue through our monthly meetings and retreats has enabled us to share what we perceive to be needs in the state and to hear what the state identifies as its needs. We can then offer technical assistance and support to meet those needs.

State education agencies often require fast action on the part of technical assistance providers. Being nimble and flexible is essential. State education agency staff often cannot wait long for information or assistance due to the demands and timelines placed upon them.

Finally, we have learned that a continual dialogue helps us maintain an ongoing feedback loop that is critical. We must be as transparent as possible with regard to what we can and cannot do. We must ask for and listen to feedback regarding our activities at the time we are conducting them. "No surprises!" is a mantra important to building and strengthening relationships and supporting the success of our work together.

K. Victoria Dimock *is a program director at Texas Comprehensive Center at SEDL.*

CHAPTER 18

"MONTANA-CIZING" A SCHOLASTIC REVIEW

Jennifer Stepanek

BACKGROUND

The Northwest Regional Comprehensive Center (NWRCC) is administered by the Northwest Regional Educational Laboratory (NWREL) in partnership with RMC Research Corporation, both located in Portland, Oregon. In its work with the state educational agencies in Idaho, Montana, Oregon, Washington, and Wyoming, NWRCC seeks to help them build their capacity to assist districts and schools in closing achievement gaps and meeting the goals of the No Child Left Behind Act (NCLB).

In Montana, the statewide system of support serves Montana's "priority schools," the state's term for schools that are in restructuring or corrective action. There are currently 33 schools identified as priority schools, and many of them have at least one characteristic in common—a large population of American Indian students. According to the Montana Office of Public Instruction (MOPI), just over 11% of students enrolled in Montana schools are American Indian. All of the priority schools have much higher proportions of American Indian students, from 50% to 100%. In 2005, 75% of districts located on reservations did not make adequate yearly progress.

Handbook on Statewide Systems of Support, pages 253–259

One of the biggest challenges in working with the priority schools in Montana is their geographic isolation. This isolation is more than just a matter of distance, according to BJ Granbery, the Title I director of MOPI's Division of Educational Opportunity and Equity, "For many of the schools we serve, there is a lack of service infrastructure. For example, there may not be motels for people who are visiting the schools. This also affects the schools' ability to have staff that live in the community. The teachers can't be there after school because they have to leave right away to make it home at night. This makes it challenging to schedule any sort of meetings. On a more positive note, there is a lot of room for growth, and there are always people who want to make the changes and get the results that we are all working for: better outcomes for students."

PROCESS AND PROGRESS

Shortly after NWRCC began operation, five staff members were assigned to serve as the state coordinator for each of the five states in the region. Their primary responsibility is to serve as the main contact for the state education agency (SEA) and to establish a scope of work for NWRCC to carry out in each state. To help determine the most appropriate capacity-building services NWRCC could provide in its first year, state coordinators developed comprehensive descriptions of the status of their states with respect to NCLB compliance. This information was used to develop state-specific work plans that matched the priorities of the SEA. Across all five states in the region, particular attention was paid to the system established to provide services to schools in need of improvement, corrective action, and restructuring.

In Montana, this emphasis proved to be timely. The development of the statewide system of support at the Montana Office of Public Instruction (MOPI) coincided with NWRCC's gearing up of its services to the states. This became the focus of the center's work in Montana. "NWRCC came on early on in our process," says BJ Granbery. "We shared our emerging plans and asked for input and advice. Robey Clark, NWRCC's Montana state coordinator, attended planning meetings and was with us every step of the way as a team member."

Scholastic Reviews and School Support Teams. To develop its statewide system of support, MOPI staff adapted the Kentucky Department of Education's model to fit their own state's needs—they call it "Montana-cized." The priority schools all undergo a scholastic review to assess three areas: academic performance, environment, and efficiency. The purpose of the review is to analyze the strengths and limitations of the school's instructional and organizational effectiveness. The findings are used to make specific recommendations to improve teaching and learning.

The scholastic reviews are carried out by school support teams. To constitute the teams, Montana recruited a group of administrators, teachers, school board members, parents, and representatives from higher education and MOPI. A total of approximately 40 people were identified to serve on nine teams, and each team worked with multiple schools. Each team included a team leader and from four to seven additional members. The teams varied in size according to the size of the schools they served. "Most of the team leaders are former teachers and administrators who recently left their schools," says Granbery. "We looked for people who had reputations for effective classrooms and schools, and who had experience with facilitating change."

The scholastic review process involves a 5-day site visit to gather data on the schools' operation. The team reviews a portfolio of documents that the school prepares prior to the start of the site visit. Some examples of the materials that go into the portfolio are school improvement plans, assessment data, policies and procedures, staff evaluation processes, professional development activities, and school board minutes.

In addition to analyzing the portfolio, the school support team conducts interviews and classroom observations. All of the administrators and teachers in the school are interviewed individually. Additional interviews are conducted with a sample of parents, support staff, and students. The team members also visit all teachers in the school to observe their instruction.

The NWRCC has played a role in helping the school support team members and in developing the scholastic review process. The staff of NWRCC helped MOPI refine the instruments and protocols that were used. This work involved a fine-grain analysis of the materials, identifying and revising items and terms that could be misinterpreted or interpreted multiple ways.

At the request of MOPI, Robey Clark, the state coordinator, participated in the initial 3-day training for the school support teams and accompanied the team leaders on practice site visits to three priority schools. "One thing I could contribute was that I have experience with collecting data in the field," Clark says, "so I knew that it was going to be harder than expected to use the rubric in a real-life setting." His field experience and background in Indian education were a resource for the team members, many of whom did not have experience with conducting observations and interviews.

The pilot testing also provided an opportunity to test the scholastic review process and instruments. "We found that the rubric had far more indicators than the observers could score in the time allotted," says Clark. "So we added another day for data collection, taking the visit up to five days rather than four. We also found that some indicators were addressing more than one issue, so some revisions were needed."

Ongoing planning discussions between NWRCC and the MOPI continued after the first round of site visits to address the unanticipated problems and needs. After the scholastic reviews were carried out, NWRCC conducted a series of interviews with the nine team leaders to identify topics for additional training. The team leaders were particularly concerned with providing ongoing support for the schools. They identified the need for a more formal intervention, anticipating that a single visit was likely to bring about only superficial changes.

Crafting a Rubric that Fits. The scholastic review process is designed to collect data based on a rubric titled "Correlates and Indicators of Effective Schools." The nine correlates are derived from the work of Larry Lezotte and are organized into three areas: academic performance (curriculum, assessment, and instruction), learning environment (school culture; student, family, and community support; and professional development and evaluation), and efficiency (leadership, organizational structure, and planning). In developing the rubric, MOPI staff knew they needed to make adaptations in order to address the needs of priority schools. They modified and added indicators specific to schools that serve American Indian students using the work of the Creating Sacred Places Project, led by Carmen Taylor for the National Indian School Board Association. Specifically, MOPI drew on the association's publication *Leadership Beyond the Seventh Generation: Creating Sacred Places for Children* (see http://nisba.skc.edu), a resource that includes indicators, tools, and strategies for school reform targeted for schools that serve American Indian and Alaska native students. Some of the topics that were added to the rubric include opportunities for authentic performances, use of native language, community involvement, integrated curriculum, and attention to Indian/tribal values and ways of knowing. For example, one of the modified indicators for instruction emphasizes students' cultural knowledge: "The implemented and fully aligned curriculum... is culturally responsive reinforcing the integrity of cultural knowledge that students bring."

In addition to the modifications to the correlates, MOPI conducted a survey of a variety of stakeholders from each of the priority schools. It used items from the Learn-Ed Nations Inventory developed by NWREL, a tool designed to assess how well the school is meeting the needs of American Indian and Native Alaskan students. The results of the survey were analyzed by the school support teams along with the other materials in the school portfolio.

Reports and Action Plans. After the data are collected and analyzed, the school support teams provide a rating for each of the indicators. All of the ratings are supported with a statement that summarizes what the team observed. The outcome of the review process is a final report that includes the team's findings and overall recommendations for each of the nine correlates. At the end of the site visit, the team holds a debriefing with the school to share its findings. The team leader gives an overview of the contents of the report and the recommendations.

After the reports are reviewed and edited at MOPI, they are delivered to the schools. The next step in the process is for the school to develop an action plan based on the recommendations and to organize a school-level leadership team to carry out the plan. The plans are developed to address from one to three of the recommendations. The school support team leaders also work with the schools to develop their plan. To help facilitate this process, the state held a series of "Call to Greatness" meetings for the schools, providing an opportunity to work with the team leaders and other MOPI staff members.

As the team leaders articulated in their interviews, there is a need for more support. "Some of the plans were not as good as we would hope," says BJ Granbery. "Some of them were too complicated. Others failed to address areas that are likely to have an impact." To help build a better support system, NWRCC recommended that Montana consult with Robert MacGregor, former assistant superintendent for school improvement from Washington state. The center sponsored a 1½-day planning meeting that brought together MOPI staff with MacGregor to develop a plan to expand and improve MOPI's system of support based on Washington's model of school improvement facilitators. MacGregor reviewed Montana's current system and made recommendations for areas of development. He advised MOPI on how to develop a system of facilitators, explaining the components of the model and the logistics of how it works.

In response to MacGregor's recommendations, MOPI is working on a plan to provide school improvement facilitators and resource people for the priority schools. The state is still developing and negotiating what this aspect of its statewide system of support is going to look like; MOPI hopes to have people on-site at the schools once or twice a month. It is also focusing in on specific areas that are likely to have the most impact for the schools. "We want to assemble an array of tools that schools can use, based on the areas of focus identified in the scholastic reviews," BJ Granbery explains. "We are creating a cadre of people who can help schools with things like data analysis, teacher mentoring, response to intervention, curriculum mapping, and helping teachers design rubrics for assessing student projects." Part of the facilitator's role will be to work with the schools on how to implement their action plans. The schools will sign a performance agreement, and the agreement and plans will be monitored by the facilitator.

LESSONS LEARNED

From the perspective of NWRCC's coordinator for Montana, Robey Clark, the state's system of support is off to a good start with the scholastic review, but it is not enough. "It's a very detailed and thorough process. We need to provide the schools with as much data as possible to inform their decisions and plans. At the same time, there are intangible things that the rubric can't capture, like the overall atmosphere and mood of the school. These are also an important part of the picture. Pulling together all of the data will help, but it is only the beginning of what the schools need in order to improve." Clark believes that Montana is moving in the right direction by developing the cadre of school improvement facilitators and resource people. "They needed a formal intervention strategy to help the schools implement their plans. That's where the facilitators come in. They can help the schools make the changes they need to make, rather than just monitoring their progress."

"Our plans are in flux," says BJ Granbery. "We've learned a lot and now we are starting 'chapter two.' One of the most important things is for MOPI to be flexible and willing to adjust. We've found that we have to see how things go, and what we develop initially may not fit what the schools need." Granbery says that this is where the comprehensive center makes a crucial contribution to the state's efforts. "The NWRCC staff brought in research and information to inform our plans. They are helping us shape the new facilitator model by serving as a resource for things like strategies for using data—not just the theory, but helping us to support the schools in actually doing it."

According to Granbery, MOPI also looks to NWRCC for advice about how to implement the statewide system of support. "They serve as a critical friend, sayings things like, 'You might want to rethink this because…' We don't want to go down a road that someone has already been down that doesn't work. NWRCC has helped us avoid some of those roads.…One of the things we've found is that some schools just really need good professional development in the subject areas, especially in reading and math," Granbery continues. "We have a tendency to think it's already out there, but the teachers may not have access to it. They may have heard about best practices, but not know how to begin. That's one of the reasons we're working with teacher mentoring. There are good teachers doing good things in all of these places. We want to build on that."

Like Montana, the NWRCC sees the need for flexibility as a key lesson derived from its work in the Northwest. Because the states in the region require different types of assistance, depending on where they are in developing and implementing their systems, NWRCC's work looks slightly different in each of the states that it serves. Because of the variation among the states, another key lesson for the center is the need to bring people from different states together. Helping MOPI to build on the work of Washington state by working with Robert MacGregor is an excellent example of how this strategy can play out. Creating opportunities for the states to learn from each other has become a key role for NWRCC throughout its work in the region.

Jennifer Stepanek *is a program advisor at Northwest Regional Comprehensive Center.*

CHAPTER 19

BUILDING SEA CAPACITY IN UTAH

Libby Rognier and Mary Peterson

BACKGROUND

The work of the Southwest Comprehensive Center at WestEd (SWCC) is organized primarily around five goal areas: assessment and accountability; district support and improvement; school support and improvement; teacher quality; and high school reform. One SWCC staff member with demonstrated expertise and experience in each goal area is assigned to be the primary point of contact for all states as they undertake work in a particular goal area. In addition, for each state, one SWCC staff member with experience, contacts, and/or residence in that state is designated as the liaison to the state education agency (SEA). Leaders of the SEAs are encouraged to channel all inquiries and new requests for technical assistance through the SWCC state liaison. The state liaison helps the SWCC leadership identify and coordinate resources that will be needed to fulfill state requests; this liaison also facilitates communication among other SWCC staff members who are working in the state.

The SWCC school and district improvement work with the Utah State Office of Education (USOE) originated with the U.S. Department of Education's January 2006 Title I Monitoring Report for Utah, which found that Utah did not have the required statewide system of support in place. As a

Handbook on Statewide Systems of Support, pages 261–267

result, the Utah superintendent of public instruction requested SWCC's assistance in developing an appropriate statewide system of school support. As the work began, USOE had only one staff person assigned to developing the system of support; that person had been on the job for less than a month when SWCC staff began to provide technical assistance in this area. As work began, USOE quickly added two additional Title I staff to provide support to schools and districts in need of improvement, among other duties. (One of these Title I specialists moved to the USOE Curriculum and Instruction Section in December 2006 and was not replaced.)

PROCESS

To assist USOE in developing its system of support, the SWCC applied its consistent approach to capacity building, which includes the following general steps:

1. access information and identify the problem;
2. disseminate essential information to create deeper knowledge;
3. identify and engage stakeholders;
4. design an actionable plan;
5. implement plan with fidelity and consistency;
6. self-assess and evaluate to refine implementation; and
7. scale-up and institutionalize implementation.

For this particular project context, SWCC staff first worked closely with USOE officials to review the U.S. Department of Education's January 2006 findings and target specific needs. The USOE–SWCC team then identified best practices and relevant research on school improvement, thus building deeper knowledge of the issues involved. This work allowed the team to develop an actionable strategy that would be appropriate for Utah. A suitable system (appraisal rubrics, data collection tools, school support teams and their protocols, etc.) was then drafted and shared with relevant stakeholders via a series of focus groups across the state. Refinements were made based on this feedback, and the system was pilot tested in spring 2007. Results from the pilots led to further reflection and refinement. An online application system for potential school support team members who will be responsible for implementing the system was developed and activated in March 2007. Applicants were reviewed and selected, and a 2-day workshop for SST members was developed. With SWCC assistance, the USOE planned and conducted SST trainings in June and August 2007, culminating in a full statewide system rollout in fall 2007. All tools will be posted online and available to all Utah schools.

Development of the statewide system of school support, outlined above, followed a rigorous timeline, discussed in the following paragraphs.

Spring 2006. The USOE–SWCC development team determined that Utah would benefit from both an improved system of Title I monitoring and a separate school support system, including school support teams, for schools identified as in need of improvement. The group reviewed examples of what other states are doing, followed by a guided discussion of what USOE would like to see developed to support schools in need of improvement and what the essential components, in terms of content and process, would be. This group discussed a sequence of events and established a timeline for developing a system.

Summer 2006. The USOE–SWCC development team split into two work groups, one focused on improving the monitoring system and one focused on developing a school support system. The latter, the school support development team (SSDT), created a detailed "Tasks and Timeline," a plan to develop and pilot a system in the 2006–07 school year and have a fully operational system for 2007–08. After reviewing research on factors affecting school improvement, and looking at systems from other states, a list of major "categories" and "constructs" for school appraisals was compiled, and draft rubrics were developed.

The SSDT and the monitoring team scheduled concurrent meeting days throughout the development of their respective projects so that they could confer on the progress of each system and co-develop plans for focus groups and communications with district Title I directors.

Fall 2006. The SSDT refined the appraisal rubrics, drafted requirements and a process for identifying SST members, and began development of data collection tools to use for a school appraisal. Both the SSDT and monitoring development team solicited feedback on rubrics and templates via focus groups with Title I directors, parents, teachers, principals, superintendents, higher education officials, and representatives of disaggregated subgroup populations. Over 120 individuals participated in focus groups that were conducted in five regions throughout the state. The rubrics and tools were revised, based on feedback from focus group participants. A School Support Team Handbook of tools and materials was also drafted.

January–May 2007. In January, the school appraisal process was piloted in two elementary schools and one middle school, each of which had been identified as in need of improvement. The pilots led to some minor changes in the tools, but also provided valuable feedback to the schools. At an April task force meeting for district improvement planning, two of the superintendents from the pilot sites spoke of the tremendous positive outcomes for the schools involved in the pilots. The superintendents reported that principals showed a refined focus and direction for their improvement efforts and that staff had increased parent involvement and interest in those efforts, both direct results of the pilots. The SSDT also developed training plans and materials for the June SST training, and completed the School Support Team Handbook, which includes the following sections:

1. System of Support Overview
2. School Support Teams—Tools for Recruiting and Selecting SST Members
3. School Appraisal Process
4. Appraisal Data Collection Tools
5. Reporting Forms
6. Post-Appraisal School Support Team
7. School Improvement Planning
8. Quarterly Progress Reports
9. Corrective Action and Restructuring
10. Ongoing Training Opportunities
11. Resources and Research

Communication strategies were developed for recruiting potential SST members statewide, and Title I directors were again updated on the progress of the system development and refinement of the tools. An online site was activated for applicants to list their qualifications and availability to serve on SSTs. In the first round of applications, 26 people applied for SST positions. The State Office of Education convened a review board, consisting of representatives from the State School Board, the Council of Minority Representatives, the Reading First director, and the Special Education Department. The review board was very pleased with the applicants and with the ease of using the online tools to access and examine their qualifications, approving 25 of the applicants.

School Support Team trainings, which SWCC helped develop and facilitate, were held in June and August 2007. The state will continue to recruit potential SST members and will hold a follow-up training for SSTs in January 2008. The system of school support will be used by schools in need of improvement in the 2007–08 school year. All tools and materials will be available on the USOE website. Beginning in spring 2008, SWCC will conduct an evaluation of the new system.

DISTRICT SUPPORT

The USOE expanded its statewide system of support to include districts during spring 2007. In preparing for the development of a statewide system of district support, USOE and SWCC hosted a meeting for all Utah superintendents, who were presented with four model options for a district support system:

1. Minimal Compliance with NCLB Model—Provide an online process to revise district improvement plans, meeting all requirements of the law, including a checklist containing essential features and links to citations, a step-by-step guide for completing the plan revision, and a resource bank of successful strategies and best practices;
2. Professional Development Model of District Support—Provide professional development modules with targeted technical assistance to district personnel involved in the improvement process. Districts will have the ability to choose one or more modules that support improvement and they may choose to present the modules in-house or send staff to USOE-sponsored trainings.
3. Expert/Consultant Model of District Support—Provide a resource list of outside experts/consultants who can provide targeted technical assistance to district personnel involved in the improvement process. One or more experts can provide examples of best practices, coaching, and/or development and implementation of plans for targeted improvements. Districts identify and hire the consultants and coordinate their assistance.
4. District Support Team Model That Parallels the School Support Model—Provide training and tools to district support teams, similar to the SST process, including a comprehensive district appraisal and ongoing assistance of a district support team.

District leaders were charged with deciding what model of support they would prefer. After consideration and discussion, the superintendents opted for two systems: (a) a minimal compliance online planning form, required for all districts identified as in need of improvement; and (b) a full support team/appraisal process (similar to that of the school support system), available to all districts and required of those districts in Year 3 of improvement. A statewide district task force, with representation from large and small districts, was assembled by USOE with the superintendents' input, to provide guidance and feedback throughout the development process. SWCC facilitated an initial meeting of the Task Force, and is continuing to assist USOE in the development and refinement of district support tools and process.

LESSONS LEARNED

Based on the experience in Utah, as well as similar work in other states, SWCC staff found three elements key to successfully assisting SEAs develop systems of support for schools and districts.

Stakeholder Buy-in. Utah is a strong local-control state, where districts had little trust in the SEA in terms of offering support and assistance to Title I schools. Holding focus groups throughout the state, and meeting twice with the district Title I directors—early in the process in focus groups, and after revisions based on stakeholder feedback—brought great credibility and support from key constituents. Including other USOE staff (representing offices dealing with curriculum and instruction, special education, accountability and assessment, English language learners, and Indian education), professors from schools of education, representatives from the State School Board and from the Coalition on Minority Affairs Council representatives, not only increased buy-in but also built collaborations for the new Title I staff. They have been invited to stakeholder meetings and asked to give input on other USOE initiatives, based on connections made through the SST development process.

Effective Use of Research and Best Practices. Both at the beginning and throughout the development of the SST process, SWCC has been responsible for sharing and implementing the use of research and best practices, including sample rubrics, processes, and handbooks from other states. SWCC helped USOE ensure that selected practices fulfilled the requirements of NCLB, and that all requirements of the law would be met through their school and district systems of support.

SEA Capacity Building. An emphasis throughout our work with Utah has been to build capacity of the SEA staff through extensive and intensive on-site coaching and through technical assistance in the area of technology. Following our modeling of facilitating focus groups throughout the state, USOE staff reported that they had run internal focus groups to solicit feedback for other work they were doing. They have also developed new presentations for stakeholder groups based on joint presentations done during the SST development process, and developed new communications to schools and districts regarding their status and requirements.

Another area of capacity-building the SWCC has provided is in the area of technology development and use. Working with the USOE's Title I and Computer Services Sections, SWCC is developing a protocol to put all tools and forms online, including an online monitoring system for Title I directors that merges several previous state-required reports and fulfills all requirements of NCLB. The Southwest Comprehensive Center is continuing and expanding this technical support to include a searchable catalog of online resources linked to school and district support tools and other online support for school and district support teams. The development of the on-line application system for potential SST members allowed USOE staff and reviewers to easily track, review, and contact applicants, as all required information and artifacts were in an easily accessible online site. Information about approved applicants is also readily available to those schools needing to form SSTs (https://usoe.edgateway.net/sst/). In addition, SWCC has made an online "live classroom" available to USOE and is completing the development and refinement of tools via this virtual community.

Libby Rognier *is a senior research associate at the Southest Comprehensive Center at WestEd.*

Mary Peterson *is a senior program associate at the Southwest Comprehensive Center at WestEd.*

PART E

TOOLS TO STRENGTHEN THE
STATEWIDE SYSTEM OF SUPPORT

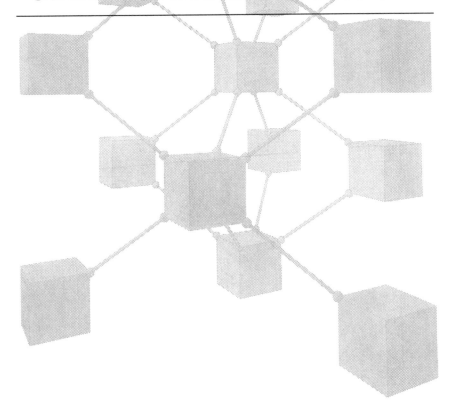

CHAPTER 20

TOOLS TO STRENGTHEN THE STATEWIDE SYSTEM OF SUPPORT

These tools enable an SEA team to self-assess its system of support and plan for its improvement. The tools are not a compliance monitoring process, a rating system, or a means of comparing one state's system with another's. The sole purpose of the tools is to guide the SEA in fully describing the statewide system of support, viewing that description within a framework, determining ways to strengthen the system, and developing a plan for improvement.

The Center on Innovation & Improvement also provides a comprehensive technical assistance manual to facilitate a self-assessment and planning process for the SEA in conjunction with a Comprehensive Center. The technical assistance provided by the Comprehensive Center is an invaluable aid to the SEA in determining the current status of its statewide system of support and planning for its improvement.

Given the great variation in SEA structures, traditions, and priorities, these tools do not present a model for a system of support, but provide a framework within which many different strategies may fulfill the same purposes. In itemizing many possible strategies in its inventories, the tools

Handbook on Statewide Systems of Support, pages 271–326

enable the SEA to develop a complete profile of its current system and consider new approaches it may choose to adopt.

This section of the *Handbook on Statewide Systems of Support* includes:

- *The Allegory of the Garden* to establish a mindset about an effective statewide system of support.
- A *Synopsis of the Framework for an Effective Statewide System of Support* as a succinct review of the framework presented in earlier chapters of the Handbook.
- *Functions of the State Education Agency* to illustrate how the statewide system of support is positioned within the overall functions of an SEA.
- List of *Key Documents* for a statewide system of support.
- *Taking Stock* to draw a critical profile of the existing statewide system of support and its functioning within the SEA and throughout the state.
- *Summary Appraisal of the Statewide System of Support* provides sets of indicators to identify areas of strength and areas that need improvement.
- *Preparation of the Plan to Strengthen the Statewide System of Support* outlines a planning process and structure for a plan.

Design Team for Tools to Strengthen the Statewide System of Support

Carol Chelemer

Susan Hanes

Bryan Hassel

Thomas Kerins

Marilynn Kulieke

Susan Morrison

Carole Perlman

Sam Redding

Lauren Morando Rhim

The Allegory of the Garden
Incentives • Capacity • Opportunities

When you want other people to do something that they may not do on their own, you may start by simply telling them that it is required. A mandate. Rules and regulations. Often that is the beginning point—clearly stating what you want done. Some will go along. Others will pretend to go along. A few will openly resist. You have to find a way to punish the offenders. You don't have much time to concern yourself with the cooperators. You may be buffaloed by the pretenders. You seek a better way.

Dad liked to plant a big garden. He was a great garden planter. He planted the garden, and then he went to work every day all summer long, leaving Mom to supervise the kids, rousting them from bed in the morning to weed and hoe and pick. The best thing about summer for a kid should be the chance to sleep in. But the garden wouldn't allow it. Mom's rule was to work before you play, and she was an early riser.

For the kids, garden work was hot, boring, and itchy. Very boring. When Mom wasn't looking, they would break the boredom by whirling a dirt clod and clobbering a sibling in the head, setting off a war. To keep them on task, Mom's first ploy was to threaten what would happen when Dad got home. That sometimes worked, but the kids knew that if they shaped up by the end of the day, Mom wouldn't report them. So they goofed around as long as they thought they could, then put in a burst of effort, placating Mom and avoiding Dad's wrath. Other times, one of the kids would push Mom beyond the limits of her patience. Then she would cut a green switch from a peach tree and shake it with resolve, until the kids buckled down to their work.

Help from a Friend

One day, when Mom was near her wit's end, a neighbor dropped by and provided sage advice: "Enforcing rules is a tough job, especially if you are enforcing rules someone else has made. Your kids need reasons to want to work in the garden. They need an opportunity to take ownership in the garden—to make it theirs. They need help in learning how to be good gardeners. Think about providing them incentives and opportunities. Then be ready to teach them. Make a plan. See how it goes. I'll be back to talk it over with you."

Offering Incentives

Mom made a plan. She introduced her new deal to the kids:

1. Sleep in if you like, but then you will have to work in the hot sun of mid-day and may miss playing with your friends. Your choice.
2. If you pick enough strawberries that we can sell for $35, we will buy a summer pass to the swimming pool, and you can go swimming when your work is done.
3. If you take care of the sweet corn, pick the ears, and sell them at the truck stop, you can keep half the money.

No more threats to tell Dad. No more green switches. Unless one of the kids screamed bloody murder when hit by a dirt clod.

Some of Mom's incentives were positive—a pass to the swimming pool or half the money from selling roasting ears. Another incentive was negative—get up early to avoid the heat and have time to play later. In other words, do the right thing and avoid a negative consequence, which is different than being punished for something you have already done that is wrong.

Building Capacity

It's easier to fill enough baskets with $35 worth of strawberries if the strawberries are big ones, and there are more of them on each plant. Full ears of sweet corn bring more money than scrawny ones, and when you get two or three ears to a stalk, you are really in business. So the kids wanted to know how to grow big strawberries and full ears of corn. Mom helped them pick out the best seeds and fertilizer and to use the best cultivation methods. Mom taught them how to garden. She built the kids' capacity, improved their capabilities as gardeners.

Providing Opportunity

Then the whole project got so exciting that the next thing you know, the boys wanted a garden of their own. Mom made space available to them. Dad showed them how to create a new plot with the garden tiller. Each of the kids discovered ways to make his or her plot more productive, and the other kids watched and learned. Fewer rules and new space provided opportunities for the kids to apply their skills as gardeners to their own garden plots. The family garden benefited from what they learned.

The Friend Returns

Throughout the summer, Mom's neighbor returned on occasion, talking things over with Mom, offering suggestions, providing encouragement. She was delighted to see thriving gardens and a happy family.

What we call school improvement is really a process of changing the behaviors of a lot of people. Not because they are bad people, although you may find a few clod throwers in the bunch, but because they don't connect the desired changes to their own interests, don't know how to successfully make the changes, or don't have the opportunity to get better at what they do. We offer incentives, build capacitites, provide opportunities. We open up new space. Incentives alone don't make for better gardens, or better schools. Neither do expanded opportunities alone. Nor efforts to teach new skills in the absence of incentives and opportunities. Behaviors change, for the better, when people are provided incentives, opportunities, and capacity. All three.

Synopsis of the Framework for an Effective Statewide System of Support

Under NCLB and related state statutes and policies, districts and schools that are labeled in need of improvement are entitled to certain state supports. State education agencies (SEAs) have long monitored districts and schools to ensure compliance with federal and state regulations. Now, to manage school and district improvement, they also partner with other state agencies, regional entities, organizations, and consultants to build local capacity. "This transition in the state role from oversight to capacity building requires states to redesign existing support systems or create new ways to ensure that districts and schools have the resources needed to bring all students to proficiency" (CCSSO Policy Brief 9-06).

NCLB Requirements for a Statewide System of Support

No Child Left Behind requires States to provide a statewide system of support to assist Title I districts and schools that are in need of improvement, corrective action, or restructuring. The statewide system of support extends beyond the SEA, including organizational partners, distinguished educators, support teams, and other consultants to assist districts and schools with expertise appropriate to the needs of the district or school.

The Framework: Incentives, Capacity, and Opportunities

Incentives and Opportunities

A successful statewide system of support depends upon more than the delivery of services by the SEA and its affiliates. A policy context that spurs change by providing incentives and opportunities must accompany the service-delivery apparatus that builds local capacity. Thus, people in districts and schools need personal and organizational incentives and opportunities alongside the capacity-building service they receive from the system of support. Incentives might include: a) financial rewards for principals and teachers who agree to work in low-performing schools, b) contingencies attached to funding to encourage desired changes, and c) giving greater autonomy to schools making exemplary progress. Opportunities would include: a) waivers from state regulation to allow greater freedom for a district or school to change, and b) creating new schools, such as charter schools, to provide a "fresh start" opportunity for school leaders, teachers, and students. Policy is largely the domain of elected officials, but helping districts and schools take full advantage of incentives and opportunities is an important aspect of a system of support.

Systemic Capacity

In addition to providing incentives and opportunities, the State builds the systemic capacity of districts and schools to achieve continuous improvement by creating and providing useful information, enhancing the supply of high-quality school leaders and teachers prepared for school improvement, and providing non-duplicative, efficient, accessible, and useful data systems to guide district and school improvement.

Local Capacity

While a policy context that provides incentives and opportunities for change contributes to the efficacy of a statewide system of support, the personnel in that system focus their efforts primarily on capacity building. As the number of schools and districts not making adequate yearly progress continues to grow, states are moving toward a triage approach for their support and are realizing the need for strong, continuous, district-directed improvement processes. These processes assist schools at all levels of current performance.

Differentiating Services to Build Local Capacity. The system of support works with the school or district to assess current performance (operations and outputs) on a variety of metrics. It also analyzes the gap between the actual and the desired, plans interventions, and provides training, consultation, and support to implement and monitor the change actions. The statewide system of support differentiates its capacity-building services for each district and school in six ways:

1. **Intensity and duration**. How much support is required and for how long?
2. **Points of impact**. Which leverage points will most likely produce desired results—district board, superintendent, district staff, principal, teacher teams, teachers, parents—and how much and what kind of support is required for each?

3. **Desired trajectory for improvement.** Will incremental improvement suffice, or is a turnaround or fresh start necessary to reach achievement goals? The choice of trajectories hinges on questions about the school's existing capacity, the availability of a strong turnaround leader and/or fresh start operator, the ability/willingness of the district to oversee a turnaround or a fresh start, and the legal regime around fresh starts (e.g., Is there a good charter law?).

4. **Areas of functioning.** What areas of school or district functioning are in greatest need of improvement, e.g., decision-making processes, curriculum, instruction, formative assessment? To achieve its purpose of providing an education that enables each student to master learning standards and acquire knowledge and skills beyond basic proficiency (as the student's abilities, talents, and interests dictate), the district and school operate with their own areas of functioning that include:

Leadership and Decision Making
- Allocation of resources to address learning goals
- Decision-making structures and processes
- Information and data systems

Curriculum and Instruction
- Alignment of curriculum, instruction, and assessment with standards
- Curriculum
- Formative and periodic assessment of student learning
- Instructional delivery (teaching and classroom management)
- Instructional planning by teachers
- Instructional time and scheduling

Human Capital
- Performance incentives for personnel
- Personnel policies and procedures (hiring, placing, evaluating, promoting, retaining, replacing)
- Professional development processes and procedures

Student Support
- English language learners—programs and services
- Extended learning time (supplemental educational services, after-school programs, summer school, for example)
- Parental involvement, communication, and options
- Special education programs and procedures
- Student support services (tutoring, counseling, placement, for example)

The statewide system of support needs methods and metrics to assess the adequacy of each of these areas of functioning in order to apply targeted assistance and monitor improvement.

5. **Mode of delivery.** Which mix of delivery methods—consultation, expert guidance, training, coaching—is most likely to achieve sustainable improvement?
6. **Service providers.** Which service providers—consultants, SEA staff, distinguished educators, support team members, partner organizations—are most likely to achieve results with a particular district or school? What specific expertise is required to address the areas most in need of improvement?

Providing Support to Districts and Schools. In providing support to districts and schools, the statewide system of support:

1. Determines the level of operational and performance adequacy and the desired trajectory for improvement
2. Assesses the status of each potential point of impact and each area of school or district functioning
3. Analyzes the gap between an efficacy standard and the status of each point of impact and each area of functioning
4. Aligns gaps with remedies
5. Provides services to close gaps
6. Monitors effectiveness of its own services
7. Monitors results of interventions
8. Plans for sustainability

For each case (school or district), the statewide system of support must make the following decisions:

1. What are the available resources?
2. What is the most efficacious delivery mode?
3. Who are the most efficacious partners for delivery of services?
4. What is the likelihood of making an impact?
5. How soon can there be an impact?
6. How sustainable will this impact be?

Sustaining Improvement. Sustainability is a critical concern in school improvement efforts, including the capacity-building endeavors of the statewide system of support. SEAs are most accustomed to helping districts and schools assess their needs and plan their improvement strategies. The plan's implementation is often left to the school or district. Successful improvement, whether directed solely by the district or school or aided by the system of support, requires careful monitoring of the implementation of planned strategies, with pre-determined checkpoints and benchmarks as outlined in the plan. Monitoring must access data at each point of impact for the planned implementation. For example, a plan to strengthen instruction should provide checkpoints and benchmarks at each stage from the delivery of training (professional development), to sampling of teachers' lesson plans, to observations of classroom teaching, to results in student learning. The statewide system of support carries conventional SEA operations beyond planning to careful monitoring of implementation, suggesting changes in course as need is detected.

An improvement plan, based on data that assesses the strength of various district or school functions, as well as outcome data (student learning), aligns objectives and strategies to the areas of need, provides timelines, and assigns responsibilities. As implementation is monitored, the improvement team continually asks: Are we implementing the right strategies? Are we implementing the strategies well? Are we hitting our timeline targets? Are we achieving the expected outcomes?

When implementation is carefully monitored, adjustments in course can emphasize aspects of the intervention that are showing results, modify approaches that show need of "tweaking," and abandon dead-end strategies that are yielding no effect after reasonable effort and time have been devoted to them. Changes in course require changes in the plan, so the underlying improvement plan becomes a "living" document that is modified to improve its effectiveness.

To achieve efficiencies in use of its own resources as well as to ensure sustainability of improvement, the statewide system of support must know when to begin withdrawing its supports and must consult with the local district and school to plan for sustainability of the improvement processes. Early successes can be encouraging, but they can also produce a slacking of effort or weakening of the ongoing processes of improvement. Early failures can be discouraging, also contributing to a loss of focus, energy, and devotion to the work. The statewide system of support gradually reduces the intensity of its services, with checkpoints for ensuring that the improvement processes maintain their vitality as supports are lessened.

Sustainability is planned and monitored, beginning with the initial meeting of statewide system of support personnel with the district or school rather than tacked on to the end of the period of primary service delivery. At each step along the way, the statewide system of support assists the district or school to internalize systems, processes, and capacities that will ensure continued devotion to the difficult work of continuous improvement.

REFERENCE

Council of Chief State School Officers (2006, September). *State support to schools in need of improvement.* Washington, DC: Author. Retrieved May 15 from: http://www.ccsso.org/content/pdfs/SSSNI_FINAL.pdf

Functions of the State Education Agency

The statewide system of support does not replace the traditional functions of the SEA; it expands the SEA's functions and must be structured for compatibility to fit within the broader functions of the SEA and integrated within those functions.

The SEA's Functions

Though state education agencies vary in organizational structure and how they relate to districts and schools, they commonly perform the following six functions:

1. provide information
2. set standards
3. distribute resources
4. monitor compliance
5. assist with improvement
6. intervene to correct deficiencies

Variance in Function

America is a nation with a history of local control of schools. The balance of authority among the school, the local district, and the state has evolved differently within each state, and the state's own traditions influence the type and degree of state involvement in each of the functions listed above. The way the state organizes its interface with districts and schools—directly or through intermediate agencies and/or external partners, for example—affects the manner in which the state supports districts and schools. For instance, in states with an existing infrastructure of regional extensions of the state education agency, a ready framework is available on which to embed a statewide system of support. By contrast, in states with no regional structure or with semi-autonomous regional units, SEA leaders must build a more coordinated infrastructure while simultaneously engaging LEA (local education agency) personnel to ensure their receptivity to an evolving state role. Further, the size of the district and the nature of the school—elementary or high school, regular or charter school, for example—also impact their relationship with the SEA and the degree to which the district appreciates the potential value of a statewide system of support.

Purposes and Processes

Within each of the six primary functions of an SEA, several processes are required to fulfill each function's purposes. Table 1 outlines each function's processes and expresses the purposes as questions that are answered through the process. For example, an SEA provides information to LEAs through the processes of notification, expectation, announcement, and enrichment, answering the questions: How does the SEA notify districts and schools of state statute and policy requirements? How does the SEA communicate its expectations of districts and schools that go beyond those requirements? How does the SEA announce services, opportunities, and resources that are available to schools and districts? How does the SEA provide evidence-based "how to" information for districts and schools?

TABLE 20.1   SEA Functions, Processes, Purposes

SEA Function	Process	Purpose: Answer to the Question…
Provide Information	Notification	How does the SEA notify districts and schools of what state statutes and policies require of them?
	Expectation	How does the SEA communicate its expectations of districts and schools that go beyond what is required?
	Announcement	How does the SEA announce services and opportunities that are available to schools and districts?
	Enrichment	How does the SEA provide evidence-based "how to" information for districts and schools?
Set Standards	Certification (input)	What is required for a person to hold an employment position such as teacher, principal, or superintendent? How are districts and schools accredited by the state?
	Programming (output)	What programs must districts and schools provide; for whom, for how much time, and in what manner?
	Assessment (outcome)	What are students expected to learn, and how is their learning assessed?
Distribute Resources	Prioritization	How does the SEA determine district/school eligibility for specific funds or resources?
	Conditioning	How does the SEA determine the conditions under which the districts/schools receive and use funds or other resources?
	Allocation	How does the SEA determine which districts/schools receive how much money or other resources?

TABLE 20.1 SEA Functions, Processes, Purposes

SEA Function	Process	Purpose: Answer to the Question...
Monitor Compliance	Assurance	How does the district/school assure the state its acceptance of responsibility for the mandate of the statute/policy and guarantee compliance?
	Documentation	How does the district/school report that it has complied with the statute/policy?
	Confirmation	How does the SEA monitor compliance and check the accuracy of documentation?
Assist with Improvement	Status Assessment	What is the district/school doing?
	Gap Analysis	Where do the district's/school's actions fall short of the operational standards?
	Planning	How does the district/school plan to meet and exceed the operational standards?
	Organizational Development	What district/school policies, structures, and procedures must change to meet and exceed operational standards?
	Training/Prof. Development	What improvements in skills and knowledge of district/school staff are necessary to meet and exceed operational standards?
Intervene to Correct Deficiencies	Remediation	How does the SEA intervene to address the district's/school's deficiencies in compliance?
	Corrective Action	What actions does the SEA take when the district's/state's outcomes are inadequate?
	Restructuring	What actions does the SEA take when the corrective actions do not result in adequate outcomes by the district/school?

Differentiation of SEA Functions

While many of the SEA's functions apply to all schools and districts in the state, some focus primarily on schools and districts that demonstrate inadequacy on operational indices and/or performance outcomes. Thus, the SEA's functions are differentiated in their application, according to the status of the district or school, as shown in Table 20.2. Ideally, the statewide system of support targets and differentiates its services to schools and districts according to their level of need, as also shown in Table 20.2.

TABLE 20.2   SEA Functions, Processes, Supports

A "performance zone" may be applied to a school or district according to its current performance and rate of improvement in both operations and outcomes. Shaded areas indicate NCLB-related statewide system of support, and the degree of shading symbolizes the kind, intensity, and duration of support. Schools and districts in the Green Zone operate and perform well above the minimum expectations of the state. Schools and districts in the Yellow Zone make progress at a rate that is close to the line of minimum expectation, or cross the line in one direction or the other from year to year. Schools and districts in the Red Zone consistently operate or perform below the minimum expectation of the state.

Function	Process	Green (Safe) Zone		Yellow (Caution) Zone		Red (Danger) Zone	
		District	School	District	School	District	School
Information	Notification						
	Expectation						
	Announcement						
	Enrichment						
Standards	Certification						
	Programming						
	Assessment						
Resource Distribution	Prioritization						
	Conditioning						
	Allocation						
Compliance	Assurance						
	Documentation						
	Confirmation						
Improvement	Status Assessment						
	Gap Analysis						
	Planning						
	Organizational Development						
	Training/Prof. Development						
Intervention	Remediation						
	Corrective Action						
	Restructuring						

Key Documents in a Statewide System of Support

1. The statewide system of support's goals, objectives, and benchmarks
2. An organizational chart that depicts the offices and entities within the SEA and outside the SEA that make up the statewide system of support
3. Role descriptions for each person, office, or entity within the statewide system of support
4. A description of the role of distinguished educators
5. A description of the role of support teams
6. A description of the role of other consultants
7. Criteria or rubric to determine which districts and schools receive services from the statewide system of support
8. A description of the criteria and assessment methods used to determine the intensity and duration of service a district or school receives
9. A description of the criteria and assessment methods used to determine the type of service a district or school receives
10. A list of key URLs to state websites that assist schools and districts with improvement and a brief description of the purpose of each

Taking Stock

The process of strengthening a statewide system of support begins with taking an inventory of what is in place, including a look at the state education agency (SEA) and its partners in the system of support. The tools provided in this section of the Handbook help a statewide system of support assemble a profile of its current situation, identify areas of strength and areas in need of improvement, and make plans to strengthen the system.

I. FUNCTIONS OF THE SEA

The statewide system of support resides within the state education agency (SEA) and also encompasses the external partners throughout the state. State education agencies (SEAs) typically perform 6 basic functions: (1) provide information; (2) set standards; (3) distribute resources; (4) monitor compliance; (5) assist with district and school improvement; and (6) intervene to correct deficiencies. For each of these functions, the SEA maintains several processes. Listed below are statements about an SEA's functional processes.

Capacity = The SEA's resources of personnel, expertise, time, equipment, information, and budget to adequately perform the functional process.

Effectiveness = The degree to which the SEA's performance of this functional process achieves its purpose.

Please indicate your consensus rating of the capacity and effectiveness for each SEA functional process according to the following scale:
4 = High level; 3 = Medium level; 2 = Low level; 1 = Little or None

SEA Capacity and Effectiveness	Capacity	Effectiveness
The SEA . . .	4, 3, 2, 1	4, 3, 2, 1

Providing Information

	Capacity	Effectiveness
1. Notifies districts and schools of what state statutes and policies require of them.		
2. Communicates to districts and schools the SEA's expectations that go beyond what is minimally required.		
3. Announces services and opportunities that are available to schools and districts.		
4. Provides evidence-based "how to" information for districts and schools.		

Setting Standards

	Capacity	Effectiveness
5. Sets or influences the credentialing requirements for teachers, principals, and superintendents.		
6. Sets or influences the state accreditation requirements for districts and schools.		
7. Sets or influences program/curriculum/course/ graduation requirements for districts and schools.		
8. Sets or influences requirements for allocation of time for school days and school years.		
9. Sets or influences state learning standards for students.		
10. Tests students to measure their proficiency with state learning standards for students.		

Distributing Resources

	Capacity	Effectiveness
11. Determines district/school eligibility for specific funds or resources.		
12. Determines the conditions under which the districts/ schools receive and use funds or other resources.		
13. Determines which districts/schools receive how much money or other resources.		

Monitoring Compliance

	Capacity	Effectiveness
14. Requires districts/schools to assure the state of its acceptance of responsibility for compliance with state statutes, policies, and program requirements.		

SEA Capacity and Effectiveness	Capacity	Effectiveness
The SEA . . .	4, 3, 2, 1	4, 3, 2, 1

Monitoring Compliance (continued)

15. Requires districts/schools to document and report their compliance with state statutes, policies, and program requirements.		
16. Monitors district/school activities to check accuracy of district/school documentation of compliance with state statutes, policies, and programs.		

Assisting with Improvement

17. Assesses district/school operational effectiveness.		
18. Assesses district/school performance outcomes.		
19. Determines gaps between state expectations/ standards and measures of district/school operational effectiveness and performance outcomes.		
20. Oversees a district/school planning process that requires districts/schools to develop and implement plans to close gaps between state expectations and measures of district/school operational effectiveness and performance outcomes.		
21. Consults with districts/schools to help them change policies, structures, and procedures to meet and exceed operational standards and performance outcomes.		
22. Trains, coaches district/school staff to improve their skills and knowledge to meet and exceed operational standards and performance outcomes.		

Intervening to Correct Deficiencies

23. Intervenes to address the district's/school's deficiencies in compliance with state statutes, policies, program requirements.		
24. Applies corrective actions for districts not meeting state expectations for operational effectiveness and/ or performance outcomes.		
25. Assists districts in restructuring schools that perennially fail to meet state expectations for operational effectiveness and/or performance outcomes.		

II. INTEGRATION OF SSOS WITHIN SEA FUNCTIONS

The statewide system of support (SSOS) operates most effectively when well integrated within the functions of the SEA. Integration implies good coordination (including communication, cooperation, and collaboration) within the SSOS and between the SSOS and other functions of the SEA.

Coordination = Degree to which players are "on the same page," aware of roles and responsibilities, provided sufficient and consistent direction, communicate well, work together, are supportive of one another.

Please indicate your consensus rating of each integration factor according to the following scale:

4 = High level; 3 = Medium level; 2 = Low level; 1 = Little or None

Coordination Among SEA Personnel and Statewide System of Support	Coordination
Coordination Among...	4, 3, 2, 1
1. SEA personnel who are part of the statewide system of support **and** other SEA personnel who are responsible for providing information to districts and schools.	
2. SEA personnel who are part of the statewide system of support **and** other SEA personnel who are responsible for setting standards.	
3. SEA personnel who are part of the statewide system of support **and** other SEA personnel who are responsible for distributing resources.	
4. SEA personnel who are part of the statewide system of support **and** other SEA personnel who are responsible for monitoring compliance.	
5. SEA personnel who are part of the statewide system of support **and** other SEA personnel who are responsible for assisting schools and districts with improvement.	
6. SEA personnel who are part of the statewide system of support **and** other SEA personnel who are responsible for intervening to correct deficiencies.	
7. SEA personnel who are part of the statewide system of support.	
8. SEA personnel who are part of the statewide system of support **and** non-SEA personnel who are part of the statewide system of support.	
9. SEA personnel who are part of the statewide system of support **and** districts/schools receiving services from the statewide system of support.	
10. Non-SEA personnel who are part of the statewide system of support **and** districts/schools receiving services from the statewide system of support.	

III. FUNCTIONS OF A STATEWIDE SYSTEM OF SUPPORT

This section organizes information about the existing statewide system of support into an evidence-based framework for an effective statewide system of support.

A. Providing Incentives for Change

States use incentives to motivate district and school personnel to change or improve. Incentives, then, are pressures from the state rather than mandates. They may be pressures that encourage or pressures that discourage certain district or school actions. The following "incentives" are examples of pressures that states may use to influence districts and schools. Which of these incentives does your state use? (Check)

1. Publicly Disclosing Low Performance
- ☐ a. Public spotlight on districts that show continued low performance.
- ☐ b. Public spotlight on schools that show continued low performance.

2. Levying Consequences for Low Performance
- ☐ a. Corrective action for districts with continued low performance that exceeds NCLB sanctions.
- ☐ b. Corrective action for schools with continued low performance that exceeds NCLB sanctions.
- ☐ c. State approval of district plans to restructure schools that show continued low performance.
- ☐ d. Encouragement for districts to make improved student learning outcomes a condition in superintendents' contracts.

3. Providing Positive Incentives for Improvement
Recognition for Accomplishment
- ☐ a. Public recognition for districts that show improved results in student learning.
- ☐ b. Public recognition for schools that show improved results in student learning.
- ☐ c. Public recognition for superintendents in districts that show improved results in student learning.
- ☐ d. Public recognition for principals in schools that show improved results in student learning.
- ☐ e. Public recognition for teachers whose students show improved learning results.

Funding Contingencies that Encourage High-Leverage Improvement Strategies
- ☐ a. Grants and other discretionary funding or resource allocations that require districts to adopt high-leverage improvement strategies.
- ☐ b. Grants and other discretionary funding or resource allocations that require schools to adopt high-leverage improvement strategies.

Financial Rewards for Results

- ☐ a. Financial rewards for districts that show improved results in student learning.
- ☐ b. Financial rewards for schools that show improved results in student learning.
- ☐ c. Financial rewards for superintendents in districts that show improved results in student learning.
- ☐ d. Financial rewards for principals in schools that show improved results in student learning.
- ☐ e. Financial rewards for teachers whose students show improved learning results.

Financial Rewards for Working in Hard-to-Staff Districts and Schools

- ☐ a. Financial rewards for new teachers to accept positions in hard-to-staff schools.
- ☐ b. Financial rewards for talented teachers to accept positions in hard-to-staff schools.
- ☐ c. Financial rewards for talented principals to accept positions in hard-to-staff schools.
- ☐ d. Financial rewards for talented superintendents to accept positions in hard-to-staff districts.

Greater Autonomy

- ☐ a. Greater autonomy to districts over budget, staffing, governance, curriculum, assessment, and/or the school calendar for improved results.
- ☐ b. Greater autonomy to schools over budget, staffing, governance, curriculum, assessment, and/or the school calendar for improved results.

4. Providing Market–Oriented Incentives

- ☐ a. Competition for students from charter schools.
- ☐ b. Competition for students through public school choice other than that required by NCLB.

B. Providing Opportunities for Change

States provide opportunities for districts and schools to improve by removing obstacles to improvement and creating new space for schools. The following are some strategies that states may use to remove obstacles and create space. Which strategies does your state use to remove obstacles and create space?

1. Removing Barriers to Improvement

- ☐ a. Waiver/exemption processes that allow districts to request waivers from state education laws.
- ☐ b. Waiver/exemption processes that allow districts to request waivers from state education rules/regulations.
- ☐ c. Waiver/exemption processes that allow schools to request waivers from state education laws.
- ☐ d. Waiver/exemption processes that allow schools to request waivers from state education rules/regulations.
- ☐ e. Waiver/exemption processes that allow districts or schools to request waivers from provisions in teacher contracts.
- ☐ f. Alternate routes to principal certification to bring new leaders into education from other fields.
- ☐ g. Alternate routes to teacher certification to bring new teachers into education from other fields.

2. Creating New Space for Schools

☐ a.   State law that allows for the creation of new charter schools.

☐ b.   State law that allows for the creation of new pilot or lighthouse schools as models or
demonstrations of innovative practices.

C. Building Systemic Capacity

1. Creating and Disseminating Knowledge

States create, support the creation of, and disseminate knowledge relevant to district and school improvement processes and strategies as well as effective teaching practices. The knowledge disseminated includes:

- Materials created by the State (guides, manuals, syntheses, tools, etc.),
- Materials created with State support or in partnership with the State (State-financed research and practical guides, etc.), and
- Materials created by other organizations but selected by the State for wider distribution to its districts and schools.

On which of the following topics does your State: (a) create (b) financially support the creation of, and/or (c) disseminate information to districts and schools?

Check Each Box That Applies			
Creates Knowledge About	Supports Creation of Knowledge About	Disseminates Knowledge About	Topics Related to District and School Improvement
Leadership and Decision Making			
			Allocation of resources to address learning goals
			Decision-making structures and processes
			Information and data systems
Curriculum and Instruction			
			Alignment of curriculum, instruction, and assessment with standards
			Curriculum
			Formative and periodic assessment of student learning
			Instructional delivery (teaching and classroom management)

Check Each Box That Applies			
Creates Knowledge About	**Supports Creation of Knowledge About**	**Disseminates Knowledge About**	**Topics Related to District and School Improvement**
			Instructional planning by teachers
			Instructional time and scheduling
Human Capital			
			Performance incentives for personnel
			Personnel policies and procedures (hiring, placing, evaluating, promoting, retaining, replacing)
			Professional development processes and procedures
Student Support			
			English language learners—programs and services
			Extended learning time (supplemental educational services, after-school programs, summer school, for example)
			Parental involvement, communication, and options
			Special education programs and procedures
			Student support services (tutoring, counseling, placement, for example)

2. Enhancing the Supply of Personnel Equipped for School Improvement

States—through statutes, policies, and agreements/partnerships—influence university programs that prepare teachers and school leaders so that graduates of these programs understand the state's accountability system, school improvement strategies, and evidence-based teaching practices. States also encourage talented students to enter the field of education. States provide programs to directly train teachers and school leaders for service in schools and districts in need of improvement. States report to universities about the workplace experience of teachers and school leaders that have graduated from their programs. States also help channel highly qualified teachers and school leaders to districts and schools most in need of improvement. Please check each of the following statements that describes your State's practices.

Increase the Supply of Teachers and School Leaders

☐ a.   The State provides incentives for talented students to enter the field of education.

Prepare Teachers and School Leaders for School Improvement

☐ a.   The State provides special programs to train school leaders to turn around low-performing schools.

☐ b.   The State provides special programs to train teachers in effective teaching practices in low-performing schools.

Influence Universities that Prepare Teachers and School Leaders

Statutes and Policies

☐ a.   The State requires teacher preparation programs to provide pre-service instruction for teachers on the state's accountability system (standards and assessments).

☐ b.   The State requires school leader preparation programs to provide pre-service instruction for school leaders on the state's accountability system (standards and assessments).

☐ c.   The State requires teacher preparation programs to provide pre-service instruction for teachers on school improvement strategies.

☐ d.   The State requires school leader preparation programs to provide pre-service instruction for school leaders on school improvement strategies.

☐ e.   The State requires teacher preparation programs to provide pre-service instruction for teachers on evidence-based teaching practices.

☐ f.   The State requires school leader preparation programs to provide pre-service instruction for school leaders on evidence-based teaching practices.

Agreements and Partnerships

☐ a.   The State has agreements or partnerships with teacher preparation programs to provide pre-service instruction for teachers on the state's accountability system (standards and assessments).

☐ b.   The State has agreements or partnerships with school leader preparation programs to provide pre-service instruction for school leaders on the state's accountability system (standards and assessments).

☐ c.   The State has agreements or partnerships with teacher preparation programs to provide pre-service instruction for teachers on school improvement strategies.

☐ d.   The State has agreements or partnerships with school leader preparation programs to provide pre-service instruction for school leaders on school improvement strategies.

☐ e.   The State has agreements or partnerships with teacher preparation programs to provide pre-service instruction for teachers on evidence-based teaching practices.

☐ f.   The State has agreements or partnerships with school leader preparation programs to provide pre-service instruction for school leaders on evidence-based teaching practices.

Report the Experience of Graduates in the Education Workplace

☐ a.   The State provides reports to teacher preparation programs that document the experience of their graduates in the workplace.

☐ b.   The State provides reports to school leader preparation programs that document the experience of their graduates in the workplace.

Channel Highly Qualified Teachers and School Leaders to Districts and Schools in Need of Improvement

☐ a.   The State provides programs to channel highly qualified teachers to schools in need of improvement.

☐ b.   The State provides programs to channel highly qualified school leaders to districts and schools in need of improvement.

3. Providing a Strong Data System to Assist School Improvement

The information that the State provides schools and districts to assist with their improvement includes web-based access to assessment data, planning tools, and other resources. Also, the State's data collection policies and procedures determine what information can be organized and made available to schools and districts. Please check each item below that describes your State's data systems.

☐ a. The State has a data system that meets minimum NCLB requirements.

☐ b. The State has an integrated data system that reduces redundancy in data collection and reporting related to school improvement.

☐ c. The State provides timely, accurate, and integrated data that is readily available to generate customized reports for stakeholders (including parents and researchers) for analyzing student performance and school performance.

☐ d. The State provides a web-based system that guides the school improvement planning process.

☐ e. The State's web-based system that guides the school improvement planning process includes integrated retrieval of school data.

☐ f. The State's web-based system that guides the school improvement planning process includes integrated retrieval of multi-year, disaggregated student assessment data.

☐ g. The State's web-based system that guides the school improvement planning process includes suggested resources for addressing areas in need of improvement.

D. Building Local Capacity

1. Coordinating Capacity-Building Structures and Roles

The statewide system of support is indeed a system, with its own boundaries, structures, and roles. In an effective statewide system of support, someone is obviously at the helm, the players and their roles are known, and the system is coordinated, with communication among its players and a coherent approach to its function.

Size of the Statewide System of Support

a. How many SEA staff members are considered part of the statewide system of support? _____

b. How many non-SEA consultants and other personnel are considered part of the statewide system of support? _____

Please check each of the following items that describe your statewide system of support.

Organization of the Statewide System of Support

☐ a. One person within the SEA has primary responsibility for the operation of the statewide system of support. If checked, the name and title of that person are:

Name: _____

Title: _____

☐ b. The statewide system of support operates with a publicly available organizational chart that depicts the offices and entities within the SEA and outside the SEA that make up the statewide system of support. If checked, please attach a copy of the organizational chart.

☐ c. The role of each person, office, or entity within the statewide system of support is publicly available in a published document (or on a website). If checked, please attach a copy of the role descriptions.

☐ d. Personnel included in the statewide system of support receive regular, written communication about the operation of the statewide system of support.

☐ e. Personnel included in the statewide system of support meet regularly to coordinate their efforts. If checked, how frequently do they meet and what is the nature of the meetings?

_____

_____

_____

Organizational Partners in the Statewide System of Support

☐ a. State agencies other than the SEA are included in the statewide system of support.

☐ b. Intermediate educational units or regional centers are included in the statewide system of support.

☐ c. Universities are included in the statewide system of support.

☐ d. Associations (professional or business) are included in the statewide system of support.

☐ e. Unions are included in the statewide system of support.

☐ f. Non-profit groups are included in the statewide system of support.

☐ g. Businesses are included in the statewide system of support.

☐ h. Other groups are included in the statewide system of support. If checked, please list them.

_____

_____

_____

_____

Distinguished Educators in the Statewide System of Support

NCLB uses the term "distinguished educators" to describe successful teachers and principals from Title I schools that serve as consultants to districts and schools served by the statewide system of support. Individual States may use a different term (peer mentor or school improvement coach, for example) to describe a similar role.

☐ a. The statewide system of support includes distinguished educators. If checked, what are they called in your State?

_____

_____

☐ b. A description of the role of distinguished educators is publicly available. If checked, please attach.

☐ c. The distinguished educators are chosen with a selection process that matches individual experiences and capabilities with specific roles in the statewide system of support.

☐ d. The experiences and capabilities of each distinguished educator are carefully matched with the needs of the districts and schools they serve.

☐ e. The distinguished educators receive significant initial training before serving in the statewide system of support.

☐ f. The distinguished educators receive ongoing professional development while serving in the statewide system of support.

☐ g. The State evaluates the effectiveness of each distinguished educator at least once each year.

☐ h. The districts and schools served by the distinguished educators provide the State with an evaluation of the distinguished educators assigned to them at least once each year.

Support Teams

NCLB uses the term "support team" or "school support team" to describe a group of SEA staff, intermediate unit staff, organizational partner staff, distinguished educators, and other consultants who are assigned to assist a specific district or school with its improvement. Individual States may use a different term for these teams.

☐ a. The statewide system of support includes support teams. If checked, what are they called in your State?

_____

☐ b. A description of the role of support teams is publicly available. If checked, please attach.

☐ c. The experiences and capabilities of support team members are carefully matched with the needs of the districts and schools they serve.

☐ d. Support team members receive significant initial training before serving in the statewide system of support.

☐ e. Support team members receive ongoing professional development while serving in the statewide system of support.

☐ f. The State evaluates the effectiveness of each support team at least once each year.

☐ g. The districts and schools served by a support team provide the State with an evaluation of the support team assigned to them at least once each year.

Other Consultants in the Statewide System of Support

Other than organizational partners and distinguished educators, States often include other individual consultants in the statewide system of support.

☐ a. The statewide system of support includes consultants other than those from organizational partners and distinguished educators.

☐ b. A description of the role of consultants is publicly available. If checked, please attach.

☐ c. The experiences and capabilities of consultants are carefully matched with the needs of the districts and schools they serve.

☐ d. Consultants receive significant initial training before serving in the statewide system of support.

☐ e. Consultants receive ongoing professional development while serving in the statewide system of support.

☐ f. The State evaluates the effectiveness of each consultant at least once each year.

☐ g. The districts and schools served by consultants provide the State with an evaluation of the consultants assigned to them at least once each year.

2. Differentiating Support to Districts and Schools

States make choices about districts and schools receiving services from the statewide system of support, and what services each district or school receives. NCLB provides a rubric to determine priorities in serving districts and schools, and States often supplement this rubric with their own criteria. Typically, districts and schools are selected according to need as determined by their prior performance and the desired trajectory for improvement (incremental or turnaround). Please check each item below that reflects your State's policies in differentiating the services of the statewide system of support.

Selection of Districts and Schools (Prior Performance and Desired Trajectory)

- ☐ a. The State uses a publicly available rubric to determine which districts and schools receive services from the statewide system of support. If checked, please attach.
- ☐ b. The State prioritizes the services of the statewide system of support to give first attention to districts and schools in greatest need of improvement.
- ☐ c. Districts and schools for which incremental improvement is appropriate receive different services than districts and schools in need of more immediate turnaround.

Intensity and Duration of Service

- ☐ a. The statewide system of support provides more intensive services to districts and schools in greatest need of improvement.
- ☐ b. The statewide system of support provides services for a longer period of time for districts and schools in greatest need of improvement.
- ☐ c. A description of the criteria and assessment methods used to determine the intensity and duration of service a district or school receives is publicly available. If checked, please attach.

Type of Service

- ☐ a. The statewide system of support provides different types of services to districts and schools based on assessment of need.
- ☐ b. A description of the criteria and assessment methods used to determine the type of service a district or school receives is publicly available. If checked, please attach.

3. Delivering Services to Districts and Schools

Provide Services. In delivering services to districts and schools in need of improvement, the statewide system of support engages in a four-phase process. First, it must determine the district's or school's current operational and performance status. Second, it assists the district or school in planning specific interventions to address weaknesses. Third, the statewide system of support provides consultation, training, technical assistance, and professional development to support the school's or district's implementation of its planned interventions. Fourth, the statewide system of support monitors the district's or school's progress with implementation and provides advice for necessary modifications in the plan. Please check each of the items below that describe how your statewide system of support functions in delivering services to districts and schools.

Assessing Operations, Performance, and Need

☐ a. The statewide system of support uses a specific analytical tool to assess the district or school's student learning outcomes for disaggregated groups of students, grade levels, and subject areas.

☐ b. The statewide system of support uses specific analytical tools to assess the district or school's operations, including budgeting, purchasing, staffing, governance, curriculum, assessment, and scheduling.

Planning for Improvement

☐ a. The statewide system of support assists districts and schools with their improvement planning process.

☐ b. The statewide system of support provides web-based support for a district or school's planning process.

☐ c. The statewide system of support provides a model for the district or school's planning process.

☐ d. The State approves the improvement plans of districts and schools receiving services from the statewide system of support.

Implementing the Plan

☐ a. The statewide system of support provides consultation to assist the district or school in implementing its improvement plan.

☐ b. The statewide system of support provides training to assist the school or district in implementing its improvement plan.

☐ c. The statewide system of support provides professional development to assist the school or district in implementing its improvement plan.

☐ d. The statewide system of support provides coaching to assist the school or district in implementing its improvement plan.

Monitoring Progress

☐ a. The statewide system of support monitors the district or school's implementation of its improvement plan.

☐ b. The statewide system of support, with the school or district, establishes benchmarks to gauge progress in implementing the improvement plan.

☐ c. The statewide system of support produces progress reports at least twice each year to document the progress of each district or school receiving services.

To see how the delivery of services operates systematically to address key district and school functions, please check each box that describes your statewide system of support.

For *Assess*, check if the statewide system of support uses a specific instrument or analytical tool to assess this function.

For *Plan*, check if the statewide system of support includes this item in its improvement planning document.

For *Implement*, check this item if the statewide system of support provides direct assistance (consultation, training, professional development, coaching) to improve this function.

For *Monitor*, check this item if the statewide system of support includes this function in its monitoring reports to document school or district improvement in implementing their plan.

SERVICES TO IMPROVE SCHOOL AND DISTRICT FUNCTIONS

School				District				Key Functions of a School or District
Assess	*Plan*	*Implement*	*Monitor*	*Assess*	*Plan*	*Implement*	*Monitor*	
								Leadership and Decision Making
								Allocation of resources to address learning goals
								Decision-making structures and processes
								Information and data systems
								Curriculum and Instruction
								Alignment of curriculum, instruction, and assessment with standards
								Curriculum
								Formative and periodic assessment of student learning
								Instructional delivery (teaching and classroom management)
								Instructional planning by teachers
								Instructional time and scheduling
								Human Capital
								Performance incentives for personnel
								Personnel policies and procedures (hiring, placing, evaluating, promoting, retaining, replacing,
								Professional development processes and procedures
								Student Support
								English language learners—programs and services
								Extended learning time (supplemental educational services, after-school programs, summer school, for example)
								Parental involvement, communication, and options
								Special education programs and procedures
								Student support services (tutoring, counseling, placement, for example)

Allocate Resources for Services

In addition to directly providing services to districts and schools, the statewide system of support may allocate resources that enable districts and schools to secure their own services from other providers. Please check each item that describes your State's allocation of resources to enable districts and schools to secure their own services from other providers.

- ☐ a. The State provides financial support to enable districts and schools to secure their own services from other providers for purposes of improvement.
- ☐ b. The State provides requirements or guidelines for the use of funds provided to districts and schools to secure their own services from other providers for purposes of improvement.
- ☐ c. The State monitors the use of funds provided to districts and schools to secure their own services from other providers for purposes of improvement.
- ☐ d. The State requires districts and schools receiving financial support to secure their own services from other providers for purposes of improvement to evaluate their satisfaction with the services received.
- ☐ e. The State requires districts and schools receiving financial support to secure their own services from other providers for purpose of improvement to document the effectiveness of the services received.
- ☐ f. The statewide system of support provides assistance to districts and schools to analyze their budgets and available resources to reallocate to address learning goals.
- ☐ g. The districts and schools served by consultants provide the State with an evaluation of the consultants assigned to them at least once each year.

E. Evaluating and Improving the Statewide System of Support

To continuously improve the statewide system of support, the system itself needs clear goals, objectives and benchmarks, a process for monitoring its progress and for evaluating its effectiveness. Please check each item below that describes your methods for monitoring and evaluating your statewide system of support.

1. Monitoring Progress of the Statewide System of Support

- ☐ a. The statewide system of support operates with publicly available goals, objectives, and benchmarks. If so, please attach a copy.
- ☐ b. The statewide system of support monitors and reports its progress toward its operational goals, objectives, and benchmarks.
- ☐ c. The statewide system of support monitors and reports the implementation progress of districts and schools receiving its services.

2. Evaluating and Improving the Statewide System of Support

- ☐ a. The statewide system of support has completed an evaluation of its effectiveness within the past year.
- ☐ b. The statewide system of support evaluates its effectiveness with established criteria.

☐ c. The statewide system of support makes modifications in its operation as a result of its periodic evaluations of its effectiveness.

☐ d. The statewide system of support prepares and distributes a written report of its evaluation results and the modifications in its operation made in response to the evaluation.

☐ e. The statewide system of support includes district and school evaluations of services received as part of the evaluation of its effectiveness.

☐ f. The statewide system of support includes measures of student learning outcomes in districts and schools served as part of the evaluation of its effectiveness.

Summary Appraisal to Inform Plan to Strengthen the Statewide System of Support

Reviewing the responses in Taking Stock, please check one box in each Indicator row below.

A. Summary Appraisal of Offering Incentives

Please check the box in the column that best describes the State's current status for the indicator in Column 1.

Indicators	No Development or Implementation	Limited Development or Partial Implementation	Functional Implementation but no Evidence of Impact	Full Implementation and Evidence of Impact
A.1 Public disclosure of low performance	☐ Not a priority or interest. ☐ Will include in plan.	☐	☐	☐
A.2 Consequences for low performance	☐ Not a priority or interest. ☐ Will include in plan.	☐	☐	☐
A.3a Recognition for accomplishment	☐ Not a priority or interest. ☐ Will include in plan.	☐	☐	☐
A.3b Funding contingencies for high-leverage strategies	☐ Not a priority or interest. ☐ Will include in plan.	☐	☐	☐
A.3c Financial rewards for results	☐ Not a priority or interest. ☐ Will include in plan.	☐	☐	☐
A.3d Financial rewards for working in hard-to-staff districts and schools	☐ Not a priority or interest. ☐ Will include in plan.	☐	☐	☐
A.3e Greater autonomy for improved results	☐ Not a priority or interest. ☐ Will include in plan.	☐	☐	☐
A.4 Market-oriented incentives	☐ Not a priority or interest. ☐ Will include in plan.	☐	☐	☐

Comments:

B. Summary Appraisal of Providing Opportunities

Please check the box in the column that best describes the State's current status for the indicator in Column 1.

Indicators	No Development or Implementation	Limited Development or Partial Implementation	Functional Implementation but no Evidence of Impact	Full Implementation and Evidence of Impact
B.1a Waiver/exemption of state rules and regulations	☐ Not a priority or interest. ☐ Will include in plan.	☐	☐	☐
B.1b Waiver/exemption of provisions in teacher contracts	☐ Not a priority or interest. ☐ Will include in plan.	☐	☐	☐
B.1c Alternate routes to certification	☐ Not a priority or interest. ☐ Will include in plan.	☐	☐	☐
B.2a State law that allows formation of charter schools	☐ Not a priority or interest. ☐ Will include in plan.	☐	☐	☐
B.2b State law that allows formation of pilot or lighthouse schools	☐ Not a priority or interest. ☐ Will include in plan.	☐	☐	☐

Comments:

C. Summary Appraisal of Building Systemic Capacity

Please check the box in the column that best describes the State's current status for the indicator in Column 1.

Indicators	No Development or Implementation	Limited Development or Partial Implementation	Functional Implementation but no Evidence of Impact	Full Implementation and Evidence of Impact
C.1a Creation of knowledge	☐ Not a priority or interest. ☐ Will include in plan.	☐	☐	☐
C.1b Support for the creation of knowledge	☐ Not a priority or interest. ☐ Will include in plan.	☐	☐	☐
C.1c Dissemination of knowledge	☐ Not a priority or interest. ☐ Will include in plan.	☐	☐	☐
C.2a Increase the supply of teachers and school leaders	☐ Not a priority or interest. ☐ Will include in plan.	☐	☐	☐
C.2b Preparation of school leaders and teachers for school improvement	☐ Not a priority or interest. ☐ Will include in plan.	☐	☐	☐
C.2c1 Statutes and policies to influence universities that prepare teachers and school leaders	☐ Not a priority or interest. ☐ Will include in plan.	☐	☐	☐
C.2c2 Partnerships and agreements that influence universities that prepare teachers and school leaders	☐ Not a priority or interest. ☐ Will include in plan.	☐	☐	☐
C.3 Report experience of graduates in the workplace	☐ Not a priority or interest. ☐ Will include in plan.	☐	☐	☐
C.4 Channel highly-qualified teachers and leaders to districts and schools in need of improvement	☐ Not a priority or interest. ☐ Will include in plan.	☐	☐	☐
C.5 Data system to support school improvement	☐ Not a priority or interest. ☐ Will include in plan.	☐	☐	☐

Comments:

D. Summary Appraisal of Building Local Capacity

Please check the box in the column that best describes the State's current status for the indicator in Column 1.

Indicators	No Development or Implementation	Limited Development or Partial Implementation	Functional Implementation but no Evidence of Impact	Full Implementation and Evidence of Impact
D.1a Organization of the statewide system of support	☐ Not a priority or interest. ☐ Will include in plan.	☐	☐	☐
D.1b Organizational partners in the statewide system of support	☐ Not a priority or interest. ☐ Will include in plan.	☐	☐	☐
D.1c Distinguished educators in the statewide system of support	☐ Not a priority or interest. ☐ Will include in plan.	☐	☐	☐
D.1d Support teams in the statewide system of support	☐ Not a priority or interest. ☐ Will include in plan.	☐	☐	☐
D.1e Other consultants in the statewide system of support	☐ Not a priority or interest. ☐ Will include in plan.	☐	☐	☐
D.2a Selection of districts and schools	☐ Not a priority or interest. ☐ Will include in plan.	☐	☐	☐
D.2b Intensity and duration of service	☐ Not a priority or interest. ☐ Will include in plan.	☐	☐	☐

D.2.c Type of service	☐ Not a priority or interest. ☐ Will include in plan.	☐	☐
D.3a Assessing operations, performance, need	☐ Not a priority or interest. ☐ Will include in plan.	☐	☐
D.3b Planning for improvement	☐ Not a priority or interest. ☐ Will include in plan.	☐	☐
D.3c Implementing the plan	☐ Not a priority or interest. ☐ Will include in plan.	☐	☐
D.3d Monitoring progress	☐ Not a priority or interest. ☐ Will include in plan.	☐	☐
D.4a Allocating resources for school and district improvement	☐ Not a priority or interest. ☐ Will include in plan.	☐	☐
D.4b Analyzing budgets to reallocate resources toward learning goals	☐ Not a priority or interest. ☐ Will include in plan.	☐	☐

Comments:

E. Summary Appraisal of Evaluating and Improving the Statewide System of Support

Please check the box in the column that best describes the State's current status for the indicator in Column 1.

Indicators	No Development or Implementation	Limited Development or Partial Implementation	Functional Implementation but no Evidence of Impact	Full Implementation and Evidence of Impact
E.1a Goals, objectives, benchmarks	☐ Not a priority or interest. ☐ Will include in plan.	☐	☐	☐
E.1b Evaluation criteria	☐ Not a priority or interest. ☐ Will include in plan.	☐	☐	☐
E.1c Evaluation process	☐ Not a priority or interest. ☐ Will include in plan.	☐	☐	☐
E.2a Modification in response to evaluation	☐ Not a priority or interest. ☐ Will include in plan.	☐	☐	☐
E.2b Communication of evaluation and modifications	☐ Not a priority or interest. ☐ Will include in plan.	☐	☐	☐
E.2c District and school evaluation of services received	☐ Not a priority or interest. ☐ Will include in plan.	☐	☐	☐
E.2d Evaluation of effects on student learning	☐ Not a priority or interest. ☐ Will include in plan.	☐	☐	☐
E.2e Monitoring and reporting ongoing progress of SOS toward goals, objectives, benchmarks	☐ Not a priority or interest. ☐ Will include in plan.	☐	☐	☐
E.2f Monitoring and reporting progress of districts and schools receiving services	☐ Not a priority or interest. ☐ Will include in plan.	☐	☐	☐

Comments:

Preparing the Plan to Strengthen the Statewide System of Support

This plan is based upon the thorough review of the existing system in Taking Stock and in the Summary Appraisals.

1. Begin the *Plan to Strengthen the Statewide System of Support* with a statement of mission and purpose for the statewide system of support.
2. Identify two sets of objectives to include in the *Plan to Strengthen the Statewide System of Support:* (a) Quick Win Objectives and (b) Longer-Term Objectives. Follow these steps to identify the objectives:
   a. Carefully review the Taking Stock inventory of the existing system.
   b. From each of the five Summary Appraisal tables, select the items marked "No Development or Implementation—Will Include in Plan" and those marked "Limited Development or Partial Implementation." Check these items on the Priority/Opportunity Index tables.
   c. For each of the five Priority/Opportunity Index tables, rate each item by priority of importance, scoring 3 for highest priority items; 2 for medium priority; and 1 for lowest priority.
   d. For each of the five Priority/Opportunity Index tables, rate each item by opportunity for improvement, scoring 3 for low-hanging fruit—relatively easy to address; 2 for realistic opportunity—accomplished within current policy and budget conditions; and 1 for challenging—requiring changes in current policy and budget conditions.
   e. For each of the five Priority/Opportunity Index tables, calculate a Priority/Opportunity Index score for each item by multiplying the priority score times the opportunity score.
   f. With the Index score for each item as a guide, list the items under the following categories for each of the five Priority/Opportunity Index tables:

Priority/Opportunity Index

Category 1: Low-Priority and/or Challenging Opportunity (low scores). These items may be dropped from the plan or put on the back burner.

Category 2: Medium Priority and/or Opportunity (medium scores). These items may be included in Longer-Term Plan.

Category 3: High Priority and/or Opportunity (high scores). These items may be included in the Quick Win Plan.

g. Develop two sets of objectives—Quick Win Objectives and Longer-Term Objectives. The total number of Quick Win Objectives, from all five Priority/Opportunity Index tables, should probably not exceed 3 to 5 items. Relate each objective to a specific item from a table.

3. For each objective, establish an indicator for determining success, develop action steps to lead to its completion, designate persons with primary responsibility, and establish a target date for achievement of the objective. For longer-term objectives, benchmarks toward achievement of the objectives will be useful.

4. Develop a concise narrative of the intent of the plan's objectives, aligned with the framework components.

5. Review the Functions of an SEA in Taking Stock. For each of the functional categories, consider how the plan's objectives might affect and be affected by the operations of that functional category. How might personnel performing the function for the SEA best support the plan? How can the plan be communicated to those personnel and their support enlisted? How can the SSOS be optimally coordinated with the overall functions of the SEA?

6. Establish follow-up expectations, including the meeting with the commissioner/superintendent and future meetings of the self-assessment team.

PRIORITY/OPPORTUNITY INDEX
FROM SUMMARY APPRAISAL

Note: Record here the results of the previously completed Summary Appraisal. Complete the Priority and Opportunity ratings only for items marked "Will Include in Plan" or "Limited Development or Partial Implementation." Multiply each item's Priority score by its Opportunity score to produce a Priority/Opportunity Index score.

Priority = 3 for highest priority items; 2 for medium priority; and 1 for lowest priority.

Opportunity = 3 for low-hanging fruit—relatively easy to address; 2 for realistic opportunity—accomplished within current policy and budget conditions; and 1 for challenging—requiring changes in current policy and budget conditions.

A. Incentives Priority/Opportunity Index
(from Summary Appraisal of Offering Incentives)

Indicators	Will Include in Plan or Limited Development or Partial Implementation	Priority Score	Opportunity Score	Priority/ Opportunity Index Score
A.1 Public disclosure of low performance	☐ Yes ☐ No			
A.2 Consequences for low performance	☐ Yes ☐ No			
A.3a Recognition for accomplishment	☐ Yes ☐ No			
A.3b Funding contingencies for high-leverage strategies	☐ Yes ☐ No			
A.3c Financial rewards for results	☐ Yes ☐ No			
A.3d Financial rewards for working in hard-to-staff districts and schools	☐ Yes ☐ No			
A.3e Greater autonomy for improved results	☐ Yes ☐ No			
A.4 Market-oriented incentives	☐ Yes ☐ No			

Comments:

B. Opportunities Priority/Opportunity Index
(from Summary Appraisal of Providing Opportunities)

Indicators	Will Include in Plan or Limited Development or Partial Implementation	Priority Score	Opportunity Score	Priority/ Opportunity Index Score
B.1a Waiver/exemption of state rules and regulations	☐ Yes ☐ No			
B.1b Waiver/exemption of provisions in teacher contracts	☐ Yes ☐ No			
B.1c Alternate routes to certification	☐ Yes ☐ No			
B.2a State law that allows formation of charter schools	☐ Yes ☐ No			
B.2b State law that allows formation of pilot or lighthouse schools	☐ Yes ☐ No			

Comments:

C. Systemic Capacity Priority/Opportunity Index
(from Summary Appraisal of Building Systemic Capacity)

Indicators	Will Include in Plan or Limited Development or Partial Implementation	Priority Score	Opportunity Score	Priority/ Opportunity Index Score
C.1a Creation of knowledge	☐ Yes ☐ No			
C.1b Support for the creation of knowledge	☐ Yes ☐ No			
C.1c Dissemination of knowledge	☐ Yes ☐ No			
C.2a Increase the supply of teachers and school leaders	☐ Yes ☐ No			
C.2b Preparation of school leaders and teachers for school improvement	☐ Yes ☐ No			
C.2c1 Statutes and policies to influence universities that prepare teachers and school leaders	☐ Yes ☐ No			
C.2c2 Partnerships and agreements that influence universities that prepare teachers and school leaders	☐ Yes ☐ No			
C.3 Report experience of graduates in the workplace	☐ Yes ☐ No			
C.4 Channel highly qualified teachers and leaders to districts and schools in need of improvement	☐ Yes ☐ No			
C.5 Data system to support school improvement	☐ Yes ☐ No			

Comments:

D. Local Capacity Priority/Opportunity Index
(from Summary Appraisal of Building Local Capacity)

Indicators	Will Include in Plan or Limited Development or Partial Implementation	Priority Score	Opportunity Score	Priority/ Opportunity Index Score
D.1a Organization of the statewide system of support	☐ Yes ☐ No			
D.1b Organizational partners in the statewide system of support	☐ Yes ☐ No			
D.1c Distinguished educators in the statewide system of support	☐ Yes ☐ No			
D.1d Support teams in the statewide system of support	☐ Yes ☐ No			
D.1e Other consultants in the statewide system of support	☐ Yes ☐ No			
D.2a Selection of districts and schools	☐ Yes ☐ No			
D.2b Intensity and duration of service	☐ Yes ☐ No			
D.2.c Type of service	☐ Yes ☐ No			
D.3a Assessing operations, performance, need	☐ Yes ☐ No			
D.3b Planning for improvement	☐ Yes ☐ No			
D.3c Implementing the plan	☐ Yes ☐ No			
D.3d Monitoring progress	☐ Yes ☐ No			
D.4a Allocating resources for school and district improvement	☐ Yes ☐ No			
D.4b Analyzing budgets to reallocate resources toward learning goals	☐ Yes ☐ No			

Comments:

E. Evaluation Priority/Opportunity Index
(from Summary Appraisal of Evaluating and Improving
the Statewide System of Support)

Indicators	Will Include in Plan or Limited Development or Partial Implementation	Priority Score	Opportunity Score	Priority/ Opportunity Index Score
E.1a Goals, objectives, benchmarks	☐ Yes ☐ No			
E.1b Evaluation criteria	☐ Yes ☐ No			
E.1c Evaluation process	☐ Yes ☐ No			
E.2a Modification in response to evaluation	☐ Yes ☐ No			
E.2b Communication of evaluation and modifications	☐ Yes ☐ No			
E.2c District and school evaluation of services received	☐ Yes ☐ No			
E.2d Evaluation of effects on student learning	☐ Yes ☐ No			
E.2e Monitoring and reporting ongoing progress of SOS toward goals, objectives, benchmarks	☐ Yes ☐ No			
E.2f Monitoring and reporting progress of districts and schools receiving services	☐ Yes ☐ No			

Comments:

Table of Contents for the Plan to Strengthen the Statewide System of Support

I. **Mission and Purpose of the Statewide System of Support**
II. **Quick Win Objectives**

Note: Include at least one objective from *E. Evaluation Priority/Opportunity Index.*

SSOS Functions Category (Index table title):
SSOS Functions Item (Index table indicator):
Objective:
Indicator of success (measure of evidence of objective's completion):
Action Step 1:
Action Step 2:
Primary Responsibility:
Target Date for Completion:

SSOS Functions Category (Index table title):
SSOS Functions Item (Index table indicator):
Objective:
Indicator of success (measure of evidence of objective's completion):
Action Step 1:
Action Step 2:
Primary Responsibility:
Target Date for Completion:

SSOS Functions Category (Index table title):
SSOS Functions Item (Index table indicator):
Objective:
Indicator of success (measure of evidence of objective's completion):
Action Step 1:
Action Step 2:
Primary Responsibility:
Target Date for Completion:

SSOS Functions Category (Index table title):
SSOS Functions Item (Index table indicator):
Objective:
Indicator of success (measure of evidence of objective's completion):

Action Step 1:
Action Step 2:
Primary Responsibility:
Target Date for Completion:

SSOS Functions Category (Index table title):
SSOS Functions Item (Index table indicator):
Objective:
Indicator of success (measure of evidence of objective's completion):
Action Step 1:
Action Step 2:
Primary Responsibility:
Target Date for Completion:

III. Longer-Term Objectives

Note: Include at least two objectives from *E. Evaluation Priority/Opportunity Index.*

SSOS Functions Category (Index table title):
SSOS Functions Item (Index table indicator):
Objective:
Indicator of success (measure of evidence of objective's completion):
Action Step 1:
Action Step 2:
Benchmarks:
Primary Responsibility:
Target Date for Completion:

SSOS Functions Category (Index table title):
SSOS Functions Item (Index table indicator):
Objective:
Indicator of success (measure of evidence of objective's completion):
Action Step 1:
Action Step 2:
Benchmarks:
Primary Responsibility:
Target Date for Completion:

SSOS Functions Category (Index table title):
SSOS Functions Item (Index table indicator):
Objective:
Indicator of success (measure of evidence of objective's completion):

Action Step 1:
Action Step 2:
Benchmarks:
Primary Responsibility:
Target Date for Completion:

SSOS Functions Category (Index table title):
SSOS Functions Item (Index table indicator):
Objective:
Indicator of success (measure of evidence of objective's completion):
Action Step 1:
Action Step 2:
Benchmarks:
Primary Responsibility:
Target Date for Completion:

SSOS Functions Category (Index table title):
SSOS Functions Item (Index table indicator):
Objective:
Indicator of success (measure of evidence of objective's completion):
Action Step 1:
Action Step 2:
Benchmarks:
Primary Responsibility:
Target Date for Completion:

SSOS Functions Category (Index table title):
SSOS Functions Item (Index table indicator):
Objective:
Indicator of success (measure of evidence of objective's completion):
Action Step 1:
Action Step 2:
Benchmarks:
Primary Responsibility:
Target Date for Completion:

SSOS Functions Category (Index table title):
SSOS Functions Item (Index table indicator):
Objective:
Indicator of success (measure of evidence of objective's completion):
Action Step 1:
Action Step 2:
Benchmarks:

Primary Responsibility:
Target Date for Completion:

SSOS Functions Category (Index table title):
SSOS Functions Item (Index table indicator):
Objective:
Indicator of success (measure of evidence of objective's completion):
Action Step 1:
Action Step 2:
Benchmarks:
Primary Responsibility:
Target Date for Completion:

SSOS Functions Category (Index table title):
SSOS Functions Item (Index table indicator):
Objective:
Indicator of success (measure of evidence of objective's completion):
Action Step 1:
Action Step 2:
Benchmarks:
Primary Responsibility:
Target Date for Completion:

SSOS Functions Category (Index table title):
SSOS Functions Item (Index table indicator):
Objective:
Indicator of success (measure of evidence of objective's completion):
Action Step 1:
Action Step 2:
Benchmarks:
Primary Responsibility:
Target Date for Completion:

IV. Summary of the Plan's Objectives

To draw the objectives together into a succinct, narrative statement of the plan's intent, develop the following three concise paragraphs for each framework component below:

Paragraph 1: the current situation, as summarized from the *SSOS Self-Assessment Report*

Paragraph 2: areas to be strengthened (if any), as addressed in the objectives relative to this topic

Paragraph 3: strategies for change (if any), as expressed in the objectives relative to this topic and including the indicators of success

Framework Components

A. Incentives—State incentives that encourage school and district improvement

B. Opportunities—State policies and SSOS practices that create opportunity for school and district improvement

C. Systemic Capacity—SSOS policies, procedures, and practices that build systemic capacity for improvement

D. Local Capacity—SSOS policies, procedures, and practices that build local capacity for improvement

E. Evaluation of the statewide system of support, including monitoring its operation and assessing its effectiveness

V. Coordination of SSOS with Functions of the State Education Agency

For each of the functional categories, consider how the plan's objectives might affect and be affected by the operations of that functional category. How might personnel performing the function for the SEA best support the plan? How can the plan be communicated to those personnel and their support enlisted? How can the SSOS be optimally coordinated with the overall functions of the SEA.

A. Provide information.

B. Set standards.

C. Distribute resources.

D. Monitor compliance.

E. Assist with improvement.

F. Intervene to correct deficiencies.

VI. Monitoring Implementation of the Plan

The *Plan to Strengthen the Statewide System of Support* includes target dates for completion of objectives, with benchmarks along the way and indicators of success. To put the plan in place, the following steps are essential:

Step 1: The self-assessment team meets with the commissioner/superintendent to review the drafted plan, make modifications suggested by the commissioner/superintendent, and enlist the commissioner's/superintendent's involvement in communicating the plan to others and establishing a mechanism for monitoring its implementation.

Step 2: The commissioner/superintendent disseminates the plan to SEA personnel, SSOS partners, and other key constituents such as the state board of education, governor's office, and legislators.

Step 3: The monitoring mechanism agreed to with the commissioner/superintendent monitors the plan's implementation and periodically reports on its progress.

The mechanism to monitor implementation of the plan may include, for example, the continued oversight by the self-assessment team or the appointment of a new leadership team consisting of key staff appointed by the commissioner/superintendent. Establish below follow-up meeting dates, conference calls, and e-mail exchanges for the self-assessment team. This schedule can be updated and expanded at regular intervals.

Follow-Up By Self-Assessment Team

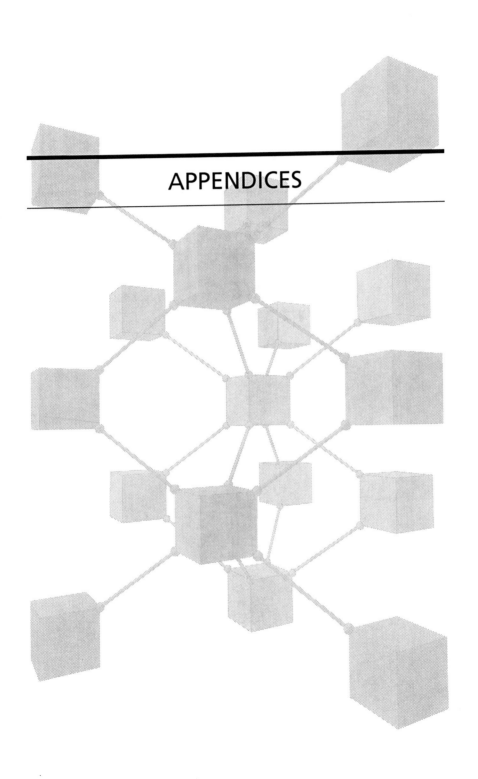

APPENDICES

THEORY OF ACTION OF
THE FRAMEWORK FOR AN
EFFECTIVE SYSTEM
OF SUPPORT

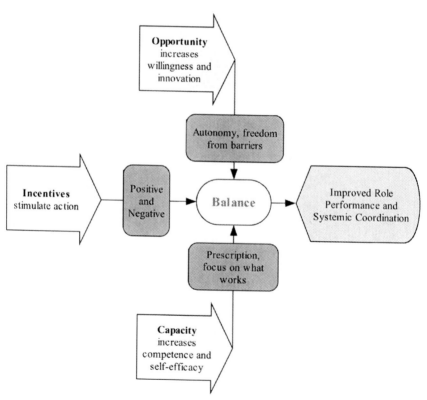

APPENDIX B

FRAMEWORK FOR AN EFFECTIVE STATEWIDE SYSTEM OF SUPPORT

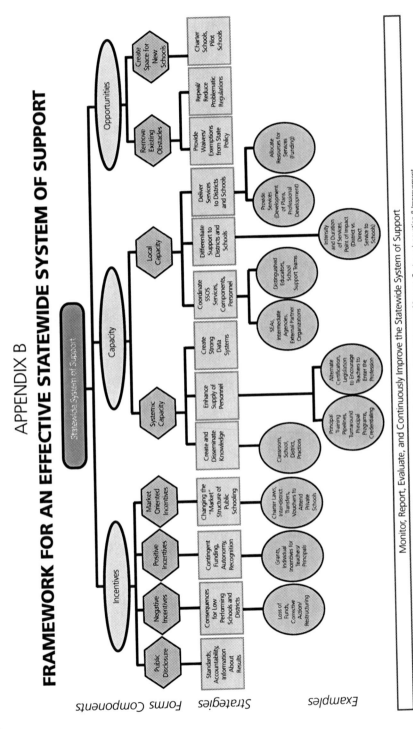

Framework for an Effective Statewide System of Support from *Handbook on Statewide Systems of Support*, Center on Innovation & Improvement Graphic created by JT Lawrence and Danette Parsley, Great Lakes West Comprehensive Center at Learning Point

Printed in the United States
103228LV00001B/4-6/A